Edward M. Lancaster

A manual of English history

For the use of schools

Edward M. Lancaster

A manual of English history
For the use of schools

ISBN/EAN: 9783741166594

Manufactured in Europe, USA, Canada, Australia, Japa

Cover: Foto ©ninafisch / pixelio.de

Manufactured and distributed by brebook publishing software (www.brebook.com)

Edward M. Lancaster

A manual of English history

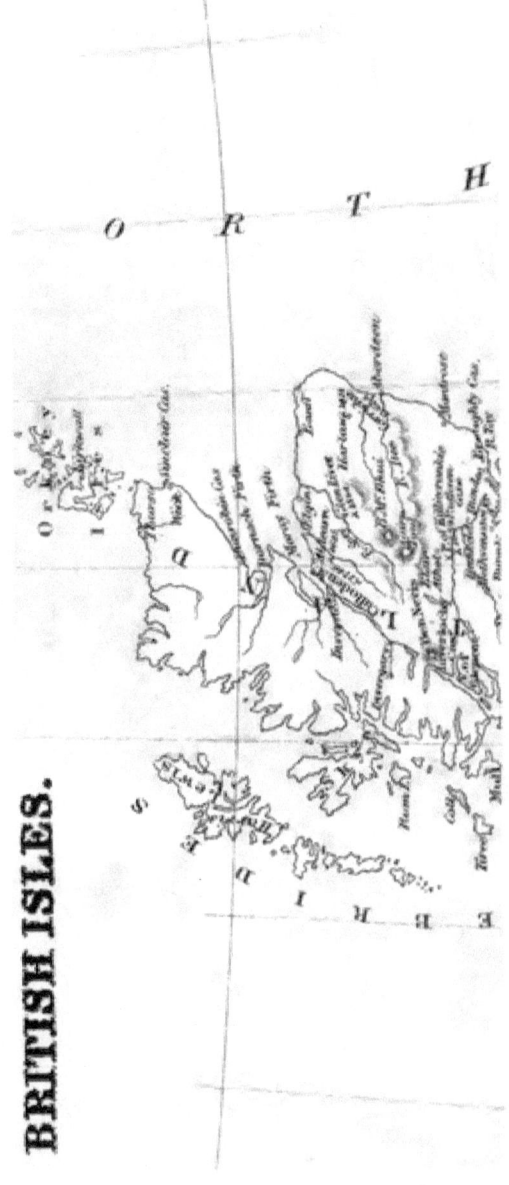

BRITISH ISLES.

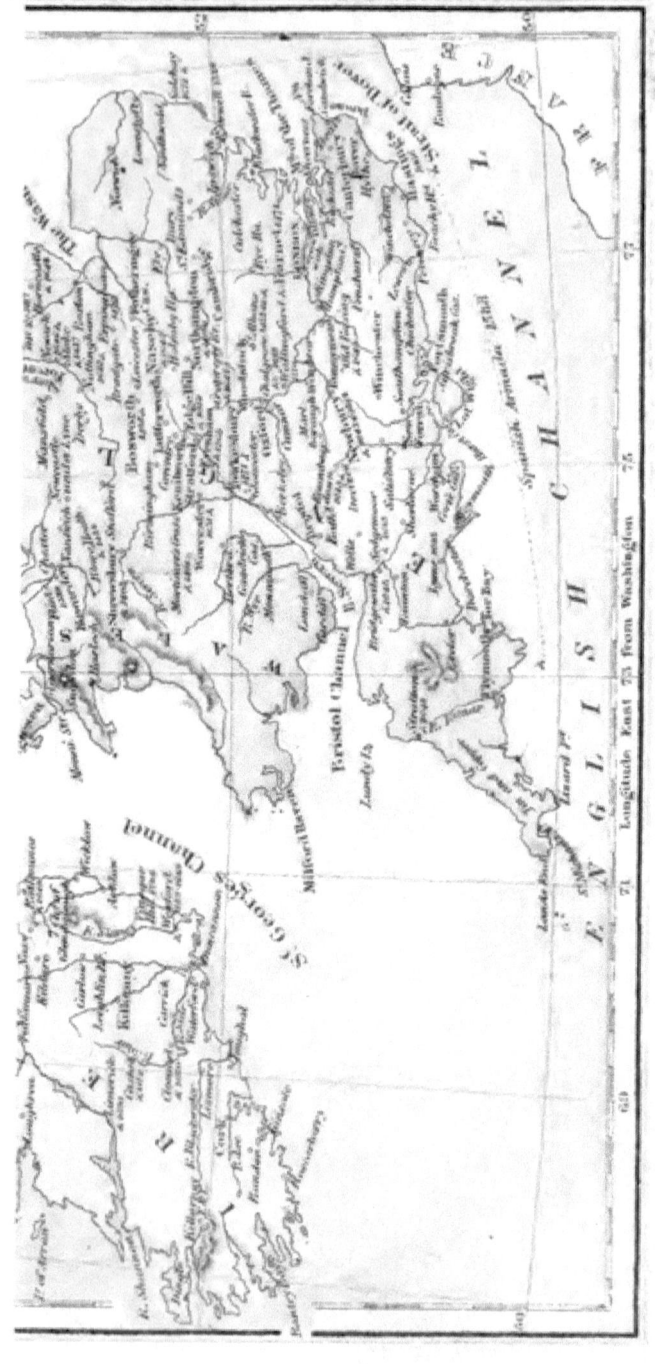

A MANUAL

OF

ENGLISH HISTORY,

FOR THE USE OF SCHOOLS.

BY

EDWARD M. LANCASTER,

PRINCIPAL OF THE STOUGHTON SCHOOL, BOSTON, MASS.

A. S. BARNES & COMPANY,
NEW YORK, CHICAGO, AND NEW ORLEANS.

PREFACE.

This "Manual of English History" has been prepared to meet the wants of those schools whose limited time forbids an extended course of study. The mere committal to memory of the names of kings and isolated events, however important, is in no proper sense a *study of history*. There should be enough of explanation and detail to make intelligible the relation which one event bears to another, that is, the *cause and effect* of events. The author has sought, therefore, in the preparation of this Manual, to arrange, in the briefest manner consistent with clearness, the essential facts of English History.

The most valuable lesson to be learned by American youth from the history of the Mother Country, is the worth of *liberty*, civil and religious. The struggle between the king and the people, the one striving to maintain the Royal Prerogative and the other to secure their Natural Rights, was happily over long before we became an independent nation. The principles, established by the Revolution of 1688, stand an enduring monument of the triumph of the people. Our constitution is but the matured product of that long and painful struggle, and a just conception of the one can be gained only by a careful study of the other.

If the youth of our land, however few in number, shall be aided, by the use of this brief work, in forming a just estimate of the free institutions under which they live, the highest object of the author will have been accomplished.

Among the many works consulted in the preparation of this Manual, special acknowledgments are due to "Knight's Popular History of England," valuable for its fulness of detail; and "Green's Short History of the English People," which, in the masterly comprehension and vivid expression of the *spirit* of English history, stands absolutely without a peer.

The author remembers thankfully the assistance of numerous friends. He takes great pleasure in mentioning the name of his esteemed friend, Henry B. Miner, Master of the Dorchester-Everett School of this city, to whom he is especially indebted for many valuable suggestions.

E. M. L

BOSTON, Feb. 22, 1877.

KINGS OF ENGLAND.

SAXON LINE.

Egbert	827— 838—11
Ethelwolf	838— 857—20
Ethelbald	857— 860— 3
Ethelbert	860— 866— 6
Ethelred I	866— 871— 5
Alfred	871— 901—30
Edward the Elder	901— 925—24
Athelstan	925— 941—16
Edmund I	941— 948— 7
Edred	948— 955— 7
Edwy	955— 959— 4
Edgar	959— 975—16
Edward the Martyr	975— 978— 3
Ethelred II	978—1016—38
Edmund II	1016—1017— 1

DANISH LINE.

Canute I	1017—1036—19
Harold I	1036—1039— 3
Canute II	1039—1041— 2
Edward—Saxon	1041—1065—24
Harold II—Saxon	1065—1066— 1

NORMAN LINE.

William I	1066—1087—21
William II	1087—1100—11
Henry I	1100—1135—35
Stephen	1135—1154—19

PLANTAGENET FAMILY.

Henry II	1154—1189—35
Richard I	1189—1199—10
John	1199—1216—17
Henry III	1215—1272—56
Edward I	1272—1307—35
Edward II	1307—1327—20
Edward III	1327—1377—50
Richard II	1377—1399—22

HOUSE OF LANCASTER.

Henry IV	1399—1413—14
Henry V	1413—1422— 9
Henry VI	1422—1461—39

HOUSE OF YORK.

Edward IV	1461—1483—23
Edward V	1483. 74 days
Richard III	1483—1485— 2

TUDOR FAMILY.

Henry VII	1485—1509—24
Henry VIII	1509—1547—38
Edward VI	1547—1553— 6
Mary	1553—1558— 5
Elizabeth	1558—1603—44

STUART FAMILY.

James I	1603—1625—22
Charles I	1625—1649—24
Commonwealth	1649—1660—11
Charles II	1660—1685—25
James II	1685—1688— 3
William & Mary	1689—1702—13
Anne	1702—1714—12

HOUSE OF BRUNSWICK.

George I	1714—1727—13
George II	1727—1760—33
George III	1760—1820—60
George IV	1820—1830—10
William IV	1830—1837— 7
Victoria	1837—

NAMES OF KINGS AND LEADING TOPICS.

Roman Conquest and Occupation — the first four centuries.
Saxon Conquest and Heptarchy — the next four centuries.
Reign of Saxon Kings and Danish Invasions — the ninth and **tenth centuries.**
Danish Conquest and Reign of Danish and **Saxon** Kings — the **eleventh** century.

Eleventh Century.

| NAMES OF KINGS. | LEADING TOPICS. |

William I. — Norman Rule — Saxon Rebellion — The Feudal System.
William II. — Beginning of the Crusades — The System of Chivalry.
Henry I. — First Charter of Liberties — Union of Saxon and Norman Families — Robert, Duke of Normandy.
Stephen — Usurpation — Civil War and Anarchy — Compromise with Henry.

Twelfth Century.

Henry II. — Plantagenet Rule — Establishment of Order — Constitutions of Clarendon and Thomas à Becket — Courts of Justice.
Richard I. — The Knight and Crusader — Usurpation of John.
John — Contest with the Pope — Rebellion of Barons — *Magna Charta*.

Thirteenth Century.

Henry III. — Rebellion of Barons — Simon de Montfort — *House of Commons* — Prince Edward and the Holy Land.
Edward I. — **Conquest** of Wales — War with Scotland — **Arbitrary Taxation** Forbidden.
Edward II. — War with Scotland — Rebellion — **Deposition of Edward.**

Fourteenth Century.

Edward III. — War with Scotland — War with **France for the Crown** — Chivalry and the Black Prince.
Richard II. — Wat Tyler's Rebellion — Chaucer — Wickliffe **and** the First Reformation.

Henry IV. — House of Lancaster — Rebellions — Persecution of Reformers.
Henry V. — Reformation Suppressed — *Conquest of France* — The Navy.
Henry VI. — Joan of Arc and the Loss of France — Jack Cade's Rebellion — *Wars of the Roses.*

Fifteenth Century.

Edward IV. — House of York — Wars of the Roses — William Caxton and the Art of Printing.
Edward V. — Usurpation of Richard, Duke of Gloucester.
Richard III. — Wars of the Roses ended with the death of Richard at Bosworth.

| NAMES OF KINGS | LEADING TOPICS. |

Sixteenth Century.

Henry VII. — Tudor Family — Union of York and Lancaster — Simnel and Warbeck — *Discovery of America* — Revival of Learning.

Henry VIII. — Catherine of Aragon and Cardinal Wolsey — Progress of Learning — Separation from Rome and the *Reformation*.

Edward VI. — Reformation Continued — Duke of Northumberland and Lady Jane Grey.

Mary — Reconciliation with Rome and Persecution of Protestants — Philip of Spain — Calais.

Elizabeth — Church of England — Mary, Queen of Scots — Philip and the Armada — Maritime Supremacy — Great Names.

Seventeenth Century.

James I. — Stuart Family — Union of Crowns — Gunpowder Plot — Translation of the Bible — Settlement of America.

Charles I. — *Illegal Taxation and Civil War* — *Petition of Right* — Trial and Execution of Charles.

The Commonwealth. — *The Monarchy Abolished* and *Commonwealth Established* — Cromwell and the Protectorate.

Charles II. — *The Restoration* — Plague and Fire — *Habeas Corpus Act* — Popish and Rye House Plots.

James II. — Monmouth's Rebellion — Attempt to Restore Catholicism — The *Revolution*.

William and Mary. — Rebellion in Ireland — War with France and Peace of Ryswick — Bill of Rights — English Constitution.

Anne. — War of Spanish Succession and Peace of Utrecht — Union of England and Scotland — The Augustan Age of English Literature.

Eighteenth Century.

George I. — House of Brunswick — The Elder Pretender — The South Sea Scheme.

George II. — Walpole and his Policy — War of Austrian Succession and Peace of Aix-la-Chapelle — The Younger Pretender — Seven Years' War — William Pitt — India.

George III. — Peace of Paris —— Canada — *American Revolution* — French Revolution — Second War with the United States.

Nineteenth Century.

George IV. — Independence of Greece — Catholic Emancipation Act.

William IV. — Reform Bill of 1832 — Abolition of Slavery.

Victoria. — Repeal of the Corn Laws — the Navigation Acts — and the Laws against Jews. Passage of Laws disestablishing the Irish Church — extending the Elective Franchise — substituting the Ballot for open voting — and founding a System of Public Schools. Wars with China and the Opening of Ports — the Crimean War — the Sepoy Rebellion — Civil War in the United States and the Alabama Claims.

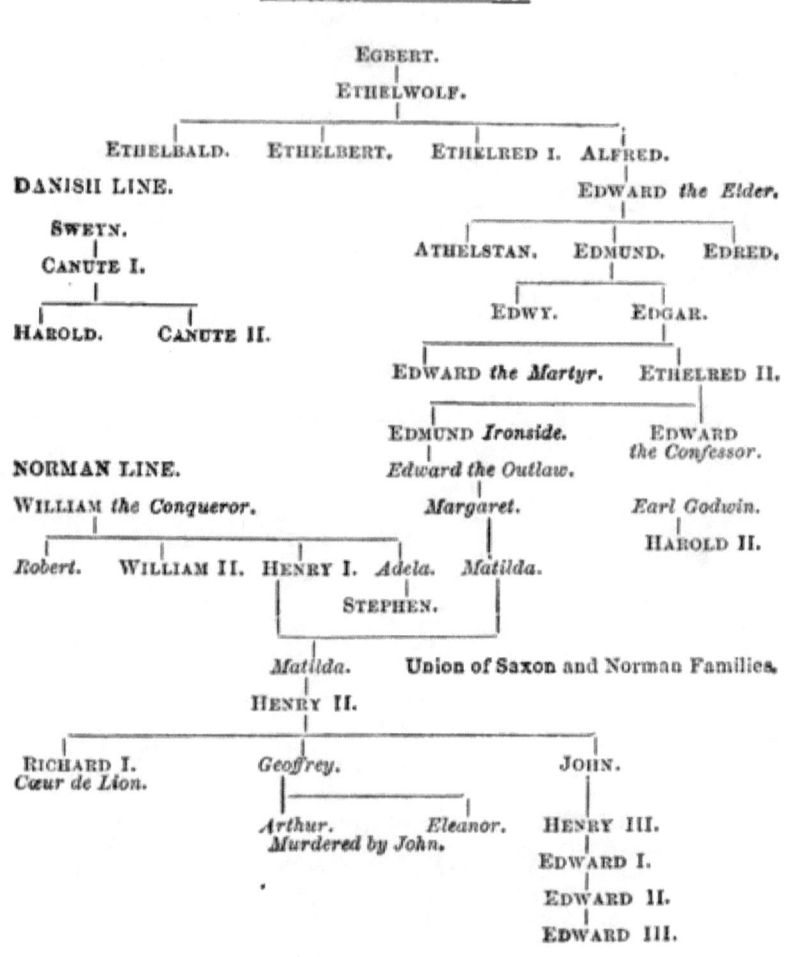

GENEALOGICAL TABLE.

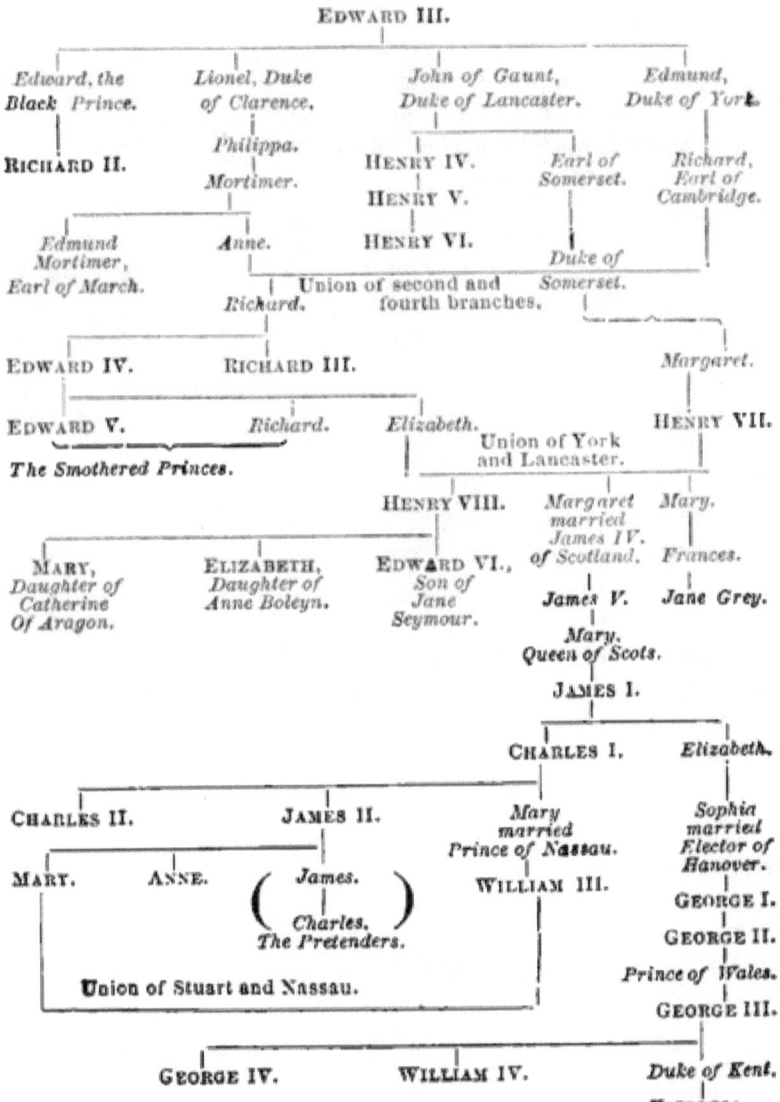

THE BRITISH EMPIRE.

The British Empire includes the Kingdom of Great Britain and Ireland and all its colonies and dependencies, having a population of more than 250,000,000, and an area of more than 8,300,000 square miles.

EUROPEAN.

The British Islands, the Channel Islands, Heligoland, Malta, Gozo, and Gibraltar.

ASIATIC.

British India, Ceylon, Aden, Malacca, Singapore, Prince of Wales' Island, Hong-Kong, Sarawak, Labuan, and Cyprus.

AUSTRALIAN.

Australia, Tasmania, Norfolk Islands, New Zealand, Chatham Islands, and the Fiji Islands.

AFRICAN.

Cape Colony, Natal, Gambia and the Gold Coast, Sierra Leone; the single Islands — Ascension, Mauritius, and St. Helena; and the groups — Seychelles, Amirante, and the Chagos.

NORTH AMERICAN.

British America including Nova Scotia and Cape Breton Island, New Brunswick, Prince Edward's Island, Quebec, Ontario, Manitoba, British Columbia, the Northwest Territory, and Newfoundland, all, except the last named, being united under the title of the Dominion of Canada; Balize, and the Bermudas.

SOUTH AMERICAN.

British Guiana, and the Falkland Islands.

WEST INDIAN.

Jamaica, the Bahamas, Trinidad, and most of the Lesser Antilles.

CHAPTER I.

The Britons. We know little of the early history of Britain. From rude relics found in the soil, we conclude that the island was once inhabited by a race of savages who disappeared before a superior people that, at some unknown period, crossed from the Continent of Europe. These Celtic invaders were found in sole possession when the Romans first visited the island, about half a century before Christ. They were a barbarous people, divided into numerous tribes, whose principal employment was war. Their weapons were spears and broadswords, with blades of bronze, and they also used wicker shields covered with skins, and chariots armed with projecting scythes, in which, drawn by trained horses, they rode at full speed into the very midst of their foes. Their homes were huts and caves in the forests which, at that time, covered nearly all the land. They subsisted upon their flocks and herds, and the products of the chase, and wore little clothing, painting their bodies blue, and covering them with hideous tattooes to make themselves terrible to their enemies in battle. But those occupying the southwestern corner of the island were superior to the rest, having been visited, from time immemorial, by other nations, for the tin found in the mines of that section. Even the merchants of ancient Tyre and Sidon, occasionally sent ships to barter Phœnician wares for British **tin**.

Druidism. The Britons professed a religion called Druidism. They worshiped one Supreme Being, of whom they had no just conception, and numerous inferior deities, to whom they offered human sacrifices. The heavenly bodies occupied a prominent place among these inferior deities. They believed in a future state of existence, in which rewards and punishments were meted out according as men's conduct had been good or bad in this life. Much of the power and all the learning were confined to the priests, called Druids. They made the laws, administered justice, and were the sole instructors of the young. Nothing was committed to writing, and education consisted in receiving from the lips of the Druids and committing to memory a great number of verses on Geography, Astronomy, and Religion. The priests performed their mystic rites in temples, each formed of a circular row of huge stones standing upright with the altar in the centre, open to the heavens above, and located in groves of their sacred tree, the oak. Remains of these temples still exist in various places, the most notable at Stonehenge on Salisbury Plain. Their most holy place was the Island of Mona, now Anglesea, just across the Menai Strait. Their most solemn festival occurred on the sixth day of the moon nearest the tenth of March, their New Year's day, when the chief Druid, clothed in white robes, with a golden knife cut the sacred mistletoe from the oak to which it clung. There were three other festivals of special interest to the English people, since to them may be traced the festivities of May-day, Mid-summer-eve, and Harvest-home, celebrating respectively the sowing of the seed, the ripening of the crops, and the gathering of the harvests.

First Roman Invasion. Britain, lying to the west of the continent, and separated from it by quite an expanse of water, was too insignificant to excite either enmity or cupidity, and long escaped the notice of Rome, the "Mistress of the World." It was only when the tide of Roman conquest had reached the western shore of Europe, that the scheme of its addition to the Empire was first conceived. Julius Cæsar, having nearly completed the subjugation of the Gauls, crossed the Channel with two legions, and landed just beyond the cliffs of Dover, B.C. 55. The Britons, warned of the purpose of Cæsar, had gathered in large numbers to oppose his landing. Though they were driven back, and repeatedly beaten, so stubborn were they, that Cæsar did not venture far from the coast, and was glad to accept their offers of peace and return to Gaul. But the next year he returned with a much larger force, five legions or thirty thousand foot soldiers, and two thousand horse. Having conquered the country for some distance beyond the Thames, compelling the chiefs to pay tribute and give hostages, Cæsar again withdrew from British soil.

Second Roman Invasion. Occupied with weightier matters, the Romans soon practically forgot their distant and worthless conquest, and the Britons were left for nearly a century to take care of themselves. During this period, a growing trade and a better acquaintance with their neighbors on the continent, had done something towards their civilization, attracting the attention of the Emperor Claudius, who began, in the year of our Lord 43, a second and more difficult conquest.

Caractacus. Caractacus, the most important of the chiefs at that time, putting himself at the head of the inland tribes, for eight years held the Romans at bay, when he was captured and taken to Rome to grace the triumph of his captor. "Is it possible that a people possessed of so much magnificence at home could covet my humble cottage in Britain," exclaimed the wondering barbarian as he gazed on the glories of Rome! His kingly bearing won the respect of the Emperor, who restored him to liberty, and this is the last we hear of the noble Briton.

Slaughter of the Druids. The Druids possessed almost unlimited power over the people, and this power they had used to the utmost, to arouse them to bitter hostility to Roman authority. Suetonius, the Roman general and governor, resolving to strike a decisive blow, in the year 61, crossed the strait of Menai and landed on the sacred shore of Mona. For a moment even Roman soldiers faltered, as they listened to the shrieks and imprecations of frantic priests and priestesses, and beheld the host of painted warriors gathered to defend their altars; then pressing resolutely forward, this stronghold of British superstition and British power was soon in their possession, and Druidism received a fatal blow in the slaughter of its priests, and the destruction of its groves and temples.

Boadicea. During the absence of Suetonius a fresh insurrection broke out under Boadicea, widow of the King of the Icenians. Stung to madness by shameful abuse,

when protesting against the seizure of all her wealth by
Roman officials, she went from tribe to tribe exciting
the warriors to phrensy with the story of her wrongs.
Under her lead they suddenly fell upon the Roman
settlements, and seventy thousand soldiers and citizens
were put to the sword. Suetonius hurried back from
Mona to wreak a terrible vengeance on the Britons in
arms. In a great battle fought near London, eighty
thousand warriors sealed with their blood their devotion to their country, and the spirited queen, unwilling
to survive the slaughter of her people and the destruction of her hopes, put an end to her own life.

The Roman Conquest. But the Britons were still
unsubdued, and it remained for Agricola (who became
Governor in the year 78), by the practice of justice and
humanity as well as soldierly skill, to reconcile them to
Roman authority. Under the firm but liberal policy of
Agricola and his successors, the Britons rapidly improved.
They gave up their heathenish rites and savage customs,
and adopted the manners, dress, and, to some extent,
the language of the Romans. They became peaceful
and industrious. Wide stretches of gloomy forests
gave place to fields of waving grain; and the mines of
tin, lead, and iron began to be worked in earnest. Their
surplus products found a ready market abroad, giving
rise to a moderate but increasing commerce. The construction by the Romans of a system of public roads
not only facilitated the transportation of troops to
needed points, but hastened the development of the
country and the civilization of its inhabitants. A
wall of solid stone, twelve feet high and eight feet thick,

running from the mouth of the Tyne to the Solway Firth, a distance of sixty-eight miles, was built by the Emperor Severus to protect the Britons from the incursions of the Scots and Picts, wild and warlike tribes occupying the highlands of Caledonia. Rome continued in undisturbed possession of Britain until the year 420, when she recalled her soldiers to repel the Goths, who were pouring from their German homes into Italy in vast numbers, threatening even Rome itself.

The Saxon Conquest. The Romans had no sooner left the island than the Scots and Picts, boldly crossing the wall of Severus, renewed their ravages in the northern districts. The Britons, weakened by long subjection to Rome, were unable to defend themselves; and, after a vain appeal to the Emperor Honorius for help, called to their aid the Saxons, Angles, and Jutes.

These were fierce people inhabiting the peninsula of Jutland and the country around the mouths of the Elbe and Weser rivers, who, roaming about the waters of the North and Baltic seas in their pirate boats, had long been the scourge of all the adjoining coasts. They entered Britain under the command of their brave chieftains, Hengist and Horsa, in the year 449, and quickly compelled the northern marauders to retire to their native highlands.

But, attracted by the mildness of the climate and the beauty and fertility of the country, and finding, in connection with the promised reward, a pretext for a quarrel, they soon turned their arms against the Britons themselves. The latter, compelled to fight in defence of their homes, gradually recovered their ancient valor. For a century and a half the struggle for mastery in the island went on, fresh hordes of Germans pouring in, from time to time, to the help of their countrymen.

The battle of Chester, fought in the year 607, established, beyond a doubt, the supremacy of the invaders. The districts still occupied by the natives being severed one from another, could no longer act in concert, and the struggle, though lingering, ceased to have a national character. The brave but hapless Britons, beaten on all sides, and pursued with fire and sword, at last found a safe retreat among the mountain fastnesses of Wales and Cornwall. There, animated by a burning love of liberty, they continued in almost unbroken war for six hundred years, defying the whole power of England to subdue them; and there, their descendants, the Welsh, live to-day, a hardy, vigorous race, and at one with the English, who have long since shared with them the blessings of a common country.

During the Roman occupation, Christianity had supplanted the native religion. The Latin language, too, had gradually come into use, especially among the upper classes and in the larger towns. The entire disappearance of Christianity, and both the Latin and native languages, attests the thoroughness of the German or Anglo-Saxon conquest. A few slaves held for the pleasure or profit of the conquerors were all that were left of the native population.

King Arthur. Of the many heroic Britons, who struggled against the German conquest, the most famous, whose name has come down to us, is Arthur, chief of one of the tribes in the West. But so much of fable has been woven into the story of this patriot Briton and his sixty "Knights of the Round Table," that we can only say with confidence, that such a prince lived and bravely fought the enemies of his country.

The Heptarchy. The conquerors gradually established separate kingdoms as they won new territory, each having its independent king. Seven of these, from their greater prominence, have been called, in history, the Heptarchy.* After the Saxons had become firmly established in their new homes, and the sharpness of the struggle with the Britons had begun to decline, jealousy and ambition for pre-eminence involved them in wars with each other. Constant changes, therefore, took place in the number and boundaries of the kingdoms. The stronger gradually absorbed the weaker, until Wessex, under its vigorous king Egbert, brought them all under one government in the year 827.

Introduction of Christianity. Britain first became Christian under Rome, but how or when is not known. Possibly, a Christian soldier in a Roman legion told the story of the Cross at a native fireside, or some nameless but devoted priest, going on a mission to heathen Britain, achieved a conquest under the banners of the Cross, more glorious than that of Roman arms. St. Alban is recorded to have suffered martyrdom as early as the year 304. With the advent of the Anglo-Saxons

---

* KENT, or Cantia, was founded by Hengist, in 457. SOUTH SAXONY, or Sussex, by Ella, in 490. WEST SAXONY, or Wessex, by Cerdic, in 519. EAST SAXONY, or Essex, by Ercewin, in 527. NORTHUMBERLAND (North of the Humber) by Ida, in 547. EAST ANGLIA, comprising Norfolk (North folks) and Suffolk (South folks) by Uffa, in 575. MERCIA (Marchmen, or people on the march or frontier) by Cridda, in 582.

the Christian religion disappeared, and, for a century and a half, Britain remained under a paganism more debasing than that of the Druids.

Christianity was introduced, a second time, by Augustine* and a band of forty monks from Rome, in the year 597. Ethelbert, king of Kent, who married Bertha, a Christian lady, and daughter of the king of Paris, was the first convert. His people followed his example and accepted Christianity. Augustine became Archbishop of Canterbury, the head of the church of England, and his successors have retained their superiority ever since. Ethelbert's daughter Ethelburh, married Edwin, king of Northumbria, and through her influence and that of her priest Paulinus, Edwin and his people were converted. The other kingdoms became Christian during the next century.

Anglo-Saxon Religion. The principal deity of the Anglo-Saxons was Woden, the God of war, from whom all their royal families claimed descent; the next in rank being Thor, or Thunder, the God of storms. Each day of the week was dedicated to a particular deity, from whom it received its name — a name it still continues

---

* The venerable Bede, our principal authority for early English history, tells how Christianity was now introduced into Britain. Gregory, a priest, one day saw in the market-place of Rome, some very beautiful boys for sale, and asked who they were and whence they came. He was told they were heathen boys from the Isle of Britain. He then asked the name of their nation. "*Angles,*" was the answer. "*Angles,*" said Gregory, " they have the faces of *Angels*, and they ought to be made fellow-heirs of the Angels in Heaven. But of what tribe of Angles are they?" "Of *Deira,*" was the reply. "*Deira!*" said Gregory, " then they must be delivered from the wrath of God. And what is the name of their king?" "*Ælla.*" "*Ælla!* then *Alleluia* shall be sung in his land." Sometime afterwards Gregory became pope and sent Augustine and forty other monks to convert the English.

to bear.* Like barbarous tribes in general, making the future existence a realization of their highest ideal of the present life, they filled their Valhalla or Heaven with scenes of war, where happy Saxons would live forever, occupying the days in the slaughter of their enemies, and the nights in wild carousals of victory.

Anglo-Saxon Government. The king was assisted in the government by a great council, called Witenagemot, or "Assembly of the Wise," composed of the great nobles, the Ealdormen or Earls, and, after the introduction of Christianity, Bishops and Abbots. This council met regularly at Christmas, Easter and Whitsuntide, and on special occasions when summoned. At the death of the king it assembled to elect his successor, who was taken from the royal family, but was not always the next in line. Besides the *Earls*, who acted as judges and rulers in their districts, there was an inferior class of nobles, called *Thanes*, men who had risen to nobility by personal attendance on the king. The *Churls* were freemen of the middle and lower classes, the lowest class of all being the *Serfs*, or slaves, who composed about two-thirds of the inhabitants.

---

*SUNDAY, (Sun's day), or day for the worship of the sun. MONDAY (Moon's day) or day for the worship of the moon. TUESDAY (Tiw's day) the day of the Dark God Tiw, to meet whom was death. WEDNESDAY (Woden's day) the day of Woden, the War God. THURSDAY (Thor's day) the day of Thor, the God of storms. FRIDAY (Frea's day) the day of Frea, the goddess of peace and fruitfulness. SATURDAY (Saturn's day) the day of Saturn, a God borrowed from Roman Mythology.

CHAPTER II.

The Saxon Line, 827 to 1013 — 186 years.

EGBERT.
ETHELWOLF.
ETHELBALD.
ETHELBERT.
ETHELRED I.
ALFRED THE GREAT.
EDWARD THE ELDER.

ATHELSTAN.
EDMUND I.
EDRED.
EDWY.
EDGAR.
EDWARD THE MARTYR.
ETHELRED II.

Egbert — 827 to 837 — 10 years. Saxon.

The Danish Invasions. Egbert called the country England from the Angles, the most powerful of the three tribes. This is generally regarded as the beginning of the English monarchy. No sooner were the different kingdoms united under one government and at peace among themselves, than a new danger appeared from without. Inroads began to be made by the Danes, a piratical people of Denmark, who, descending upon the eastern coast during the summer, would load their boats with plunder, and retire for the winter to their strongholds on the shores of the North and Baltic Seas. They came year after year in ever increasing numbers, until at last, from pirate bands in search of plunder, they grew into invading armies bent on conquest. They planted themselves at various points along the coast, and waged perpetual war with the English in the interior.

They even colonized the coast of Ireland, forcing the inhabitants back to their native bogs. From the reign of Egbert to that of Ethelred the Unready, a period of nearly two hundred years, the struggle between Saxon and Dane went on, ending as we shall see a little later, in the establishment of Danish rule.

Egbert was succeeded by Ethelwolf, a good and pious king, who was followed by his four sons in succession; Ethelbald, who died lamented by his people; Ethelbert, a vicious and unworthy king; Ethelred I, a brave soldier, under whom Alfred learned the art of war, and whom he succeeded.

Alfred the Great, 871 to 901 — 30 years. Saxon.

War with the Danes. During the early part of his reign, Alfred was engaged in constant warfare with the Danes. Defeated in battle after battle by the overwhelming number of his foes, he was compelled, for a time, to hide in a secluded spot in the swamps and forests of Somersetshire, still known as Athelney, or Prince's Island.* Wishing to learn the strength and arrangement of the Danish camp, he presented himself before Guthrum, the Danish king, disguised as a minstrel.

---

* Alfred, while a **refugee**, found temporary shelter in a herdsman's cottage. The herdsman's wife one day set him to watch some **cakes** that were baking over the fire; but Alfred, intent on mending his bow, let the cakes burn, and was sharply reproved by the indignant woman when she returned. The whole story may be a mere legend or come from an ancient ballad. There are two old Latin verses that quaintly express the good woman's alleged reproof:—

"*Urere quos cernis panes gyrare moraris,
Quum nimium gaudes hos manducare calentes.*"

"There, don't you see the cakes on fire? Then wherefore turn them not? You are glad enough to eat them when they are piping hot."

For several days he amused the unsuspicious Danes with harp and song, when, having gained the desired information, he disappeared as mysteriously as he had come. Putting himself at the head of his trusted followers, he made a sudden attack on the Danish camp and gained a signal victory.

By treaty, Guthrum and his followers received baptism, withdrew from Wessex, Alfred's native kingdom, and settled in the eastern districts as nominal vassals of the English king. Peace was broken after an interval of ten years by the arrival of Hastings, the famous sea-king, with a great fleet. Alfred once more took the field, and by his skill and genius the Danish fleet was captured, its army routed, and Hastings compelled to take refuge in France.

Alfred's Government. Peace being restored, Alfred devoted the few remaining years of his life to the better organization of his kingdom and the elevation of his people. He invited wise men of other nations to his court, and founded schools of learning, among them the University of Oxford. He translated into the English tongue, portions of the Scriptures, the history of Bede, the early English chronicler, and Latin works of merit, and thus gave an impulse to learning. He compiled a code of laws, chiefly from the systems of his predecessors, containing principles of the greatest value in modern jurisprudence. He organized a militia, and divided the country into counties, hundreds, and tens, after the old Saxon system, making each section responsible for the good behavior of its inhabitants. So complete and successful was his system of government, that violence and disorder disappeared from the land.

The boast is handed down to us that gold and jewels, left unguarded by the roadside, would remain untouched by dwellers or passers-by. As a soldier, statesman, and scholar, Alfred has never been surpassed by any English sovereign.

Alfred's Successors. He was succeeded, in order, by Edward the Elder, who first assumed the title of King of England,—Athelstan, a good and valiant king, who caused the Bible to be translated into Anglo-Saxon, and a copy placed in every church in the kingdom,—Edmund, who was stabbed at his own table by the banished robber, Leolf,—Edwy, whose romantic marriage with his beautiful cousin Elgiva brought upon both the vengeance of Dunstan the Abbot, Elgiva dying by violence, and Edwy with grief,—Edgar the proud but peaceable,—Edward the Martyr, young and promising, who was killed at the gate of Corfe Castle, by order of his step-mother,—and then by Ethelred the Unready.

Massacre of Danes. Ethelred, afraid to fight the Danes in an open and manly way, purchased peace by promising to pay them an annual tribute, called Danegelt, raised by a tax on land, the first on record in England. This tax proving very unpopular, Ethelred planned a massacre of all the Danes in the kingdom as the easiest way of getting rid of both Danegelt and Danes.

The Danish Conquest. This massacre took place on the Festival of St. Brice, in the year 1002, and so enraged Sweyn, king of Denmark, whose sister, a hostage of peace, was among the slain, that he assembled a large army, transported it to the English coast, and commenced the work of vengeance. Through and through the kingdom of Wessex went the furious Dane, "lighting his war beacons as he went," leaving behind him only the bodies of the dead and the ashes of their dwellings. Ethelred fled to France, and Sweyn became king of England, establishing the Danish line in the year 1013. Sweyn died before coronation, and for a short time, the Saxon line was restored in the person of Ethelred, and then in that of his son Edmund, called Ironside. Between the latter and Canute, son of Sweyn, there was a short and furious war to decide which should be king, ending in the division of the country between them. The death of Edmund soon after, led to the submission of all England to the rule of Canute.

Comparison between Saxon and Danish Conquests. A brief comparison should be made between the Saxon and Danish conquests. The Saxons and Danes were of the same Teutonic stock, and in their German homes spoke the same language with dialectical differences. They worshiped the same heathen gods, and had essentially the same laws and customs. The Saxons had, long before their invasion of Britain, roamed about the waters of the German ocean in fleets of black pirate-boats, swarming up all the rivers and scouring all the coasts in search of plunder. It was while they were on just such a piratical raid, that the Britons first obtained their help against the Scots and Picts.

So clouds of Danish pirates hovered about the English coast before the Danish invasion, plundering their somewhat civilized and christianized Saxon kindred. The Saxons were a century and a half in completing their conquest, the Danes somewhat longer in effecting theirs. There was the same savage ferocity in battle, and the same ruthless slaughter of the conquered. The Danes regarded the Saxons as renegades from their ancient faith, and so it was, in either case, a war of heathenism on Christianity.

But the final results were widely different. There was nothing in common between Briton and Saxon, and the war they waged was, on the part of the latter, one of extermination. But there was much in common between Saxon and Dane, and they could easily assimilate. The barbarism of the conquering Dane yielded to the civilization of the conquered Saxon, so that, in process of time, the former became, as it were, transformed into the latter.

CHAPTER III.

Danish Line, 1017 to 1042 — 25 years.

CANUTE THE GREAT. | HARDICANUTE.
HAROLD.

Canute the Great, 1017 to 1036 — 19 years. Danish.

The Reign of Canute. Canute well deserved to be called the Great. He enlarged his kingdom, then comprising England and Denmark, by bringing under his sway Norway and Sweden. But his chief claim to greatness rests not on his exploits in war, but his achievements in peace. Coming to England from his native Denmark a fierce and blood-thirsty savage, he became in time a good, wise, and great king, * impartial in his sway over Saxon and Dane. Peace and the welcome sounds of industry soon took the place of war and its horrid din. By wise and popular laws, rigidly but impartially executed, he united and harmonized the discordant kingdoms, and healed the animosities of the

---

* His courtiers, wishing to flatter him by exalting his power, once told him that he was lord alike of sea and land, and would be obeyed by both. Wishing to show them how foolish as well as impious these praises were, he gave orders that his throne should be carried to the sea-shore at Southampton, and sat down upon it while the tide was coming in. " Now," said he, " O sea, I am thy lord; come no nearer, presume not to wet my feet!" The waves, of course, instead of attending to him, rolled on, till they flowed around his throne and washed over his feet. Turning to his attendants, he bade them remember that there is only One who can say to the deep, "So far shalt thou go, and no further; and here shall thy proud waves be stayed." He afterwards hung up his crown over the altar in Winchester Cathedral, and never wore it again.

[YONGE.

different races, laying, for the first time, the foundations of national unity and greatness.

Canute and the Christian Church. Canute's treatment of the Christian church is worthy of notice. The barbarous Danes had been merciless in the destruction of churches and monasteries, and in the slaughter of their inmates; and, in consequence, all the powers of the church had been arrayed against them. Canute, on coming to power, instead of taking vengeance on the Christian church, yielded his heart to its holy faith, and became its friend and patron. He re-built and re-endowed the religious houses which he and his father had burned, and even protected Christian pilgrims journeying to Rome, from the robbers of the Alps. On the other hand, with a keen sense of justice, he protected his people from the exorbitant demands of the church itself. He died in 1036, lamented by all his people, and was succeeded by his son Harold, called Harefoot, whose only claim to fame was his swiftness in running; and then by his second son Hardicanute, or Canute II., who died of intemperance after a reign of two years. The people, disgusted with their later Danish rulers, then called to the throne Edward the Confessor, brother of Edmund Ironside, and son of Ethelred II., thus restoring the Saxon line.

Edward the Confessor, 1041 to 1066. — 25 Years.
Edward had spent all his early years in exile in Normandy, and thus naturally had become Norman in his tastes and habits. On coming to the English throne he surrounded himself with Norman companions, whom he appointed to the principal offices of church and

state, greatly to the discontent of the English people. But he had the wisdom to appoint, as his principal adviser, Godwin, Earl of Wessex, an Englishman, and the ablest statesman in the kingdom. Edward being in feeble health, Godwin became the virtual ruler of England, and by his skill and wisdom kept peace between the jealous English and the haughty Norman. Once exiled, he was soon recalled; and at his death, which occurred shortly after his return, his son Harold, who had inherited all his father's greatness, took his place at the head of the affairs of state.

Character of Edward. Edward was a wise and pious king, and caused England to be governed by just and equal laws. For generations afterwards the people, when ground down by tyranny, would look back with longings to the "good laws of Edward." His time was chiefly spent in deeds of charity and in the exercises of religion, and he attained to a purity and sanctity of character that, about a hundred years after his death, placed his name among those of the Saints in the calendar of the church, and that have hallowed his memory, even to this day. Edward was popularly believed to have the miraculous power to cure the scrofula, or "king's evil," by a touch,—a strange superstition in connection with the sovereign of England that found credence among the masses of the people, even down to the reign of Queen Anne. Edward had married a daughter of Godwin, but died without heirs in the year 1066. On his death-bed he named Harold as his successor, and the Witan the same day elected him as king.

William, Duke of Normandy. William, Duke of

Normandy, had been planning for years to take the English throne at the death of Edward. He affirmed that Edward, with whom he had been educated at his father's court, had even promised him the kingdom, and that Harold, when once wrecked on the coast of Normandy and thrown into William's power, had sworn to support his claim. However this may be, on hearing of Harold's election, William, "speechless with rage," at once commenced the most vigorous preparations to enforce his claim. He built a great fleet, and gathered about him an army of sixty thousand knights, the flower of the chivalry of Normandy; and having first obtained the Pope's sanction to the enterprise, crossed the channel, and landed on the coast of England, the last of September.

Battle of Hastings, A. D. 1066. William's merciless ravages of the adjoining country brought Harold to battle at Senlac,* near Hastings, about the middle of October. After a desperate struggle of nine hours' duration, just at dusk, Harold fell, pierced to the brain with an arrow, and his broken and panic-stricken army fled away during the night. William entered London in triumph, two months later, and was crowned, on Christmas day, at Westminster. This is called, in history, the Conquest.

* In commemoration of his victory, William built a Monastery called Battle Abbey, on the very spot where Harold's standard had been planted. Although this has long since passed away, its successor, in ruins, reminds the traveller of the famous battle of Hastings.

CHAPTER IV.

Norman Line, 1066 to 1154 — 88 Years.

WILLIAM I., the Conqueror.	HENRY I., Beauclerk.
WILLIAM II., Rufus.	STEPHEN.

William the Conqueror — 1066 to 1087. — 21 Years.

Rolf, the Dane. William was descended from Rolf, a Danish pirate, who, in 912, just after the time of Alfred the Great, had planted himself with his pirate crew, at the mouth of the river Seine. The king of France, being unable to dislodge him, finally, by treaty, gave him his daughter in marriage and a title to Normandy, in return for which Rolf agreed to receive baptism and acknowledge himself a vassal of France. In process of time, the same change befell the Danes in France that had befallen them in England; they were absorbed by the more civilized people among whom they settled. As in England the Dane became an Englishman, so in France he became a Frenchman.

Revolt of the English. Soon after William's accession to power, and during his temporary absence in Normandy, there was a wide-spread revolt of the English. The signal for the rising was the appearance on the coast, of a Danish fleet designed to restore Danish authority to the island. With a heavy bribe, the crafty William induced the Danish commanders to abandon their purpose and return to Denmark. He then turned upon the rebels in arms with a ferocity he only could show. He ravaged the sea-board so that no Dane should find either foothold or plunder in future, and laid waste with fire and sword the old district of Deira, between the Humber and the Tees, the source and centre of the rebellion. So complete was the devastation, that, for the space of sixty miles north of York, the whole district remained for half a century without an inhabitant, a barren waste, and marked only by blackened ruins. One hundred thousand human beings, who had fled to the woods at William's coming, crept back to the ashes of their homes, only to die of starvation. Although it was mid-winter when the cruel work was done, the ruthless king started at once for the West, where the revolt was still formidable. Through an unbroken wilderness, covered with drifts of snow, and crossed by swollen streams, the starving army toiled painfully on, with the tireless king ever at the head. Chester * was reached at last, and with its fall the rebellion virtually came to an end.

Confiscation of English Estates. Then commenced, under the direction of the revengeful king, a wholesale confiscation of rebel estates. These were distributed

---

* Chester is one of the most interesting as well as one of the oldest towns in England. It shows more plainly than any other the marks of the Roman occupation. It is the only town in England that has maintained its walls in their original form, the foundations of which were laid by the Romans themselves. Its long and interesting history is indicated by the following inscriptions, made from time to time upon its walls:

    A. D. 61. Walls built by Romans.
        73. Marius, King of the Britons, extended the walls.
       607. The Britons defeated by the Saxons.
       908. Rebuilt by daughter of Alfred the Great.
     1399. Henry of Lancaster mustered his troops under the walls.
     1645. The Parliamentary forces made a breach in the walls.

among the Norman knights and nobles who had fought around William's standard, while their former Saxon owners either found refuge in foreign lands, or, forming in hostile bands, waged a desultory warfare with their Norman conquerors. Hereward, a Saxon noble, retired to the isle of Ely, where, protected by almost impassable swamps, he long defied the Norman power. But William, building a causeway across the swamps, finally forced the valiant Saxon to surrender.

The Feudal System Established. The conquest of England now being complete, William turned his attention to the organization of the government, with a view to its security in the future. Normans were put into all places of power and trust. The military power of the government was based on the Feudal system that already prevailed in Spain, France, and Germany. Under this system, the great nobles were granted almost unlimited power over the persons and property of their tenants, on certain conditions, the most important of which was, that they should come to the support of the king with all their retainers in time of war. These nobles, generally living in strongly fortified castles, and constantly surrounded by devoted bodies of men-at-arms, thus became petty sovereigns, spending their time in the pleasures of the chase, or in making war on each other, and sometimes on the king himself. William erected the Feudal system in England as a bulwark to the throne; and such it was as against the conquered English. But when the spirit of disaffection crept into the Norman nobility, thus made powerful and independent, the Feudal system became its chief danger.

The Doomsday Book. For the better organization of the kingdom, and the more certain collection of its revenues, he ordered a great survey, the results of which were embodied in the "Doomsday Book," showing the ownership, extent, and productions of all the estates in the kingdom. From this register the crown dues were carefully calculated and rigidly collected.

The Curfew Bell. William established the curfew (fire-covering) bell. This was rung from every church-tower and monastery in England, at sunset in summer, and at eight o'clock in winter, as a signal for the people to cover the fires on the hearth, and retire to rest. The law of the curfew had long prevailed in various parts of Europe as a safeguard against conflagrations, which were frequent and extensive in the wood-built towns.

The Norman Language. After the Saxon rebellion, Normans had been put into all responsible places, both of church and state. Of necessity, therefore, all the business of the government and courts of justice, the services of the church, except such as regularly employed Latin, and the exercises of the schools, were conducted in the Norman language. Norman thus came largely into use, even among English people; but the English masses still continued to talk in their Anglo-Saxon tongue. It is said that William tried, though in vain, to learn the Anglo-Saxon language, that he might be the better qualified to govern his whole people.

Character of William the Conqueror. Reserved, haughty, severe in his rule, and ruthless in his revenge, "stark to baron or rebel," but "mild to them that loved God," he inspired a mingled sense of respect and awe in all about him. This sense was heightened, no doubt, by a consciousness of his great physical strength, no ordinary man being able to swing his battle-axe or bend his bow. There was a grandeur about the Conqueror that belongs to no other English king, as manifest in his fearless humanity as in his dauntless ferocity. If, with a ferocity that finds few parallels in all history, he blotted out rebellious towns, and brought the silence of death upon offending districts, with a humanity in striking contrast with the spirit of the age, he formally abolished capital punishment, and but one person suffered death for crime during his whole reign.

To gratify his love of solitude and his fondness for the chase, he laid waste an extensive tract in Hampshire, reaching from Winchester to the sea, driving out its inhabitants and burning their dwellings and churches. But he also abolished the slave trade that had long been a source of wealth to the merchants of Bristol, and became the friend and patron of the Jews, then a hated race, allowing them to build dwellings and synagogues in all the principal towns.

He was a true Catholic, and strengthened the church by the establishment of ecclesiastical courts, afterwards, in the reign of Henry II., the source of so much trouble; but he bluntly refused to obey the command of the pope to do fealty for his realm. If he removed English prelates and abbots, he required of their Norman successors the most exemplary lives, and instantly dismissed those found unworthy.

Although he could not brook opposition, and was like a raging lion to all who withstood him, there was one man, Anselm, the good abbot of Bec, in whose presence he always became gentle and patient.

William's end was characteristic. He died on an errand of vengeance. He had become corpulent during the latter part of his life; and once, when ill, had been made the subject of a silly jest on the part of the king of France. William took it to heart, and, on his recovery, commenced to lay waste the border lands of France. While riding through the burning town of Mantes, his horse reared among the hot embers that filled the road, and he received injuries from the pommel of his saddle that terminated, in a few weeks, in his death, at Rouen. He left the kingdom of England to his second son William, called Rufus or the Red King, from the color of his hair. To Robert, the eldest son, set aside on account of a rebellion in which he had engaged, he gave the dukedom of Normandy. William's wife was Matilda,* daughter of the Earl of Flanders, through whom the present royal house of England traces its descent from Egbert.

---

* Ethelwolf, eldest son of Egbert, had by his first wife four sons, Alfred the Great being the youngest. His second wife was Judith, daughter of Charles the Bald of France. He was succeeded by his son Ethelbald, who also married Judith, his father's widow. At Ethelbald's death Judith went back to her father's court and eloped with Baldwin, afterwards Earl of Flanders. Their son married Elfrida, daughter of Alfred the Great, and from them sprang Matilda, wife of William the Conqueror.

The famous "Bayeux Tapestry" was the handiwork of Matilda. This was a piece of canvas sixty-eight yards long and nineteen inches wide, on which were embroidered in wool, scenes and figures, giving a complete pictorial history of the Conquest.

William II. 1087 to 1100 — 13 years. Norman.

Rebellion of the Barons. William II. was greeted, on his arrival in England, with a rebellion of the barons in behalf of Robert. By the aid of the English, whom he rallied to his support by the promise of good laws — a promise that was forgotten as soon as the danger was past — the rebellion was quelled. Still another attempt was made by the barons, later in the reign, to dethrone the king and put in his place, Stephen, a grandson of the Conqueror; but this, too, failed, for the Red King proved himself every inch a soldier and equal to any emergency.

Character of William II. In personal courage, violence of temper, and strength of will, he was the equal of the Conqueror himself, but in all the higher moral qualities he was greatly his inferior. He was coarse and profane in speech, mean and covetous in disposition, and prodigal and licentious in his habits. He kept his ministers busy devising means to wring new taxes from his people.

By a law of the realm, the revenues of vacant sees and abbeys went to the crown. The Red King refused to fill vacancies that occurred during his reign, that he might appropriate their incomes, thus robbing the church of its rights, and the people of religious privileges. The money thus obtained went to gratify his desire for debasing pleasures, and to enrich worthless courtiers. He was twice engaged in hostilities with Malcolm, King of Scotland, compelling the latter to do him homage as his superior.

The Red King met with a tragic death while hunting in the new forest which his father had made. He was found pierced to the brain with an arrow, whether by design or accident was never known. But he is supposed to have been killed by Walter Tyrrel, one of the king's party, who immediately fled from the country. He was succeeded by his younger brother Henry, Robert the elder brother not having returned from the Holy Land, whither he had gone on a Crusade.

The Crusades. The reign of William II. marks the beginning of the Crusades. These were military expeditions, undertaken on a large scale by the Christian nations of Europe, to free the Holy Land from the rule and presence of the Saracen. Christians from all countries, since the fourth century, had made long and painful pilgrimages to the Holy Sepulchre at Jerusalem, either as a penance for sin, or as a means of attaining to greater piety; but they had been subjected to such dangers and indignities from the predatory infidel, that the Crusades were undertaken as a religious duty.

They began in the year 1096, under the lead and preaching of a monk named Peter the Hermit (who had himself suffered while on a pilgrimage), and continued, at intervals, through a period of two centuries, sacrificing, it is computed, two millions of lives, and leaving the Holy Land still in the hands of the Saracen.

The Benefits of the Crusades. Though failing to accomplish their primal object, the Crusades were productive of great good in other directions. They brought the Christian nations into greater harmony with each other by uniting them in a common cause, and into immediate contact with the East, making them familiar with its arts, institutions, and laws, and opening to them its rich and varied commerce. They caused the construction of numerous vessels for the transportation of crusaders, thus stimulating ship-building and navigation, and ultimately turning men's attention from the arts of war to those of peace. They enlisted and sent abroad the dangerous and turbulent elements, for the most part never to return, thus purifying and making society at home safer and more peaceful. They struck the first great blow at the Feudal system, by compelling the nobles to sell or divide their great estates to raise money for their outfit. Finally they gave birth to the spirit and system of Chivalry, whose value at this period, the darkest of the Dark Ages, can hardly be over-estimated.

The System of Chivalry. Christianity had to a great extent lost its power; and superstition, gross and degrading, reigned supreme. War with all its unmeasured depths of vice and crime and woe, was the pastime of kings or the mere instrument of personal ambition and passion, and even peace, when it came, instead of bringing new life to art and industry, left men to sink into a more degrading ignorance and a still grosser superstition. During the Middle Ages spiritual darkness brooded over all the nations. Sleep, like the sleep of death, rested on the human intellect. The spirit of Chivalry was light breaking upon the long and dreadful night, a clarion note awaking the world from the sleep of ages. It appealed to the nobler sentiments of the soul, inspiring the love of truth, honor, and religion, and enjoining the practice of courtesy, chastity, and humanity.

Though, with its solemn oath, imposed on all who aspired to its honors, and its iron garb, the insignia of knightly character, it could not always transform rude and brutal men into true and chivalric knights, it did place upon rudeness and brutality a needed and effective check. Who can estimate its worth to *woman*, in the protection it gave her, through those long and gloomy ages, when sensual pleasure was the chief aim, and brute force the highest law, known to most men?

The *system* of chivalry, both ludicrous and impractical in some of its features, when viewed from the standpoint of the nineteenth century, passed away before an advancing civilization; but its *spirit*, enlarged and purified by true religion, still exists in the enlightened public sentiment of modern times.

Henry I., 1100 to 1135 — 35 Years. Norman.

First Charter of Liberties. Henry I., surnamed Beauclerc the Scholar, was clearly a usurper. Being opposed by the barons, who espoused the cause of Robert, now on his way home from Palestine, Henry following the example of William, fell back on the support of the English. He gave them a Charter of Liberties, in which he restored the laws of Edward, renounced the right to plunder the church by allowing its sees and abbeys to remain vacant, and shielded the people from the unjust exactions of their lords, the barons.

To conciliate the English still further, he married Matilda, or Maud,* as the English loved to call her, a descendant of Edmund Ironside, thus uniting the Saxon and Norman families.

Robert, Duke of Normandy. The enthusiasm of the English masses, at the elevation of an English princess to the throne, was unbounded, and when Robert landed in England, and raised his standard as the rightful heir to the crown, he found himself, face to face, with sixty thousand resolute English yeomen, and surrendered to Henry without a battle. A treaty was made between the brothers, Robert yielding all claims to the crown, for a pension for himself and pardon for all his followers. And now occurs the darkest act of Henry's reign. Robert had no sooner returned to Normandy, and the barons dispersed to their castles, than commenced under Henry's direction the confiscation of the estates of all implicated in the rebellion. The chivalric Robert, indignant at the treachery of his brother, at once called his retainers to arms and renewed the war. The king, claiming that the treaty had been broken, invaded Normandy, defeated Robert's army, took Robert himself prisoner, and doomed him to life-long confinement within the walls of Cardiff Castle. It is affirmed that having once attempted to escape, Henry caused his eyes to be put out with a hot iron. This noblest of the sons of the

---

*When Canute seized the crown in 1017, he sent the infant sons of Edmund Ironside to Germany.

The Confessor on coming to the throne, twenty-four years later, invited Edward, the only surviver of these sons, to return to England. Edward died soon after his arrival, and his family, at the coming of William the Conqueror, took refuge in Scotland, where his daughter Margaret married King Malcolm. Maud was the offspring of this marriage.

Conqueror lingered twenty-nine years in sightless confinement, dying, at last, in his dungeon an old man of eighty years.

Character and Reign of Henry. Henry's character was a strange admixture of virtues and vices. He was unscrupulous, false-hearted, and revengeful, but he promoted the welfare of his people, encouraged manufactures, improved the coinage, established a system of weights and measures, repealed the odious law of the Curfew, and re-organized the courts of justice. Henry's system of justice, with modifications and improvements, is the system of to-day, both in England and America. He dealt a heavy blow at the Feudal system, and gave an impulse to liberty, when he endowed the great towns with charters of freedom.

The White Ship. The last years of Henry's life were sad and gloomy, on account of the death by shipwreck, of his only son, Prince William. They had been on a visit to Normandy, to secure the acknowledgment of the Prince as heir to the crown, and to complete his marriage contract with the daughter of the Count of Anjou. Both matters being satisfactorily arranged, they embarked for the return, on different ships. The White Ship, in which William had taken passage, being delayed, attempted to overtake the rest of the fleet by moonlight. Speeding swiftly along under the sweep of its fifty rowers, it struck on a rock in the race of Alderney and went to the bottom. Only a single soul escaped to tell the sad tale to the bereaved father, who is said never to have smiled again.

Henry left a daughter Matilda, whom he had married to Geoffrey Plantagenet, Earl of Anjou, to strengthen his possessions beyond the channel. Before she could return to England to take the crown that belonged to her, it was seized by Stephen, Count of Blois, nephew of the late king. Affable in his manners and familiar in his address, Stephen had made himself a general favorite with the people of the capital, and so paved his way to power.

– **Stephen, 1135 to 1154 — 19 years. Norman.**

Civil War. Matilda endeavored to secure her rights by force of arms. David, King of Scotland, was the first to espouse her cause. With an army of wild and lawless highlanders, he invaded the northern counties, inflicting havoc alike on the friends and foes of Matilda. Against this army of marauders, the Archbishop of York took the field, and, in the battle of the Standard, put them to utter rout and drove them across the border. Matilda herself reached England the next year with a small force, and her adherents quickly gathered to her support. In the battle of Lincoln the army of Stephen was defeated, and Stephen himself captured and sent, in chains, to Bristol Castle.

Matilda entered London and was acknowledged queen of England. But her haughty manners and violent temper, so much in contrast with the generous and good natured ways of Stephen, soon changed even her friends to foes. The rapid approach of Stephen's heroic queen at the head of an army, and the ringing of the alarm bells in London, having caused a sudden uprising of the people, Matilda fled, in haste, from the city, and took refuge within the walls of Oxford Castle.

Stephen, once more at liberty and at the head of his army, in 1142, surrounded her place of refuge, so disposing his men as, apparently, to cut off every avenue of escape. The garrison ran short of provisions, and Matilda with three devoted knights, clad like herself in white to resemble the snow that covered the ground (for it was mid-winter), passed silently through the lines of Stephen's army in the night, crossed the frozen Thames, and found refuge among the loyal people of the west, whence, four years later, she withdrew to France. Her son Henry had now grown up to manhood. Possessed, by inheritance and marriage, of the larger part of France, he collected an army of his own subjects, crossed the channel, and re-opened the war with Stephen.

Compromise Between Stephen and Henry. But the bishops of England, under the lead of Theobald, Archbishop of Canterbury, weary of a struggle that had brought such fearful waste, and to which they could see no end, finally, in 1153, effected the treaty of Wallingford. It was mutually agreed that the crown should remain with Stephen while he lived, and descend to Henry at his death. It was also decided that the grants of crown lands made by Stephen should be cancelled, the new castles demolished, and the foreign troops dismissed.

The Robber Barons. Two things influenced Stephen to consent to this arrangement, the death of his eldest son, and the defection of his principal nobles, some of whom had turned against him, while more had abandoned the contest and retired to their estates. We find here a practical illustration of the workings of the

Feudal system. To win the support of the barons, Stephen had, at the beginning of his reign, given them permission to build new castles on their estates, besides granting new titles of nobility to his chosen adherents. One hundred and twenty-six fortresses were thus erected, many of them of great strength and frowning from inaccessible heights. Secure in these, the barons lived like petty princes, defying the authority of the king, and renewing old family quarrels. They plundered the country around their estates, and taxed its inhabitants till famine stared them in the face. Even churches were robbed of their wealth. The rich were waylaid as they journeyed, and held or tortured for ransom. These nobles have gained in history the well-deserved title of Robber Barons.

The Outlaws of the Forest. Following their example, criminals and outcasts, unemployed soldiers and starving peasants, everywhere took to the woods and became outlaws, making it dangerous to travel in some districts without an armed escort. Banded together, sometimes in large numbers, they set laws and authorities at defiance, or, retreating to their hiding places in the dense recesses of the forest, were safe from pursuit. While many of these bandits were rude and ruthless men, sparing neither age nor sex, others were generous and courteous, robbing the rich to relieve the wants of the poor. Such was Robin Hood, the very prince of bandits, who, some fifty years later, in the reign of Richard I., with a hundred free and jovial companions, occupied the depths of the Sherwood forest.

It is difficult to depict the anarchy and misery to which England was reduced in the reign of Stephen.

Towns were abandoned, farms were left to decay, the sanctuaries were crowded with helpless, starving people, and thousands fled, in terror, to foreign countries.

Stephen lived but a year after the treaty of Wallingford, and Henry, quietly and unopposed, assumed the crown. Having both Saxon and Norman blood in his veins, a new name, that of his father, Plantagenet,* was given to the royal line he founded.

*The name Plantagenet is derived from *Planta Genista*, a common shrub called broom, which the first Earl of Anjou wore as an emblem, while on a pilgrimage to the Holy Land.

CHAPTER V.

Plantagenet Family, 1154 to 1485 — 331 Years.

HENRY II.	EDWARD II., of Caernarvon.
RICHARD I., Cœur-de-Lion.	EDWARD III.
JOHN., Lackland.	RICHARD II., of Bordeaux.
HENRY III., of Winchester.	HOUSE OF LANCASTER.
EDWARD I.	HOUSE OF YORK.

Henry II., 1154 to 1189 — 35 years.   Plantagenet.

The Condition of England. No king ever mounted the English throne under circumstances more peculiar, and, in some respects, more appalling, than greeted the first Plantagenet on his accession to power. During the reign of Stephen, the entire fabric of society had fallen to pieces, and both regard for law and respect for religion had been swept away in the general wreck. Beginning with the nobility, the spirit of lawlessness had permeated the priesthood and the peasantry. It is no wonder the helpless peasant either became an outlaw, or, in consternation, abandoned home and harvest-field and fled beyond seas, when priest and noble turned robber! This was the peculiar and appalling aspect of the case, that the best and highest elements in society had become, for the time being, most demoralized. Henry, though but twenty-one years of age when he ascended the throne, undertook the work of reconstruction with a courage and an intelligence that challenge our admiration. His efforts were mainly directed to the accomplishment of two distinct ends, the establishment of order, and the correction of the abuses of the church.

The Establishment of Order. The Robber Barons were, one after another, subdued, and their castles razed to the ground; and the less noble, but no worse, highwaymen, the forest outlaws, were mercilessly hunted down. The crown lands were also reclaimed, and foreign soldiers expelled. To increase the power of the crown, and weaken that of the baronage still more, two sweeping edicts were issued. One, in 1159, substituted the payment of money, called "shield money," for the personal services of the barons in time of war, enabling the king to keep a paid and standing force. The other, in 1181, restored the militia, making every freeman a soldier, always to be suitably armed, and subject to the call of the king in time of national danger.

Contest between Church and State. Henry's contest with the church was not only more difficult, but more dangerous, than that with the barons. Anciently, judges and bishops sat together on the civil benches, but the Conqueror had established separate courts for ecclesiastical cases, over which the bishops presided alone. Criminals in holy orders were thus put beyond the reach of the civil authorities, and as, by a canon of the church, the priesthood could not impose the death penalty upon one of their own order, these priestly criminals were also put beyond the reach of extreme punishment. It is not surprising that the church had grown arrogant and independent, or that one hundred murders were proved to have been committed, during the first few years of Henry's reign, by priests, who either suffered no punishment, or one not at all commensurate with the crime. They merely suffered some trifling penance or degradation in office.

The Council of Clarendon. At the summons of the king, a council of nobles and prelates met at the castle of Clarendon in 1164. It was decided by this council, among other things, that the civil courts should have a certain jurisdiction over the church courts, and that law-breaking priests, on conviction in the latter, should be stripped of their orders and turned over to the civil authorities for punishment.

Thomas à Becket and King Henry. Thomas à Becket had been Henry's bosom friend and companion. Henry had raised him from poverty to affluence, from the position of tutor to his children, to that of Archbishop of Canterbury, the highest office of the church in England. Becket at first accepted, then rejected, the "Constitutions of Clarendon;" and then began that long and bitter struggle between himself and the king, in which personal animosities are strangely mingled with the graver affairs of church and state, ending in the violent death of Becket in 1170, and the ultimate triumph of the king. The priesthood and the laity were made equal before the law. The supremacy of the state over the church was achieved. Although, after the death of Becket, the king assented to a modification of the "Constitutions," it was merely nominal, the practice of the courts and the submission of the bishops showing that the king still retained all the substantial fruits of victory.

The Death of Thomas à Becket. The death of Becket was tragic. Four knights in attendance on the king in Normandy, interpreting too seriously his rash and impatient wish "to be rid of the turbulent priest," silently left the royal presence, and secretly crossed the English Channel. Making their way to the gray old Cathedral of Canterbury,—where shortly before, on Christmas day, Becket, sad but undismayed, had preached to the peasantry from the text "I come to die among you,"— the knightly assassins, backed by their followers, murdered him before his own altar. A cry of horror arose from all Christendom. For the first time during the bitter struggle Henry bent before the storm. He disclaimed all responsibility for the crime, and afterwards publicly expressed his sorrow for its commission, by walking barefooted to the tomb of Becket, and submitting his back to the scourge of the monks; and the threatened excommunication was averted. The guilty knights went on a pilgrimage to Jerusalem, where they died; and on their tomb was inscribed this epitaph, "Here lie the wretches who murdered St. Thomas of Canterbury."

The Judiciary System. One of the most interesting works of Henry's reign was the improvement of the judiciary system founded by Henry I. England was divided into six judicial districts, each with three itinerant judges, who went regularly on their circuits, having jurisdiction alike over peasant and noble. The most radical change was made in the form of trial. The Anglo-Saxons brought with them, from Germany, a form of trial called Compurgation. A person charged with crime was acquitted or convicted, according as his kinsmen or neighbors, generally twelve, or some multiple of twelve, in number, made oath to his innocence or guilt. Another and very singular method of trial was called the Judgment of God. Among other things, if a suspected person could carry a bar of red hot iron a certain distance, or plunge his hand into boiling water, and in three days show no scar, he was pronounced innocent, otherwise, guilty. Sometimes he was thrown into deep water, and if he sank he was innocent, if he swam, guilty. The Conqueror introduced Wager of Battle, or Single Combat. An accused person was allowed to challenge his accuser to mortal combat, and if he came out of the fight victorious he was declared innocent, otherwise, guilty.

Trial by Jury. "The first clear beginnings" of Trial by Jury are found in the reign of Henry II, when, by the Assize of Clarendon, in 1166, twelve freemen chosen from the hundred, and four from each township, acting in the two-fold capacity of judges and witnesses, presented reputed criminals for the Ordeal of Battle, or the Judgment of God. By the same Assize, Compurgation was abolished.*

---

*Trial by Jury has generally been attributed to Alfred the Great, but there is every reason to believe that the Jury trials in Alfred's time were, like those of all other Saxon kings, trials of Compurgation. Haydn makes the following statement, illustrating the fact that juries of twelve men existed before Alfred's time. "In a cause tried at Hawarden, nearly a hundred years before the reign of Alfred, we have a list of twelve jurors; confirmed too, by the fact that the descendants of one of them of the name of Corbyn of the Gate, still preserve their name and residence at a spot in the parish yet called the Gate." At the Fourth Council of Lateran held at Rome in 1216, Henry III. being King of England, all Ordeals were abolished, and went rapidly out of use. † After a brief interval of uncertainty as to the method of trial and punishment in England, the *Petit* or *Trial Jury* came into use. In the reign of Edward I, persons having particular knowledge of the facts in any case, were added to the jury. In the reign of Edward IV, a division was made, the origi-

Conquest of Ireland. In this reign Ireland was conquered by Strongbow, Earl of Pembroke, and added to Henry's dominions; but the English authority was lightly regarded for a hundred years to come.

Henry's Rebellious Sons. The last years of Henry's life were greatly embittered by estrangement from his wife and children. He had five sons, William, Henry, Geoffrey, Richard, and John. Encouraged by their mother, who was a divorced wife of Louis VI., a former king of France, and also by Louis VII., the present king (whose daughter Prince Henry had married), these unnatural sons repeatedly attempted the overthrow of their father. In one of these attempts, in 1173, they were aided by William, King of Scotland. It was just at this time that King Henry, to propitiate divine favor, performed his penance at the tomb of à Becket. King William was captured the very day the royal penance

---

nal jurors ceasing to be special witnesses, though they still made use of their personal knowledge of the facts in making up a verdict, and the added witnesses ceasing to be jurors. From this time witnesses simply gave testimony, and the jurors decided whether it was sufficiently grave to warrant an indictment of the accused. This is our modern *Grand Jury*. Henry II. restored the *King's Court*. After the Great Charter this court was divided into three distinct courts, the *King's Bench*, *Exchequer* and *Common Pleas*, which in the reign of Edward I. came to have distinct judges. On account of the corruption that gradually crept into the Circuit Courts established by Henry, he authorized an appeal from their decisions to the King in Council, thus forming a *Court of Appeals*, from which has sprung the *Privy Council*, now an important element in the government.

† Though Wager of Battle was abolished by the Catholic Council, the English Statute authorizing it was not repealed, and it still remained a legal form of trial, occasionally resorted to, especially while the age of Chivalry lasted. The last instance of its use in England is of comparatively modern date. In 1817, reign of George III., a young maid was believed to have been murdered by one Abraham Thompson, who, in an appeal, claimed his right to Wager of Battle, which the court allowed. He challenged the brother of the maid to mortal combat, but the latter refusing to fight, the accused man, in accordance with the old statute, was at once set at liberty. But the next year the law of Single Combat was stricken from the Statute Book.

was completed, and was not released until he consented to acknowledge himself a vassal of the English crown. It was on this acknowledgment that Edward I., afterwards based his claim to the sovereignty of Scotland.

In their last attempt, Henry was compelled to submit to the most humiliating terms. After the treaty of peace was signed, the king, who was sick in bed, asked to see the list of rebels he had agreed to pardon, and the first name that met his eye was that of John, his youngest and his favorite son. He turned his face to the wall, heart-broken, saying, "Now let the world go as it will, I care for nothing more." He died soon after, and was succeeded by his eldest surviving son, Richard.

Richard I., 1189 to 1199 — 10 years.   Plantagenet.

Slaughter of Jews. Richard's inauguration took place in the midst of a cruel slaughter of Jews. They had come to the coronation with rich gifts to propitiate the royal favor. A cry having gone forth that the king had decreed their death, they were beset by an ignorant and blood-thirsty rabble. Blood once shed, passions once inflamed, these hated but helpless people were mercilessly slaughtered, and their dwellings burned, throughout the city. As the news spread from town to town, the same terrible scenes were enacted, the same horrible butchery of innocent people. At York, five hundred Jews, with their families, took refuge in the Castle, which was speedily surrounded by an armed force. The Jews vainly offered their wealth as a ransom for their lives. Having no hope of mercy, they plunged their daggers into the bodies of their own wives and children, rather than see them fall into the hands of their infuriated enemies. Richard had accepted their gifts, but, though he issued a proclamation in their favor, he took no adequate measures for their protection.

Richard in the Holy Land. The Christian nations were preparing for the third Crusade. Richard and Philip of France arranged to go in company, at the head of their forces. To raise sufficient money for his outfit, Richard freely offered for sale the lands of the crown, besides titles, offices, and pardons. At the rebuke of one of his friends, on account of his wholesale disposal of crown property, he is said to have exclaimed, "I would sell London, if I could find a purchaser."

His career in the Holy Land is full of the stirring incidents of battle and adventure. He captured Acre and defeated Saladin, the great Saracen, at Ascalon. Philip, jealous of Richard's growing fame, abandoned the Crusade and returned to France. John, Richard's brother, probably instigated by Philip, usurped the government of England, and was planning to seize the crown, when Richard, alarmed for the safety of his kingdom, prepared to return home. Effecting a treaty with Saladin, by which pilgrims could visit the Holy Sepulchre unmolested, Richard reluctantly turned his back upon Jerusalem, the goal of many hopes, whose walls were, indeed, in sight, but within which he was destined never to enter.

Richard a Captive in the Tyrol. Being wrecked in the Adriatic, and attempting to make his way overland to England to escape the cruisers of Philip, he fell into the hands of his enemy, the Emperor of Germany. After lying a captive for more than a year, in the Tyrol, he was released on the payment by the English people of one hundred thousand marks, as ransom. The English people were reduced to the greatest distress to raise the money, the churches even melting down their plate. Richard returned, in 1194, after an absence of **four years.** "Take care of yourself," wrote Philip to John, who hastened to leave the country. But returning at Richard's command, he confessed on his knees his traitorous designs, and humbly asked for pardon. Said Lion Heart with characteristic generosity, "I hope I shall as easily forget his ingratitude, as he will, my forbearance."

War with France and Death of Richard. Richard remained in England a few months, and then crossed the Channel to wage war with Philip. Learning that the Viscount of Limoges, one of his vassals, had found hidden treasure in one of his fields, Richard demanded its surrender, under the common law that made treasure-trove the property of the Crown. The demand was refused, and Richard at once besieged the Viscount in his castle of Chalus. During the siege he received a mortal wound, and died, as he had lived, in armor. Though ten years' king of England, he had spent less than one in his kingdom.

Character of Richard I. Richard the Lion Heart was a valiant and romantic knight, who loved tilts and tournaments better than royal courts, daring deeds on hard-fought battle-fields, than the irksome cares and dry details of government. His very name, embalmed in song and story, has become a synonym for Chivalry. In Richard, the king was subordinate to the knight, and since he made so poor a king, it would, doubtless, please the young who may read this book, could we represent him as, at least, a model knight, famous for humanity and true nobility, as well as matchless valor. But beneath Richard's iron armor there beat a hard, cold, selfish heart. Though fearless of danger and mighty in battle, courteous to a gallant enemy and generous to a fallen foe, a skilled musician and familiar with the songs of the Troubadours, Richard was brutal and unscrupulous, and stained his knightly honor by many a dark and cruel deed. He cared little for the happiness or welfare of his people, the power to gratify an inordinate love of military glory and daring adventure being the limit of his ambition. Though dazzled by his brilliant personal qualities, and proud of his world-wide renown, England mingled a sense of relief with a sigh of regret, when her roving soldier-king, whose genius had both impoverished and glorified her, rested forever at Fontevrault.

John., 1199 to 1216 — 17 years. Plantagenet.

Character of John. John, the craven-heart, was as base and cowardly, as Richard the Lion Heart was generous and knightly. He had, indeed, a brazen boldness in the midst of safety, but it quickly vanished at the presence of danger. Though grossly impious in his treatment of the sacred rites of the church, he was childishly superstitious, wearing charms and relics about his person as a safeguard against evil. Other English kings have been corrupt, but there is no king in all the list so basely licentious as he.

Loss of Possessions in France. He is generally believed to have murdered, with his own hand, his nephew Arthur, a boy of fifteen and the rightful heir to the throne, and to have kept Eleanor, sister to Arthur, in close confinement, till she wasted away and died. In retaliation for his treatment of Arthur, he was stripped of all his possessions on the continent by the king of France, and was ever after called Lackland. To recover them, he raised a large army and invaded the territories of France. When the opposing armies were on the eve of battle, John proposed peace, and ignominiously fled to England in the very midst of negotiations.

John's Quarrel with the Pope. John quarrelled with the pope about the appointment of an Archbishop of Canterbury. He had secured the election, by the monks, of John de Gray, but Pope Innocent III. appointed Stephen Langton. The monks, submitting to the decision of their superior and recognizing Langton, were turned out of doors and reduced to beggary by the enraged tyrant.

The Papal Interdict. He made light of the papal threat to lay the kingdom under an Interdict, and when it fell, in 1208, with all its horrors, upon the land, he alone seemed insensible to the blow. The pope waited one year, and then issued against John, who still remained obdurate, a bull of excommunication. Even this had no terrors for John, and in about three years more was launched against him the last and crowning decree of the church, that of Deposition. * Philip of France was specially commissioned with the execution of this final decree.

John's Submission to the Pope. For a while John continued defiant. But when Philip had assembled a great army ready for invasion, with seventeen hundred ships for its transportation across the channel, and the elements of opposition at home were beginning to gather like a dark cloud about him, his bravado forsook him, and his submission to the pope was as abject and pitiful as it was sudden and complete.

Said William the Conqueror, when Pope Gregory VII. called on him to do fealty for his realm, "Fealty I have never willed to do, nor do I will to do it now. I have never promised it, nor do I find that my predecessors did it to yours." Every true Englishman experienced a share of the national shame, when the degenerate descendant of the Conqueror, on his knees, at the feet of the papal legate, acknowledged himself a vassal, and his kingdom a fief of the Papacy. It was

---

*It is difficult to realize at this day the horrors of the Papal Interdict. To the people, it was nothing less than the curse of God. All England was at once plunged into deepest gloom, for the blessings and benedictions of religion were suddenly withdrawn from all except the unconscious infant and the dying. For four long years it was as though a pestilence had swept over the land. The churches were closed, and their bells hung motionless in the belfries. "No knell was tolled for the dead; for the dead remained unburied. No merry peals welcomed the bridal procession; for no couple could be joined in wedlock."

Excommunication adds but little to the miseries entailed by the Interdict, except to the one who suffers it. According to the tenets of the church and universal belief at that age, an excommunicated person was cut off from all hope of Heaven as well as all fellowship in the church on earth.

The decree of Deposition absolved the people from their allegiance, the throne being declared vacant. It was made lawful and Christian for any man to kill a deposed king.

the first and the last time, in its history of a thousand years, that a king of England surrendered to a foreign potentate the independence of his country.

Magna Charta, A.D. 1215. With John's submission, the papal decrees were recalled, and the French invasion stayed. Elated at the ease with which he had escaped the threatened danger, and relying on the support of the pope, whose servant he had become, John next undertook to punish the barons for refusing to join him in a fresh war with France. Three years of royal outrage brought affairs to a crisis. A league, formed in secret among the barons, culminated in a general muster of their forces, and John suddenly found himself face to face with all England in arms.

At a conference on an island in the Thames, John was forced to assent to the terms of the barons, and the next day, in the valley of Runnymede, signed the Magna Charta, the most remarkable instrument known in English history. It was not entirely new. Some of its most important principles can be traced to Anglo-Saxon origin, having been set aside by the Norman conquest. Others were brought from the reigns of the Henries, but all were made more broad and liberal and couched in more explicit terms. The two most important sections run as follows:—

Section 45. "No freeman shall be taken, or disseized, or outlawed, or banished, or anywise injured, nor will we pass upon him, nor send upon him, unless by the legal judgment of his peers, or by the law of the land."

Section 46. "We will sell to no man, we will not deny or delay to any man, right or justice."

In other sections, the royal prerogative was limited and defined; the rights of the church guaranteed; the Feudal system relieved of some of its grievances; unlawful fines and punishments forbidden; the free disposal of personal property by will allowed; the means of obtaining a livelihood, such as the tools of the mechanic and the goods of the merchant, were exempt from fine or forfeiture for crime; fines were to be proportioned to the offence; the circuit courts brought into the neighborhood of all, and the liberties and customs of free towns confirmed.

So far only freemen were benefited. The larger part of the people of England were serfs, and but two sections related directly to them. In one of these, agricultural implements were exempt from fine or forfeiture on account of crime, and in the other, guardians were charged, in the management of the property of their wards, "to make no destruction or waste of the *men* and *things.*"

Such is a partial notice of the Great Charter, called by Hallam "the keystone of English liberty." The people of England did not realize, for hundreds of years to come, all the benefits conferred by the Great Charter. Its provisions were often ignored and openly trodden under foot by John and his successors, but the great principles of justice and liberty which they embodied were never forgotten by the people. They became, amidst the oppressions of after times, the centres around which clustered national hopes, the goal towards which were directed national efforts. They were so many beacon lights in an almost shoreless sea of misrule, guiding an oppressed people in their struggle for freedom. They are to-day the basis and the bulwark of those rights and immunities that make England and America the most free and happy countries on the earth.

Patriotism of the Bishops of England. The rest of John's ignoble history is soon told. He surrounded himself with foreign soldiers, for the double purpose of taking vengeance on the barons, who had been the authors, and were now the guardians, of the Charter, and of overthrowing the Charter itself. John was assisted by the pope, who as over-lord of England annulled the Charter, and excommunicated all who sustained it. The patriotism of Archbishop Langton and most of the bishops of the English church, at this period, should never be forgotten. Langton himself became the leader of the barons in their opposition to the tyranny of John and the assumptions of the pope. He first presented to them, at a preliminary meeting, the charter of Henry I., as a basis for their demands. The bishops and the barons stood side by side at Runnymede, alike indifferent to the execrations of the king and the anathemas of the pope. In the midst of the contest, John suddenly died. Overtaken by the incoming tide, as he was crossing a treacherous place by the sea-side, called the Wash, his treasure and material were swept away, and his army thrown into confusion. Vexation and exposure, or, as some think, poison administered by a monk at the abbey where John found shelter, threw him into a fever, of which he died in a few days. His son Henry, a youth of ten years, was at once crowned King of England.

—Henry III., 1216 to 1272 — 56 Years. Plantagenet.

The Regency. The Earl of Pembroke was appointed Regent, and under his vigorous rule England was soon reduced to order. Louis, a prince of France, who, in the midst of the struggle with John, had been invited by the barons to assume the English crown, soon left the country with all his followers. The Charter was confirmed, and the severities of the forest laws mitigated, by the substitution of fine and imprisonment, instead of mutilation and death, for killing the king's deer. Unfortunately, in 1219, the able Pembroke died, and England quickly relapsed into a state of disorder. Henry had placed foreigners in all the principal offices of the state, to the great disgust of his own people. The pope, too, as over-lord of England, had filled the vacant livings with foreign priests, and had even demanded a share in the government. The king and Hubert de Burgh, the new Regent, were at variance with each other, and both at times with the pope. But in one thing king and pope were always agreed, in the mutual endeavor to wring from the poverty-stricken people their last farthing.

Redress, the Condition of a Vote of Supplies. In 1225, a great council was summoned to consider the question of supplies to the crown. A grant was made conditioned on a new confirmation of the Charter. From this time the practice prevailed of making a confirmation of the Charter, or a redress of grievances, the condition of a vote of money to the crown. Some of the most precious rights now enjoyed by the English people were retained or acquired in this way.

Henry's Attempt to Overthrow the Charter. In 1227, Henry, being twenty-two years of age, took the reins of government into his own hands. He inaugurated his full assumption of power by an attempt, in the following declaration, to make the Great Charter subordinate to the royal prerogative:

"Whenever and wherever, and as often as it may be our pleasure, we may declare, interpret, enlarge or diminish the aforesaid statutes, and their several parts, by our own free will, and as to us shall seem expedient for the security of us and our land."

This declaration was the key-note to Henry's policy for forty years, while the barons, on account of feuds among themselves, stood idly by. The history of the whole period is but a dreary and monotonous record of royal recklessness and folly, of royal beggary and extortion. The king, when in need of money, would swear on his honor as "a man, a christian, a knight, and a king," to preserve inviolate the provisions of the Charter, and the next moment, when his wants had been supplied, trample them, in mere wantonness, under his feet. Under the royal influence, even the courts of justice became but a legalized system of extortion and robbery, the judges on the circuits compounding felonies and selling justice to the highest bidder.

Rebellion of the Barons. In 1258, a crisis was reached. There had been a failure in the crops, and a famine was imminent. Corn sent from Germany to relieve the general distress, was seized and sold by the king; and being still in want, he summoned the barons to a great council at Westminster. Aroused by outrage and united at last, they obeyed the summons;

but they came at the head of their men-at-arms. As Henry entered the great hall at Westminster and looked upon the stern array of mail-clad barons, whose clanking swords alone broke the stillness, he asked in the suddenness of his alarm, "Am I a prisoner?" "No, you are our sovereign," was the answer; "but your foreign favorites and your prodigality have brought misery upon the realm, and we demand that you confer authority upon those who are able and willing to redress the grievances of the public." Henry was powerless to resist, and consented to a commission of twenty-four barons, one-half to be appointed by himself, empowered to act in behalf of the realm. But all attempts at a permanent settlement failed, and both parties finally prepared for war. In 1264, the opposing armies met on the downs of Lewes. The royal army was defeated, and the king and his gallant son, Prince Edward, taken prisoners.

Simon de Montfort and the House of Commons, A. D. 1265. The kingdom was now at the disposal of the barons. The ablest man among them was Simon de Montfort, Earl of Leicester, whose brief but brilliant career furnishes the one bright page in the black record of Henry's reign. In a Parliament, summoned by Montfort, at Westminster, in 1265, he invited representatives of the people, two knights from each county, two citizens from each city, and two burgesses from each borough (anciently a community of ten families, now a town) to take their seats side by side with prelates and barons. This was the first House of Commons. As from the tyranny of John sprang the Great Charter, the corner-stone of English liberty, so from the oppressions of Henry rose the House of Commons, its bulwark and defence.

Evesham. Prince Edward, having escaped from captivity, quickly assembled the royal forces, won the battle of Evesham, and placed the liberated king once more on the throne. Though the barons were beaten, and the noble de Montfort slain, no attempt was made to undo their one great work, the establishment of the right of the people to representation in Parliament. Order being restored, Prince Edward went on a Crusade, the last in the series, in 1270. In two years Henry died, and the same day the nobles took the oath of fealty to the absent Prince. In two years more, King Edward, having made a ten years' truce with the Saracens, returned to England, and was formally crowned at Westminster.

Edward I. 1272 to 1307 — 35 years. Plantagenet.

Conquest of Wales. Llewellyn, Prince of Wales, had repeatedly refused to acknowledge Edward as his feudal superior. In 1277, an English army was sent into Wales, and the Prince, deserted by most of his chieftains, was compelled to sue for peace and accept Edward's terms, the surrender of the sovereignty of his country. In 1282, the Welsh people, fired by patriot bards, whose stirring songs had kept alive in their hearts the love of liberty, rose in rebellion against their English rulers. Edward once more invaded the country at the head of an irresistible force, and Llewellyn being early slain in a skirmish, the Welsh chieftains quietly submitted and the country was formally annexed to England. Edward wisely gave the Welsh people the English system of courts and laws, and for a hundred years, with a single exception, they remained at peace. Edward's queen, who had accompanied him on the march, gave birth, in the castle of Caernarvon, to a son, some twenty years afterwards called Prince of Wales, a title still given to the eldest son of the reigning sovereign. Returning to England, Edward devoted himself to the administration of the government. He secured the adoption of a code of wise and wholesome laws,* thereby winning in history the name of the English Justinian.

Arbitrary Taxation Forbidden. By far the most important of these laws, was passed in the year 1297, when by excessive and arbitrary taxation, Edward had provoked a rebellious confederation of the barons. He was compelled to assent to a new confirmation of the charter, and the addition of a clause forbidding the king to tax the people without the consent of Parliament. Edward not only made wise laws, but he greatly improved the courts,† rendering the administration of justice more sure and equal.

---

* Among these were laws basing more thoroughly than ever the defence of the kingdom on an armed militia, ever at the immediate call of the king; ensuring the freedom of elections against menace or forcible interference; forbidding judges and officers receiving rewards for official services, lawyers using deceit to beguile the court, persons uttering slanders and jurors rendering a false verdict; requiring the gates of walled towns to be kept shut from sunset to sunrise, and a watch to be set; ordering every man to cut away the bushes and undergrowth on his own land, two hundred feet on each side of the principal roads, to make an ambush by highwaymen difficult; and a statute for London, forbidding armed men to appear in the streets, or taverns to sell ale or beer, after Curfew.

† The ecclesiastical courts were confined to purely spiritual matters. The county court was undisturbed, but by the appointment of "Justices of the Peace," as local magistrates, its business was somewhat limited, and the people in the rural districts better accommodated. From the Court of Appeal sprang the Court of Chancery, with the Chancellor at the head, a court gov-

Beginning of the Wars with Scotland. The King of Scotland having died, thirteen claimants appeared for the vacant throne, of whom Robert Bruce and John Baliol were the most prominent. Unable to settle peacefully the question of their claims, it was referred, in 1291, to the arbitration of Edward of England. Edward decided in favor of Baliol, on condition that the latter should acknowledge himself a vassal of the English crown. Edward's claim to superiority was based on the fact already stated on a previous page, that William, a Scottish king in the time of Henry II., being taken in battle, was held in captivity until he acknowledged the King of England as his feudal superior. Baliol received the kingdom at the hands of Edward, but soon rebelled against the humiliations imposed upon him, and thence arose those fierce and bloody wars between the two countries, that continued through successive reigns to desolate the border lands of both. The earlier ballad and legend, wild and weird like the Scotch character itself, and the later tale and song with their warp of fact and woof of fiction, have involved the whole story of the struggle between England and Scotland in the fascinations of romance.

Battle of Dunbar. In the battle of Dunbar, in 1296, the Scots suffered a signal defeat. Edinburgh was besieged, Sterling taken, and finally, at Montrose Abbey, Baliol surrendered into Edward's hands all right and title to the kingdom of Scotland. The Scottish kings were wont to be crowned at Scone, on a fragment of

erned by the principles of equity, and not common law, and designed to have jurisdiction, when the technicalities of law, and the inability of the other courts to vary from fixed methods of procedure, prevented the administration of exact justice.

rock, called the Stone of Destiny. There was a Scotch tradition that wherever that stone might be, there the Scots would reign. By Edward's order, it was taken to Westminster Abbey, then just completed, and placed beneath the Coronation Chair, in which all the kings of England are crowned.

William Wallace. But Scotland found a champion in the patriot William Wallace. Mustering an army of stalwart peasants, he put to flight the English knights at Stirling. Castle after castle fell into his hands, until all Scotland was once more free from English rule. He pushed his victorious arms across the border and ravaged the north of England. The war-like Edward, who had been abroad while these events were occurring, now returned, and putting himself at the head of a large force, brought Wallace to bay at Falkirk, in 1298. The latter had been appointed Guardian of the Realm of Scotland, but proud Scottish lords, scorning to serve under one of humble birth, forsook, if they did not betray him, at Falkirk, and Wallace was utterly defeated.

For seven years, outlawed, and with a price upon his head, hiding among his native mountains, he waged a pitiless war on the English, and was then basely betrayed by a Scotch noble. He was taken, in chains, to London, and there tried as a traitor, with a crown of oak leaves upon his head, to indicate that he was king of outlaws. Being condemned to death, he was tortured and executed in the most horrible manner. From lowland moor to highland glen, from peasant cot to lordly castle, sped the story of his cruel death. What Wallace living failed to do, Wallace dead achieved. Scotch jealousies died. The fierce resentment that united all hearts in a stern resolve to avenge his cruel death, united them in the nobler resolve to free their country from the hated English yoke.

Robert Bruce. In four months all the clans were in arms under their second champion, Robert Bruce. Edward, bowed with years, but resolute still, once more took the field. But he sank under exertion and excitement, and died just as his army, at Burgh-on-Sands, came in sight of the blue hills of Scotland. In his dying moments he enjoined upon his son to prosecute the war with vigor, and even desired that his dead body should be carried at the head of the army as it marched.

Character of Edward I. Edward I. was a wise legislator, a skilful soldier, and a gallant knight. Though a despot in disposition, and doggedly tenacious of the royal prerogative, he was just and even generous to law-abiding subjects. To others he was severe and even cruel. The Jews tampered with the coinage, and three hundred of the guilty died on the scaffold; and finally, in 1290, the whole Jewish people, numbering sixteen thousand souls, were banished from the realm. His natural sternness was tempered by gentleness and affection in his domestic relations, but he would not shield from the consequences of his crime, even his own son, who once went to prison like a common felon. Under the pressure of want, Edward at one time levied money contrary to the Charter; but, convinced of his error, he acknowledged it in tears, in the presence of his Parliament, and reformed. In this reign Parliaments became more regular and met permanently at Westminster, but as yet the Commons had no voice in matters of legislation, simply voting money.

Edward II., 1307 to 1327 — 20 Years. Plantagenet.

Character of Edward II. Edward II. was weak, though childishly wilful, and utterly destitute of the knightly qualities that shone so brightly in his father's character. He had neither vigor nor virtue enough, to be just himself, or to enforce justice among his people; and much less did he rise even to a faint conception of the one grand purpose of his father's life, the extension of English dominion over the whole island. He had but a single aim, indulgence in sensual pleasures.

Piers Gaveston. The first five years of Edward's reign were spent in contentions with his barons, on account of one Piers Gaveston, a dissolute Gascon knight, to whose corrupting influence he had wholly surrendered himself. One of Edward the First's dying injunctions to his son was, never to recall the banished Gaveston. This injunction was forgotten by the son, the moment the father was dead; and the recalled favorite acquired, besides his old influence over Edward, entire control of the government. But it was Gaveston's insolent manners, and his stinging witticisms on the barons, quite as much as his assumption of authority, that won for him their cordial hatred. Twice by force of arms they compelled him to leave the kingdom, and twice the infatuated king recalled him. He was seized by the barons on his re-appearance in 1312, and thrown into Warwick Castle, whose lord he had nick-named the "Black Dog of the Wood." After a form of trial, he was taken to Blacklow Hill, a little rise of ground a short distance from the castle, near the river Avon, and there beheaded.

The quarrel between the king and the barons over the worthless knight is only important as out of it came an advance in constitutional liberty. Parliament established the right to investigate the public expenditures and punish bad advisers of the king.

Bannockburn, A. D. 1314. While Edward and the barons were wasting their time in petty strife, the Scots under Bruce were gaining their independence. Linlithgow, Roxburgh, Edinburgh and Perth successively fell into their hands. *

Stirling Castle was besieged, and its governor, under the pressure of want, agreed to surrender on a certain day, the Feast of St. John, if not relieved by the English. Edward, roused from his lethargy by the critical state of affairs at Stirling, hastily gathered an army of a hundred thousand men and pressed forward to its relief.

He was met at Bannockburn by Bruce, at the head of thirty thousand Scots. In the battle that followed, the English suffered the most disastrous defeat, considering the disparity of the forces engaged, to be found in the history of English warfare. Edward's treasure, and all the vast material

---

* The accounts of the sieges of castles held by English garrisons are full of romantic interest. Linlithgow was taken somewhat after the manner of ancient Troy. A Scotch peasant had been in the habit of supplying the garrison with forage. He came one day with a load of hay in which Scotch soldiers were concealed. Having crossed the drawbridge, he placed his load in such a position that the gates could not be shut. The concealed soldiers, suddenly appearing, held the gates until reinforcements lying in ambush came up, and the garrison was overpowered.

of his army, fell into the hands of Bruce, while his panic-stricken soldiers were butchered without mercy. The Scots again ravaged the northern counties. Fresh armies were raised by the English, but little was accomplished.

After the battle of Bannockburn, Edward fell under the influence of two new favorites, the Spencers, father and son. It is but the story of Gaveston repeated, a brief use and abuse of power, a short but desperate struggle with the enraged barons, and a violent death at their hands.

Queen Isabella in France. In 1325, the year before the fall of the Spencers, Queen Isabella had been sent by Edward to the court of her brother, Charles IV. of France, to arrange terms of peace between the two kings. She accomplished her mission in a manner more favorable to France than to England, but declined to return at Edward's earnest entreaty, pleading her fear of the Spencers. She had little love for her husband, and had formed a violent attachment for Roger Mortimer, who had been condemned to the Tower on account of his enmity to the Spencers, but had escaped to France. He became the chief officer in Isabella's household. While abroad, the Queen, who was accompanied by her son Edward, Prince of Wales, visited the Court of William, Count of Hainault, and while there arranged a marriage contract between the Prince and Philippa, daughter of the Count.

Deposition and Death of Edward. In 1326, with a small force furnished by the Count, Isabella returned to England, and at once raised the standard of revolt, ostensibly to overthrow the Spencers, but in fact to gain for herself and Mortimer the supreme power. She was hailed as a deliverer by all classes, and soon had an overwhelming force at her command. The king, deserted and helpless, embarked for the Isle of Lundy, off Bristol Channel, but was driven upon the Welsh coast and landed at Swansea. He soon surrendered himself to his enemies, and was hurried like a felon from place to place, and finally lodged in Berkeley Castle.

Parliament, in 1327, declared the throne to be vacant; and thus was established the parliamentary right to depose the king. The young prince was crowned under the title of Edward III. To satisfy the feigned scruples of Isabella, Parliament extorted from the captive king a formal abdication of the throne. Edward never left Berkeley Castle. Its gloomy walls one autumn night rang with heart-rending shrieks, and the next day the distorted features of the dead king told only too plainly the tale of his cruel death. A few years after this, Mortimer, when about to expiate his crimes on the gallows, confessed that he sent two hired assassins to murder the hapless king.

— **Edward III., 1327 to 1377 — 50 years. Plantagenet.**

The Regency. Edward III. became a powerful monarch, and his reign was one of the longest and most brilliant in the history of England. Being crowned at the early age of fourteen, a Council of Regency, composed of twelve principal lords, was appointed to administer the government during the minority. But this Council being controlled by Queen

Isabella and Mortimer, the real power still remained in their hands.

Treaty of Northampton. The Scots under James, Earl of Douglas, continued their ravages across the border, and the young king raised an army and marched against them. But the light-armed and well-mounted Scots, skilfully avoiding battle and eluding pursuit, forced Edward to retire for want of supplies. Finally, in 1328, by the Treaty of Northampton, the independence of Scotland was acknowledged.

Fall of Isabella and Mortimer. Edward, now eighteen years of age, resolved to take the reins of government into his own hands. Isabella and Mortimer occupied a strong castle at Nottingham. Every night the keys of the castle gates were brought to the bed-side of the suspicious queen, while guards were stationed at every avenue of approach. Under the guidance of the governor, a small but trusty band of Edward's friends entered the castle at night, through a subterranean passage, and being joined by Edward himself, took its garrison completely by surprise. Mortimer was seized and borne away, the queen piteously entreating her son "to spare her gentle Mortimer." From this moment, Edward was king in fact as well as name. He summoned a Parliament, before whom Mortimer was brought charged with various offences, including the murder of Edward II. He was pronounced guilty and hanged on an elm at Tyburn, in 1330, while Queen Isabella was consigned to life-long imprisonment in Castle Risings. She lingered twenty-seven years in hopeless captivity, visited once a year by her son, the king.

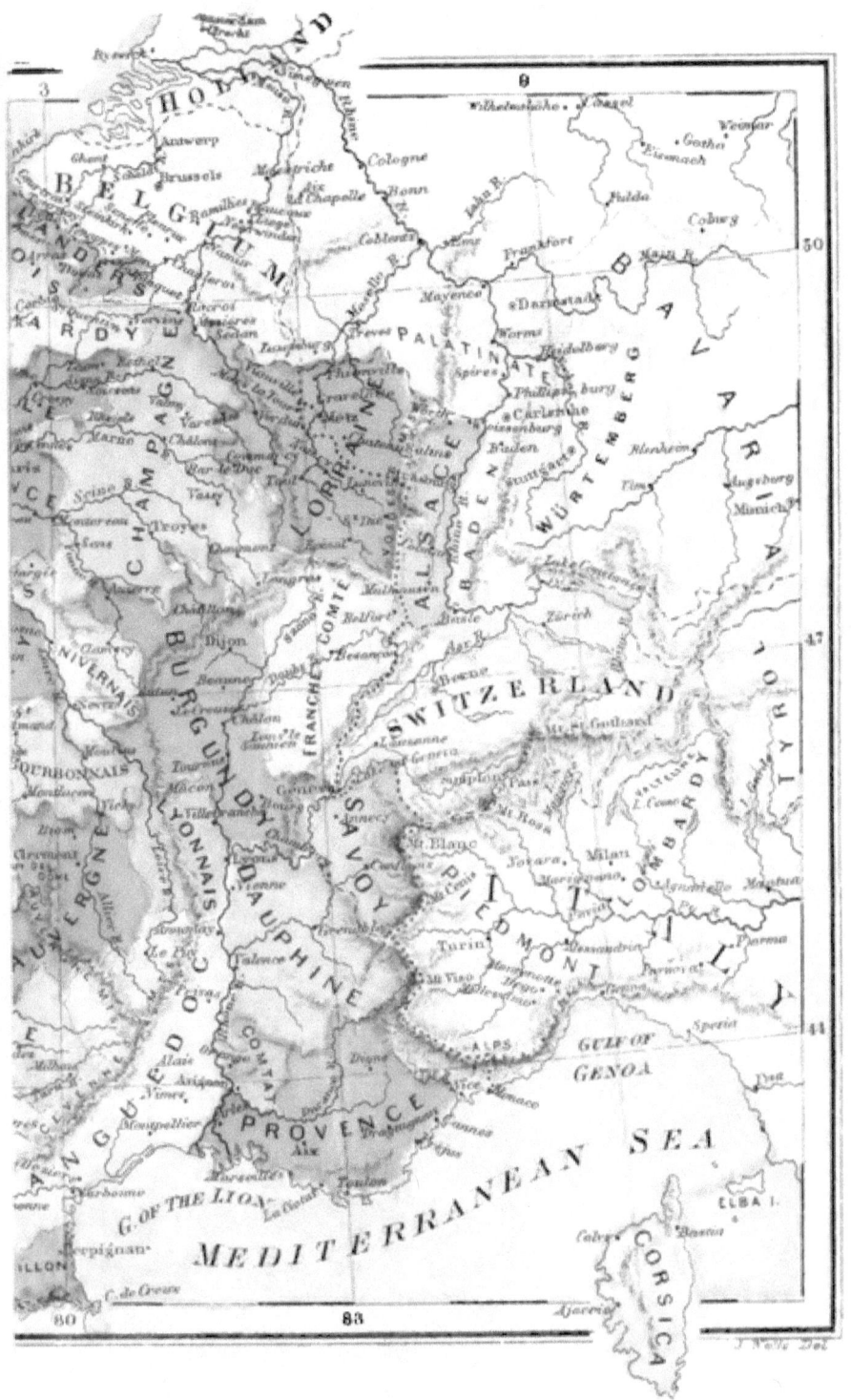

Halidon Hill. Robert Bruce, the heroic old king of Scotland, died in 1329, and the crown descended to David his son, then but seven years of age. History now repeats itself. Edward Baliol, son of John Baliol who figured in the reign of the first Edward, asserted his right to the sovereign power, as his father had done before him. Defeating the forces of Bruce, near Perth, he seized the power, while Bruce fled to France. To gain the support of Edward of England, he, too, agreed to reign as a vassal of the English crown. The indignant Scots sprang to arms and drove him from the kingdom.

After a show of reluctance, on account of the treaty still in force between the two countries, Edward pronounced in favor of Baliol. Raising a large army, he marched into Scotland, and, by one great battle at Halidon Hill, in 1333, placed Baliol again upon the throne, and compelled Bruce once more to take refuge in France. The very name of Baliol was hateful to the Scots, and upon the withdrawal of the English army, he was a second time driven from the kingdom.

The "Hundred Years' War" with France. The cause of Bruce had been warmly supported by the King of France, and Edward, convinced that English supremacy in Scotland could never be made secure, so long as the ships and soldiers of France were at the call of the Scots, resolved to strike a decisive blow at France herself. Two convenient pretexts were at hand, the encroachments of the French on the English possessions on the continent, and the claim of Edward to the French throne itself.

The war that now began between England and France is known as the " Hundred Years' War," because, with intervals of peace, it continued for a hundred years.* Though English kings won a world-wide renown, and English soldiers covered themselves with glory, during its progress, it ended in the loss to the English people of all their possessions in France, except Calais.

Cressy, A. D. 1346. The first conflicts were indecisive. Edward gained a great naval victory over the French, off Sluys, in the English Channel. Landing some years afterwards on the French coast, he won the famous field of Cressy. It was in this battle that Edward, Prince of Wales, called the Black Prince, from the color of his armor, bravely won his spurs, entering upon a career that, for brilliancy of achievement and the splendid exhibition of knightly qualities, finds no parallel in the annals of chivalry.

Calais. Five days after the battle of Cressy, Edward laid siege to Calais, a strongly fortified town on the seaboard, opposite the cliffs of Dover, which French privateers had long made their haunt, while lying in wait for unguarded English traders. In

---

* The ground of Edward's claim will be seen in the following statement:— Philip IV., predecessor of the present King Charles IV., of France, left three sons and a daughter, Isabella, who became the wife of Edward II. of England. The daughter was the youngest. The sons left only female issue, while the daughter left male issue, Edward III. of England. Edward was thus the nearest male heir. It was maintained by the French that Edward's claim was barred by the Salic law, a law that had long prevailed in France, forbidding female succession. Edward sought to evade the force of this law by asserting that, though a female could not inherit the power, she could transmit it to her male descendants. To this the French replied that a female could not transmit a right she did not herself possess. The French practice was in strict accordance with their theory, for on the death of Philip's sons, his heirs direct being females, or the issue of females, were passed over, and the crown was given, without opposition, to Charles, a nephew of Philip.

twelve months it was starved into surrender, but the fortitude of its inhabitants, and the heroism of the immortal six, who offered their lives as a ransom for the people, will challenge the admiration of all ages. Though Edward's army had been greatly wasted during the siege, and he had threatened to put the whole city to the sword, on account of its obstinate defence, he promised, at last, to spare the lives of its inhabitants, if six principal citizens, bare-headed, barefooted, and with halters about their necks, would bring to him the keys of the town and castle, and deliver themselves up to his will. Six noble men offered themselves for the sacrifice. They presented to Edward the keys, and were ordered to instant death. But Edward's gentle Queen Philippa, falling on her knees before him, begged their lives, and they were spared.

Neville's Cross. The Scots, who were in alliance with France, taking advantage of Edward's absence, appeared in large force in the north of England, under the command of Bruce, their king. They were defeated by Philippa (who had not yet joined her husband in France), in the battle of Neville's Cross, Bruce himself being taken captive. The exhaustion of an expensive foreign war, and the ravages of a fearful plague, called the Black Death, forced Edward to make a temporary peace with France.

Poictiers, A.D. 1356. But war was renewed in 1355, by the Black Prince, who marched from his Duchy of Aquitaine with a small but well-appointed force, and penetrated to the very heart of France. When about to return laden with spoils, he found himself opposed, a few miles from the city of Poictiers, by the French king at the head of an overwhelming army. By a wise choice of ground and a skilful disposition of his little force, he inflicted upon the French host a terrible defeat. Among the prisoners was John, the French king, who was brought by the gallant prince to London. Edward now held two captive kings. Bruce was released in 1357, after a period of eleven years, and, by the peace of Bretigny, in 1360, John was ransomed for three million gold crowns. Failing to raise the ransom money, the chivalric king returned to a life-long captivity. By the same treaty, Edward relinquished his claim to the French crown, holding his French possessions, no longer as a vassal, but as an independent sovereign. Up to this period his career had been one of brilliant success.

Loss of French Possessions. A few years of peace, and disasters came thick and fast. The Black Prince, broken in health by a fruitless expedition into Spain, returned to England, a mere wreck of his former self; and the war being renewed by the French king at a favorable time, one after another of the English possessions on the continent was wrested away, until, in 1374, nothing remained but Calais, Bordeaux and Bayonne. Spanish fleets had all but destroyed the navy of England, and swept the seas of her commerce.

Internal Disorder. At home were misrule and discontent. Edward's noble consort, Philippa, having died, the enfeebled old king fell under the influence of an infamous favorite, one Alice Perrers. John, Duke of Lancaster, one of the king's sons, having got control of the government, the people were ground down with taxes, the courts of justice overawed, and the elections corrupted. The Catholic church at this time owned about one-third of the real estate of England, and the taxes for church purposes exceeded all other taxes put together. Although more money was annually raised in England for the pope than for the king himself, the former had demanded the payment of the tribute money, 1000 marks a year, promised by John when he made England a fief of the Papacy, now in arrears thirty-three years.

The Good Parliament. The Good Parliament, summoned by Edward to consider this claim, promptly rejected it, and then proceeded to reform the many abuses that had crept into the affairs of the state. It was nobly supported by the Black Prince, who, though slowly dying with disease, devoted his last remaining energies to the work of reform. Officers of the crown were impeached and removed, and the Duke of Lancaster, the source of many of the prevalent abuses, was forced to retire. The death of the Black Prince, closely followed by the return of the Duke to power, and the election of a new Parliament in his interest, brought the work of reform to a sudden close.

John Wickliffe. In one thing the Duke had been in harmony with the Good Parliament and the people, in resisting the demands of the pope. He had a powerful ally in John Wickliffe, an Oxford professor, who, beginning with a denunciation of the exactions and corruptions of the Church of Rome, ended, as we shall see in the next reign, in a bold attack on its doctrines, thus inaugurating the first Reformation. There was little in common between the Duke of Lancaster and John Wickliffe, the former being selfish and unscrupulous, caring little for the corruptions of the Church, but coveting its wealth; the latter, of exalted purity of character, opposing the Church on account of its abuses and assumptions. Lancaster is said to have planned a sweeping confiscation of church property.

The English Language. There are several important landmarks in the reign of Edward III. The Anglo-Saxon had always been the language of the peasantry, Latin the language of business and the graver literature, and French the language of society and the lighter literature. During this reign a marked change took place. The Anglo-Saxon, with an admixture of both Latin and French, was slowly becoming the national tongue. The writings of Wickliffe, sent broadcast over the land, gave both shape and impetus to the movement. Wickliffe may be called the morning star of English prose, as Chaucer has been of English poetry. Towards the close of Edward's reign, the English language was taught in the schools instead of French, and a statute, passed in 1357, required its use in the courts of justice. Even French romances began to be translated into English.

The English People. There had always existed feelings of hatred and jealousy among the people of the different races. The native Briton could never forgive his Saxon conqueror, and both alike detested the proud and domineering Norman. The reign of Edward witnessed the blending of these discordant races into one harmonious people. They fought, side by side, at Cressy and Poictiers, and their animosities melted away amidst rejoicings of victory. From that time they looked back with a common pride to a glorious past, and forward with a common hope to a more glorious future.

Change in the Methods of Warfare. A change was gradually taking place in the methods of warfare. Hitherto, mail-clad knights had been the main reliance in battle, but Edward, following the example of William Wallace at Falkirk, had won his most brilliant campaigns with English archers. At Cressy and Poictiers, the knights of France were first thrown into confusion by clouds of arrows sped with unerring aim by English bowmen. It is said that cannon were first used on the battle-field, at Cressy; but heavy cannon, throwing stones, were used before, for siege purposes.

The Two Houses of Parliament. Edward had increased the number of towns allowed to send representatives to Parliament, making the latter so large, that it was found necessary to divide it into two distinct bodies, the one composed of lords and bishops, called the House of Lords, and the other, of representatives of towns and counties, called the House of Commons. And thus was perfected the legislative branch of the government. The Witenagemot of the Saxons had developed into the Great Council of the Normans, and that, first into the single Parliament of Earl Simon, and now into its perfected form of two independent Houses. From this moment, the Commons, who had been overawed in the presence of lords and bishops, assumed a more independent character. It is a significant fact, in this connection, that Edward, forced by his necessities during the French wars, confirmed the Great Charter thirteen times.

Death of Edward. Enfeebled by age, and overwhelmed by the disasters that had befallen him, Edward survived the Black Prince but a year, dying in 1377. His last years were gloomy, and his death peculiarly sad, and a striking commentary on the vanity of human glory. As the end drew near, he was utterly forsaken. Even Alice Perrers snatched a ring from his unresisting finger, and fled. At the last moment, a compassionate priest entered the silent chamber, and held a crucifix before the fast glazing eyes of the dying king. It is difficult to realize, that *this* is the Edward who was the very prince of that proud race, the Plantagenets, the hero of the French wars, and the pride of England. Chivalry was then at its zenith, and Edward's court had been Chivalry's capital. Hither gallant knights had been wont to gather from all parts of Europe, to mingle in the scenes of Feudal splendor, that constantly dazzled the eyes of the wondering people. But, whether in the friendly lists of the tournament, or the deadly shock of battle, Edward's plume had always been pre-eminent.

Richard II., 1377 to 1399 — 22 years. Plantagenet.

The Regency. No king ever came to the English throne more heartily welcomed, or left it less regretted, than Richard II. The fact that he was the son of the Black Prince, that mirror of Chivalry and idol of the people, opened all hearts to him. He was handsome, but effeminate, a mere lover of pleasure and royal display. His retinue numbered ten thousand persons, and its passage through the country was dreaded little less than that of an invading army. Being but eleven years of age when he inherited the crown, a regency was appointed.

Causes of Wat Tyler's Rebellion. Four years after his accession, the Peasants' Revolt, or Wat Tyler's Rebellion, broke out. This revolt is worthy of very brief mention, considered alone in the incidents attending it. It had none of the "pomp and circumstance of war," and was little better than tumultuous gatherings of ill-organized mobs, whose subsidence was as sudden as their uprising. But the social and political questions involved lift it into a plane of grave importance. It was a revolt founded on social distinctions, the beginning of an irrepressible conflict between the poor and humble oppressed, and the rich and noble oppressor; of an antagonism between labor and capital, that, in one form or another, has continued unabated to this day.

Emancipation. During the preceding reigns, the serfs had, in various ways, gradually risen to the condition of freemen. The work of emancipation had been hastened by the necessities of the lords themselves, who, to maintain the pomp and splendor of Chivalry, expensive even in time of peace, but doubly so in time of war, resorted to every artifice to raise money. It was a ready and productive way, to commute the services of the serfs for their estimated value in money. Edward himself, to raise funds for the French wars, sent agents to all the royal estates to sell to the serfs their freedom. So that by the middle of the fourteenth century, free labor had, to a considerable extent, taken the place of slave labor, and was then abundant and cheap.

The Black Death. In 1348, in the reign of Edward III, a terrible plague, called the Black Death, originating in Asia and traversing the continent of Europe, swept England as with the besom of destruction. One-half its inhabitants were carried off, but it was especially malignant among the lower classes. At its close, labor was scarce and high, and as it naturally sought the best market, in some sections harvests could not be gathered for want of help.

The Statute of Laborers. The landowners appealing to Parliament for relief, an Act, called the "Statute of Laborers," was passed, re-establishing the old low price of labor, and compelling the laboring classes to seek employment within the limits of their own parishes. This virtually restored the old and odious system of serfdom, creating the most intense discontent among the peasantry. They gathered in large numbers at the different centres, to listen to the harangues of their leaders depicting in bitter language the wretched condition of the poor, and the luxurious estate of the rich. By the close of Edward's reign, the oppressed peasantry were ripe for revolt.

The Breaking out of the Rebellion. In the fourth year of Richard's reign, a tax of one shilling was imposed on every person in the kingdom, above fifteen years of age. It was not the amount of the tax, but the fact that the poor were taxed as heavily as the rich, that kindled the smouldering spark into a flame of rebellion. The most formidable rising took place in Kent, where a hundred thousand peasants gathered under Wat Tyler, and taking up their line of march for London, poured into the city in a vast disorderly mass. Many excesses were committed, but the fury of the multitude was chiefly directed against those concerned in the odious tax and previous oppressive legislation. The king, who at first had taken refuge in the Tower, met them by appointment at Mile-end, just out of London. During the conference, Tyler placed his hand on the dagger at his side, and was instantly stricken down by one of the king's attendants. The lives of the royal party were in imminent peril, for the bows of the enraged insurgents were already bent, when the king, riding hastily forward, exclaimed, "Tyler was a traitor; I will be your leader." They quickly gathered about their new and youthful leader, praying for liberty for themselves and their children. This achievement of Richard's seems almost heroic, and is all the more conspicuous from the long and ignoble career that followed it. Richard professed to yield to their prayers, and thirty clerks were set to work preparing and distributing free papers. The pacified insurgents began to break up and return home. In the meantime the nobles were assembling their forces and hastening to the support of the king. The latter, false to his word, quickly cancelled all the free papers he had issued, and caused the leading rebels in all the towns to be tried and punished.

Though the revolts were suppressed and the peasants nominally returned to a state of serfdom, the newly awakened desire for personal liberty could not be extinguished, and the work of emancipation went slowly but surely forward, until, in a century and a half, serfdom may be said to have disappeared from England.

Wickliffe and the First Reformation. The Peasants' revolt, charged, as it was, by Romanists, to the seditious teachings of Wickliffe and his followers, was a serious blow to the reformation.* Wickliffe was forsaken by his most powerful friends, including the Duke of Lancaster himself. But there was another reason for this defection,—Wickliffe's extreme views in regard to some of the tenets of the church. So long as he merely exposed its corruptions, he was applauded by all classes; but when he assailed its cardinal doctrines, he lost the sympathy of all good Catholics. It was in this emergency that Wickliffe displayed the real grandeur and versatility of his genius. Instead of the scholarly arguments in classic Latin he had hitherto addressed to the great and learned, he now directed his appeals in plain Anglo-Saxon to the masses of the English people. Pamphlet after pamphlet against both the doctrines and the practice of the church, issued from

* The teachings of some of the leaders, and so the tendency of the times, are clearly indicated in the following sentiments, attributed to John Ball, the "mad priest of Kent":—"Good people, things will never go well in England so long as goods be not in common, and so long as there be villains (simply vassals) and gentlemen. By what right are they, whom we call lords, greater folk than we? On what grounds have they deserved it? Why do they hold us in serfage? If we all came of the same father and mother, of Adam and Eve, how can they say or prove that they are better than we, if it be not that they make us gain for them, by our toil, what they spend in their pride? They are clothed in their velvet and warm in their furs and their ermines, while we are covered with rags. They have wine and spices and fair bread, and we eat oat-cake and straw and water to drink. They have leisure and fine houses. We have pain and labor, the rain and the wind in the fields. And yet it is of us and of our toil that these men hold their state." The following couplet is also attributed to Ball:—

"When Adam delved and Eve span,
Who was then the gentleman?"

It is hardly to be wondered at, that multitudes of ignorant men, bitterly conscious of their own wretchedness and the sumptuous estate of their masters, both equally undeserved, in their minds, should enlist in an enterprise that promised to make them all more equal.

his prolific pen, and was sent broadcast over the land. An order of preachers, called the Simple Priests, was instituted to disseminate his doctrines. Such progress was made, that "every other man you met was a Lollard," * to use the bitter language of a careful observer of the times. The crown, at last, came to the aid of the church: Wickliffe was banished from Oxford, and his writings condemned as heretical and ordered to be burned. Retiring to Lutterworth, he devoted his energies to the last and grandest work of his life, the translation of the Bible into English. December 30th, 1384, he had a stroke of paralysis, while attending mass in the parish church, and passed peacefully away the next day.

Otterburn and Chevy Chase. There is little of interest in the foreign relations of this reign. The border lands of both England and Scotland were wasted by hostile incursions. In 1388, occurred the battle of Otterburn, a mere border-fight between two hostile noblemen, Percy and Douglas, and their retainers, but made forever memorable by that celebrated ballad, "Chevy Chase."

Chaucer. In the reigns of Edward III. and Richard II. lived Chaucer, the "Morning Star of English poetry," whose "Canterbury Tales," the most famous of his works, is still read with delight. Thirty pilgrims from all classes in society are represented as travelling together from London to Canterbury, to visit the shrine of St. Thomas, and whiling away the tedium of the journey

---

* The name Lollard, derived from the old German *lollen* or *lullen*, *to sing*, was first applied to the Reformers as an epithet of derision, from their practice of singing hymns in their meetings.

by telling stories, which furnish the most accurate picture of the manners and customs of the times that has come down to us.

Tyranny of Richard. Richard was in a constant quarrel with his uncles and guardians. When twenty-two years of age, he assumed entire control of the government. After reigning a few years with moderation and justice, he became more despotic than any of his predecessors. By a cunningly devised statute, granting him a life income, and placing the legislative power in the hands of a select number of lords and burgesses, Parliament was virtually abolished. Though the king now seemed more secure in the possession of power than ever, his downfall was near at hand.

Deposition of Richard. A personal quarrel having arisen between two young noblemen, an appeal was made to "wager of battle." On the day appointed for the contest, and in the presence of the multitude gathered to witness it, Richard banished both from the kingdom, and soon after seized the estates, to which one of them, Henry Bolingbroke, his own cousin, had fallen heir. Taking advantage of the absence of the king in Ireland, Henry landed at Ravenspur, in Yorkshire, and raised the standard of revolt. His twenty followers increased to sixty thousand fighting men by the time he reached London.

Richard hastened back to England, only to fall into Henry's hands, suffer dethronement by Act of Parliament, and disappear within the walls of the Tower. With Richard, end the Plantagenet kings, on the whole an able though a tyrannical race. But the worst of these kings were the best for England in the end, for with intolerable tyranny came rebellion, and ultimate relief. Rebellion founded in a just cause does not often end in mere bloodshed and anarchy, but in a permanent advance in justice, liberty, and law.

CHAPTER VI.

House of Lancaster, 1399 to 1461 — 62 years.

HENRY IV., Bolingbroke. | HENRY VI. of Windsor.
HENRY V. of Monmouth.

Henry IV., 1399 to 1413 — 14 years.

Henry's Title. Henry IV. gained the crown by his prowess. Conscious that his title* was defective, and his possession of power precarious, he sought to win to his support those most powerful elements in the State, the nobility and the church. To the nobility, flushed with pride at the memories of Cressy and Poictiers, but burning with shame at the loss of Aquitaine, he held out the gains and the glory of another French campaign. To the church, fully conscious of the steady growth of reformed ideas, especially among the

---

* To explain:—The four eldest sons of Edward III. were Edward, the Black Prince; Lionel, Duke of Clarence; John of Gaunt, Duke of Lancaster; and Edmund, Duke of York. Edmund, Earl of March, was descended from Lionel the second, and Henry IV., from John of Gaunt, the third son of Edward III., so that when the eldest branch of the royal family became extinct, as it did at the death of Richard II., son of the Black Prince, the crown belonged of right to the Earl of March, the representative of the second branch. This usurpation of Henry IV. was all the more glaring, since it really occurred before the death of Richard II., and it led, some sixty years later, in the reign of Henry VI., to a series of wars, called the "Wars of the Roses." One other fact ought to be mentioned in this connection. Shortly after this usurpation, the second and fourth branches of the royal family were united by the marriage of their two surviving representatives, Anne, and Richard of Cambridge. Richard, Duke of York, the issue of this marriage, was the one, in the reign of Henry VI., to press the claims of his house to the throne.

masses, he promised persecution of the reformers. Incessant domestic troubles prevented his renewing the war with France, but his promise of persecution was fulfilled with terrible fidelity.

The First Martyr at the Stake. By an Act of Parliament, called the "Statute of Heretics," the bishops were empowered to imprison all writers, teachers, and preachers of heresy, and, on their refusal to abjure, to hand them over to the civil authorities to be burned. William Salter, a London preacher, was the first martyr at the stake. Being condemned by the bishops, he was handed over to the civil authorities and burned, in accordance with the statute, in 1401.

Henry IV. has the unenviable reputation of being the first king of England to impose on his subjects, by statute, the penalty of death, and that, the awful death by fire, solely on account of their religious belief. And thus was inaugurated the system of horrible intolerance that blackens, for so long a period, the page of English history, of which Catholics and Protestants were alike guilty, and whose only palliation is the spirit of the age. To the prayer of the House of Commons, that the cruel statute might be repealed or mitigated, Henry replied that "he wished one more severe had been passed," and gave a terrible proof of his sincerity by immediately signing the death warrant of another reformer.

Revolt in Behalf of Richard II. Henry's reign witnessed a constant succession of revolts. Three of these will be noticed. The first was in behalf of King Richard, who was rumored to have escaped from confinement, and to be still living in concealment in Scotland. This was quickly suppressed, and in less than a month a report was current that Richard had died at Castle Pontefract. His body was even brought to London and exposed to the public gaze, that all might see that he was really dead. Strange and conflicting stories were told of the manner of his death, but nothing is positively known. He is supposed to have been consigned by Parliament to an unknown dungeon, and to have died a violent death, at the instigation of Henry himself.

Revolt of the Welsh. Another revolt broke out in Wales, under Owen Glendower, who claimed descent from the royal line of Llewellyn and the ancient Britons. As in the times of Edward I., patriot bards, journeying from place to place with song and story of the early heroes of Welsh history, fired the Welsh heart anew with its old love of liberty. Glendower, being defeated in the open field, retired to the fastnesses of Snowdon, and throughout Henry's reign defied the whole power of England. What became of him was never known. He lived for some time after Henry V. came to the throne, a wanderer and an outlaw, refusing all overtures of peace, and making his home in hidden caves among his native hills. A cave still called "Owen's Cave" is to be seen on the coast of Merioneth.

Revolt of the Percies. But the insurrection most dangerous to Henry's throne suddenly broke out under the Percies, who had hitherto been its most powerful supporters. The cause of their defection is not clear. It may have been Henry's inability to pay the expenses of their previous campaigns in his behalf, or his unwillingness to ransom the elder Mortimer, Hotspur's brother-in-law, who was a prisoner to Glendower; but its declared object was to place upon the throne the Earl of March, whom Henry held as a state prisoner at Windsor. They were assisted by Glendower and Douglas, each at the head of a band of his countrymen. Henry gained a complete victory over all these foes at Shrewsbury, in 1403, Hotspur, the younger Percy, being killed on the field of battle. The elder Percy perished in a subsequent revolt.

The Poet-King of Scotland. Prince James, a youth of twelve, and heir to the Scottish throne, had embarked for France, to escape the perils that menaced the royal family of Scotland. His ship was taken by an English cruiser, and the young prince remained a state prisoner in England for nearly nineteen years, two of which were spent in the Tower, and sixteen in the Keep of Windsor Castle. He was provided with good instructors, and became the famous "Poet-king of Scotland." When released, he assumed the crown to which he had fallen heir, and made one of the noblest of Scottish kings. He married Lady Joanna Beaufort, an English princess, to whom he had become attached while in prison.

Henry's Troubles. Henry lived in constant dread of the Lollards, who were known to be active in fomenting insurrections. He was conscience-smitten, too, it is said, at the part he had taken in their persecution, as well as at the means he had used to attain to power. Forced to be ever on the alert against the friends of the dead Richard on the one hand, and the living Mortimer on the other; morbidly jealous of the growing popularity of the Prince of Wales, and in constant fear lest the latter should snatch the crown from his head; distressed at the Prince's wild and reckless conduct; and shattered in mind and body by epileptic fits to which he was subject, no wonder he grew morose and unpopular towards the end of his reign, and was hurried prematurely to his grave. He died in a fit, while praying before the shrine of St. Edward's at Westminster. "Uneasy lies the head that wears a crown," was Shakspeare's sage reflection on the stormy years of Henry's reign.

Henry V., 1413 to 1422 — 9 years. Lancaster.

The Wise Beginning of Henry's Reign. The reign of Henry V. was short but brilliant, happily disappointing those who feared that the reckless prince would make a reckless king. Calling together his old companions in folly, he told them of his purpose to change his life, and forbade them to enter his presence until they should follow his example and reform. In proof of his sincerity as well as wisdom, he selected as his principal advisers in the government, men of known integrity of character. Among them was Gascoigne, who, as Chief Justice, once sent Prince Henry himself to prison, for interfering with the course of justice. Several just and noble acts, at the very outset of his career, did much to disarm the enemies of his house. He pacified the York family by setting free the long imprisoned Earl of March, and by giving to the bones of Richard II. a truly royal burial among the kings of England at Westminster. He gained the support of the powerful family of the Percies, by restoring to them their forfeited estates.

Suppression of the First Reformation. Henry's attention was early called to the Lollards. Their doctrines had been gradually spreading, during the preceding reign, not only in England, but on the continent. John Huss, rector of the University of Prague, had become, through the influence of Wickliffe's writings, a convert to Lollardism, which he openly preached, until silenced at the stake.

The Catholic clergy, early in this reign, saw the necessity of acting with more vigor against the "new heresy," and marked as their first victim, Sir John Oldcastle, the leader of the Lollards in England, whose castle they had made a place of refuge.

The king, inspired by an old friendship, sought to save him from death; but Oldcastle, refusing to recant, was cast into the Tower, and, after trial and condemnation by the prelates, was turned over to the civil authorities to be burned. The king again interposed, granting a respite of fifty days, during which Oldcastle made his escape, and planned, so it was said, and so the king believed, an immediate rising of the Lollards. Henry at once took decided ground against the Reformation, and the most violent persecution followed. The severest statutes were enacted, commanding the arrest of all persons, even if suspected of heresy, and entailing forfeiture of estate and blood on all convicted. Oldcastle and many others perished, and the first Reformation, in all that was outward and visible, was soon at an end. Elsewhere allusion has been made to the decline of the Reformation among the influential classes, on account of its connection with the "Peasants' Revolt." A word more seems proper before leaving the subject. Some of the leaders of the Reformation, lacking the singleness of purpose that inspired its founder, Wickliffe, sought, as we have seen, to bring within its sweep the removal of social distinctions and the equalization of property,— our modern communism. At the time of its suppression, it also rested under the odium of conspiring to subvert the government. The Reformation, branded on the one hand as communistic, and so, dangerous to society; on the other as revolutionary, and so, destructive to public order, gradually arrayed against itself not only the rich and powerful, but also the more thoughtful and conservative. Outwardly, the Reformation ceased to exist, but in the hearts of many there was all the while taking root a simpler and a purer faith, based on the open Bible that Wickliffe had put into their hands. As Knight has beautifully said, "Out of Wickliffe's rectory, at Lutterworth, seeds were to be borne upon the wind which would abide in the earth till they sprang up into the stately growth of other centuries."*

*Thirty years after Wickliffe's death, and in the early part of Henry's reign, the Council of Constance, the same that condemned John Huss, issued a decree that Wickliffe's remains should be disinterred and burned. This was done, and his ashes were cast into a little brook that runs past Lutterworth, into the Avon. The Avon leads into the Severn, the Severn into a narrow sea, and the sea into the ocean. In the following beautiful lines the poetic fancy of Wordsworth makes the scattering of Wickliffe's ashes an emblem of the spreading of his doctrine:—

> "As thou these ashes, little brook, wilt bear
> Into the Avon—Avon to the tide
> Of Severn—Severn to the narrow seas—
> Into main ocean they—this deed accurst,
> An emblem yields to friends and enemies,
> How the bold teacher's doctrine, sanctified
> By truth, shall spread throughout the world dispersed."

Renewal of the "Hundred Years' War." During the reigns of Richard II. and Henry IV., there had been an intermission in the "Hundred Years' War" with France. It was renewed by Henry V., a year after he became king, by a revival of the old claim to the French throne. The time was a favorable one. The French King, Charles VI., was insane, and his son, the Dauphin, too young to rule; while the Dukes of Burgundy and Orleans had involved the nation in a bloody war to decide which should be regent during the Dauphin's minority. Henry crossed the channel and captured Harfleur, near the mouth of the Seine, but with a loss, by sickness and death, of two-thirds of his army. Against the advice of his nobles, he formed the daring purpose of marching through the country to Calais, following the old route of Edward III. He had about ten thousand men. The French factions, startled at the new danger, ceased their fratricidal strife, and prepared to meet the common foe.

Agincourt, A. D. 1415. The French army, estimated at one hundred thousand men, planted itself directly across Henry's path, near the village of Agincourt. The hostile armies joined battle about noon, October 25th. In three hours, the battle won added new glory to English arms, and fresh laurels to her kings. Considering all the circumstances of the day, it was the most brilliant victory English soldiers ever gained over those of France.

Agincourt at once took its place in history by the side of Cressy and Poictiers, but outshone them both; Cressy in the fearful odds against which the English contended, and in the brilliant personal achievements of England's king; Poictiers, in the amazing fortitude with which that little band of sick and starving men encountered the flower of the chivalry of France. Seven princes of the blood, above a hundred noblemen, and eight thousand knights, fell on the side of France that day.

Henry then made his way unopposed to Calais, and soon after crossed the channel to England. What a joyful welcome the English people gave their warrior-king when he returned from his brilliant campaign! They rushed into the water, as he neared the land, and bore him on their shoulders to the shore. Throngs of delighted people went out to meet him from all the towns, strewing flowers in his path. His entrance to London finds no parallel except in the magnificent Triumphs the people of ancient Rome were wont to give their returning victors.

Siege of Rouen. All attempts at a permanent peace were futile, and, in 1417, Henry again entered France with a well-appointed force of forty thousand men. Towns and castles surrendered at his summons, or fell before his assaults. The siege of Rouen lasted six months. Its inhabitants, variously estimated at from one hundred and fifty to two hundred thousand, refusing to open their gates, were at last reduced to the most dreadful extremities. "War," said Henry, "has three handmaidens, Fire, Blood and Famine, and I have chosen the meekest maid of the three." And while the merciless king was slowly drawing his lines closer around the devoted city, this meek but pitiless handmaiden, Famine, was executing her horrible commission within its walls. One half its inhabitants had perished, and the survivors, in despair, had resolved to burn the city and die in battle before its walls, when Henry, fearful that Fire and Blood would, at the last, snatch from his hands the coveted prize, offered them terms of capitulation.

Conquest of France and Treaty of Troyes. An event soon happened that hastened and completed the conquest of France. The Duke of Burgundy was assassinated in the very presence of the Dauphin himself, and probably with his connivance. The Duke's son, Philip, in revenge, allied himself with Henry, and the whole Burgundian party threw itself into the scale against the Dauphin. A treaty was made at Troyes, in the presence of the king and queen of France, in 1420, bestowing on Henry the hand of Princess Catherine, and securing to him the regency of France during the life of its maniac king, and its sovereignty at his death. The States-General solemnly ratified the treaty. While engaged in bringing the kingdom to order, in the very prime of life and at the height of his power and glory, Henry was attacked by an incurable disease, and died, August 21st, 1422. He left an infant son at Paris, now king of England and France.

Henry's widow, Catherine, afterwards married Owen Tudor, a Welsh chieftain, one of her attendants, and from them sprang the Tudor sovereigns.

Beginning of the Navy. The first ship of war ever owned by the English government was built in Henry's reign. Before this period, the maritime towns had furnished all the ships needed for war or national purposes.* The House of Commons took but a single step in advance during Henry's reign. It settled the principle that no law should be valid without the assent of the House of Commons.

— **Henry VI., 1422 to 1461 — 39 years. Lancaster.**

The Dauphin of France Assumes the Crown. Henry VI. was crowned King of England and France at the age of nine months, his uncles, the Dukes of Gloucester and Bedford, being appointed, in accordance with the wish of his father, the one Protector of the Realm of England, and the other Regent of France. The Dauphin of France had never consented to the "Treaty of Troyes," setting aside his claims to the throne, and, at the death of his maniac father, shortly after that of Henry V., assumed the title of Charles VII. The town of Orleans, lying on the north side of the Loire, and the country south of the Loire, were loyal to Charles, never having come under the sway of England. Bedford, who, as a soldier, was little inferior to Henry V. himself, laid siege to Orleans, with the design of extending the English dominion. The French were in consternation; for, with the fall of Orleans, the country south of the Loire would be open to invasion.

Joan of Arc. The amazing success of the campaigns of Edward III. and Henry V. had given the French an exalted idea of English valor and a great

---

* The dependence of the government on maritime towns, for ships of war, continued for a long time, even after it began to own vessels of its own; for the growth of the English Navy was very slow. The fleet with which Elizabeth, many years later, destroyed the Invincible Armada, was mainly contributed, all manned and equipped, by maritime towns and wealthy individuals.

distrust of their own. There is no other explanation of the ease with which a mere handful of English soldiers could repeatedly overrun the most populous districts of France. It was at this moment, when French despondency was deepest, that help appeared from a most unexpected quarter. A simple peasant girl of Domremy, on the eastern confines of France, believing that she was destined by Heaven to free her country from foreign rule, presented herself at the Court of Charles. She told the story of the angel visions she had seen, and the voices she had heard, commanding her to go to the succor of her king. The French people had unlimited faith in Joan's divine commission, and Charles himself, believing, or professing to believe, her story, paid her the greatest honor. The belief in sorcery and witchcraft was all but universal in that age. To allay the alarm of their superstitious soldiers, the English commanders assured them that Joan was not a messenger of Heaven, but this only forced them to the belief that she was sent by the Evil One, and was a witch, and their dismay was complete.

Joan, clad in white armor and mounted on a snow white horse, with a great white banner borne before her, on which were embroidered the lilies of France, directed her march towards Orleans. Crowds of excited soldiers joined the strange procession that passed unopposed through the lines of the awe-stricken English, and entered Orleans. Under her lead, the French soldiers, restored to confidence in themselves, soon drove the besieging army from its intrenchments, and Orleans was saved.

Joan, called from this time the "Maid of Orleans," then commenced her triumphant march on Rheims, where, according to the prophetic "voices," the king was to receive his crown. Town after town was taken on the way, sometimes without a blow, the English soldiers flying in dismay as the dread banner came in sight. At Rheims, the garrison was driven out by the inhabitants, and the gates opened wide to receive the advancing host. In the old cathedral that had witnessed the coronation of so many of his ancestors, Charles was formally crowned King of France in 1429.

Joan, with tears of joy, declared that her work was done, her mission ended, and desired to return at once to the care of her father's flocks. There were other cities to be conquered, and the king detained her; but her enthusiasm was gone, her counsels became timid and vacillating, and the spell of her power over the soldiery was soon broken. Captured in the defence of Compiegne, she was sold to the English by Burgundy, and, after a year's captivity at Rouen, basely handed over to the church courts for trial. Being condemned as a witch and a heretic, she was burned to death in the ancient market-place at Rouen, in 1431. Whatever credit we may give to the "visions" and "voices" Joan professed to have seen and heard, we cannot doubt her heartfelt sorrow for her crownless king and fallen country, her sincere faith in her mission, or her devotion in fulfilling it, her purity, her piety, and her martyr's death. Though her ungrateful king made no effort to rescue or ransom her, and took no interest in her fate, her name is held in grateful remembrance among her countrymen, and excites a tender respect wherever her strange, sad story is told. These will form a monument more enduring than that erected to her memory on the spot where she died.

Loss of all France, except Calais. The English rule in France was hastening to its close. The Dukes of Burgundy and Orleans had been reconciled, and their united forces hurled against the English. Fighting bravely, but defeated on every side, they retired to Normandy in the hope that that province, at least, might be saved. There was a truce and then a treaty, but both were powerless to stop the war. Normandy rose in rebellion in the north, and Guienne in the south. Though the English fought with desperate valor, they were steadily driven towards the sea-board, and finally within the walls of Calais, and the "Hundred Years' War," that long, fitful dream of an English empire in France was over. Such an empire was impossible.

The campaigns of Edward III. and Henry V. were brilliant, but unsubstantial, feeding the national pride, but exhausting the national resources. As soon as those great captains retired from the scenes of their conquests, those conquests melted away like mist before the morning sun. The French crown was but a bright and tempting "Will-o'-the-wisp," luring on ambitious kings, but ever eluding their grasp.

English Discontent. The loss of France caused intense disappointment in England, and as the vengeance of the people could not be visited on the royal person. it fell on the heads of his advisers. The Duke of Suffolk had brought about the marriage of Henry with Margaret of Anjou, consenting, in the contract, to the cession of Maine and Anjou to Margaret's father. To satisfy popular clamor, Suffolk was impeached by Parliament, and hurried by the king into exile, to save him from a worse fate at home. But Suffolk's enemies were not to be cheated out of their prey. He was pursued and overtaken on the high seas by a large ship, called the "Nicholas of the Tower." Being ordered on board the Nicholas, he was greeted, as he reached its deck, with the salutation, "Welcome traitor." Two days afterwards, he was let down into a small boat and beheaded with a rusty sword, on a block of wood. The Duke of Somerset was held responsible for the more recent losses in France. But, being a relative of the king and a favorite of the queen, he continued for a while to defy all his enemies.

Jack Cade's Rebellion. Shortly after the death of Suffolk, a revolt broke out under one Jack Cade, an old soldier in the French wars. It grew out of the general discontent at the mismanagement of the government at home and abroad. Cade's grievances were embodied in a "Complaint" sent to the Royal Council, of which bad counselors to the king, interference of the nobles in the elections, extortion of the royal officers, and the Statute of Laborers, formed the chief burden. It is interesting to note that this revolt was chiefly located in Kent, Wat Tyler's old home, and among the very classes implicated in Tyler's old rebellion.* Cade, advancing towards London with a

---

*Tyler's principal grievance was serfage, and his chief demand freedom. The fact that neither serfage nor freedom was mentioned in Cade's Complaint is strong incidental proof that slavery, though still on the statute book, had virtually died out, especially in its more odious features. The sumptuary laws of this period also show the improved condition of the lower classes, and the gradual passing away of social distinctions. Although the Statute of Laborers was still unrepealed, it had ceased to be executed, the labor question

motley crowd of twenty thousand men, met and scattered the royal forces at Sevenoaks. The king fled to Kenilworth, and Cade entered London. Three days he held the city, putting to death obnoxious persons, and, at the last, plundering private property. Retiring at night to Southwark, the citizens held London bridge and prevented his return. On a promise of pardon and redress of grievances, the pacified insurgents began to return to their homes, while Cade himself, with a price on his head, and almost without a follower, was pursued into the country and put to death.

Events Preceding the Wars of the Roses. Cade's rebellion is supposed by some to have been incited by Richard, Duke of York, who returned from his government in Ireland, in a short time, only to increase still more the general confusion. He demanded the dismission of the Duke of Somerset from office. The violent quarrel that now began between the ambitious Dukes soon ripened into open war. Henry, although a man in years, was but a child in intellect. The real government lay in the hands of the Queen, the friend of Somerset. At this juncture Henry sank into utter imbecility, and Parliament appointed York, Protector. Somerset went into the Tower. The king recovered, and York retired to his estate, while Somerset returned to power. The most powerful noble in England was the Earl of Warwick, who took the side of York. In the spring of 1455, York and Warwick marched towards London, with

being left, for the most part, to the natural laws that govern it, the laws of supply and demand. In comparing the two revolts, *Tyler's* was an outburst of despair on the part of men whose wrongs had become unendurable; *Cade's* a mere political outbreak, inaugurated by men dissatisfied with the management of public affairs.

professions of loyalty to the king, but with a peremptory demand for the surrender of Somerset. The battle of St. Albans, in 1455, left Somerset dead on the field; that of Northampton, in 1460, witnessed the complete overthrow of the royal forces and the capture of the king himself.

Hitherto, the Duke of York had professed loyalty to the king and enmity only to his bad advisers, but he now revealed the hidden purpose that had inspired all his movements from the beginning. Boldly entering the House of Lords, he pronounced Henry VI. a usurper, and claimed the crown as his own by right of inheritance.* The Lords, compelled to act, acknowledged the justice of his claim, but decided that, since the House of Lancaster had held the sceptre for sixty years and the nation had sworn fealty to its present king, with him the sceptre should remain while he lived, and then descend to the House of York.

— **Wars of the Roses.** Henry's spirited Queen, indignant at an arrangement that disinherited her son, summoned all the friends of the House of Lancaster to the field. The conflicting claims of the two Houses had been discussed at every hearth-stone and camp-fire in England, and the sympathies of civilians as well as soldiers were warmly enlisted on the one side or the other. The adherents of the House of Lancaster wore as a badge the red rose, and those of the House of York, a white rose; hence the name "Wars of the Roses." Though there was actual warfare less than two, these wars covered a period of thirty, years, sacri-

* See note on page 90.

being nearly all the members of both royal families, and more than half the ancient nobility of England. In the first conflict, at Wakefield, in 1460, the Red Rose triumphed over the White, the Duke of York being captured and brought to the block, on the field of battle. His head was placed on the walls of York, adorned, in mockery, with a paper crown. In the second, at Mortimer's Cross, the White triumphed over the Red, Edward, the young Duke of York, being in command. In the third, at St. Albans, the Red was again victorious, and King Henry, who had been brought, a prisoner, upon the field by Warwick, being left behind in the rush of retreat, was restored to liberty.

The true qualities of most minds are best seen in emergencies. Some men are never so little to be feared as when victorious; others never so dangerous as after a defeat. While the Lancastrian generals, instead of following up their advantage at St. Albans, allowed their men to scatter over the country to pillage, Edward, spurred to promptitude and boldness by failure, pushed straight on to London. As the young and handsome prince rode through the streets of the capital, he was greeted by the people with shouts of "Long live King Edward." A council of peers, prelates, and citizens, was hastily convened, before whom Edward boldly demanded the crown. The council declared that Henry had forfeited his life-lease by taking sides with the Queen, and that Edward was the rightful King. The formal coronation took place at Westminster, June 29th, 1461.

CHAPTER VII.

House of York, 1461 to 1483 — 22 years.

EDWARD IV.
EDWARD V.
RICHARD III.

Edward IV., 1461 to 1483 — 22 years. York.

Towton, A.D. 1461. Edward put himself at the head of all the forces he could muster, and set out in pursuit of the Lancastrians, now hurrying northward. He overtook them at Towton, about eight miles from York. Each army numbered sixty thousand men. It was in the midst of a snow storm, about four o'clock in the afternoon of Palm Sunday, that the struggle began. All night long and part of the following day the dreadful battle raged, and when the Lancastrian army, panic-struck, fled from the field, thirty-three thousand men lay dead in the snow. It had been the practice, from the very beginning of the war, for either party, when victorious, to execute the nobles of the other, and confiscate their estates. After Towton there was a sweeping confiscation of Lancastrian estates, many of which went to reward the Earl of Warwick, the main pillar of the House of York. So rich and powerful did this nobleman become, it is said he could muster an army of men from the vassals on his own estates, and he has come down to us in history as the

King-maker, from his ability, as we shall presently see, to make and unmake kings.

Two risings occurred within the next two years, only important as one of them left Henry a prisoner in the hands of Edward, and the other made Margaret a friendless fugitive, attended only by her little boy of eleven.*

Tewkesbury, A.D. 1471. King Edward was growing jealous of the overshadowing power of Warwick. The romantic and secret marriage of Edward to Elizabeth Grey (widow of a Lancastrian knight who fell on the field of St. Albans), against Warwick's wishes, the elevation of the queen's family to power, and the removal of Warwick's friends, one after another, from office, — led, first to estrangement, and then to open war, between them.

Fortune was fickle. Edward a prisoner to Warwick, and the betrothal of Edward's infant daughter to Warwick's heir, as the price of liberty, — Warwick a fugitive at the Court of France, his reconciliation with Margaret, and the betrothal of Margaret's son to Warwick's daughter, on condition that Warwick should restore the House of Lancaster to power, — the return of Warwick to England, the flight of Edward to the Court of Burgundy, and the transfer of Henry from

---

* In the midst of so much barbarity and so little chivalry, it is refreshing to read of the noble conduct of an outlaw of the forest. Margaret, having fled for safety to the woods, was discovered by a band of robbers. While they were quarrelling over her gold and jewels, Margaret, taking her little boy by the hand, plunged into the depths of the forest, and into the very presence of another outlaw. Throwing herself upon his generosity, she exclaimed, "This is the son of your king; to your care I commit him; I am your queen." The outlaw, touched at the pitiful state of the queen, and the confidence she reposed in him, took them under his protection, and guided them in safety across the border.

Tower to the Throne,—the landing of Edward on the western coast, the death of Warwick on the field of Barnet, and the utter and final overthrow of the House of Lancaster at Tewkesbury, where Margaret herself was taken captive, and her son stabbed, while crying for mercy,—are events which followed each other in rapid and confusing succession. Henry returned to the Tower, never to leave it again; and his high-spirited queen, who had been the very soul of the war, ransomed by the King of France, after five years of captivity, returned to her native Anjou, and died in a few years, broken-hearted at the disasters that had befallen her family.

Character and Government of Edward. Edward had a superior mind and was a good soldier. So long as his crown was in jeopardy, he continued vigilant and active; but when the last enemies of his house had been silenced, in the dungeon, in exile, or in death, he gave himself unreservedly to the gayeties and excesses of his court. Handsome and affable, he made himself a favorite in society; but sagacious and unscrupulous in matters of state, he became a tyrant and established a despotism.

He attempted to revive the old thread-bare claim to sovereignty in France. Parliament voted large sums for a French war, and raised and transported to French soil an immense army. Advancing from Calais a short distance, negotiations were opened with King Louis, resulting in a treaty, Edward yielding his claims for an annual pension.

The odious spy system was a device of Edward's, and was made so thorough, that the lightest court gossip as well as the gravest state intrigue found its way to the king's ear. Another invention of Edward's was called a "benevolence." This was a gift of money which he would invite his rich subjects to make him, and which they dared not refuse,—an ingenious way of keeping the letter, but violating the spirit, of the law against arbitrary taxation.

Results of the Wars of the Roses. We are now at the close of Edward's reign, and although the last battle of the Wars of the Roses has not yet been fought, the main part of the struggle is over, and it seems proper here to allude briefly to its general results. These may be summed up as follows:— 1st. The destruction of the ancient nobility of England and the fall of the Feudal System. 2nd. The loss of constitutional liberty. 3rd. The decline of civilization.

The Destruction of the Ancient Nobility. The Wars of the Roses were peculiarly the wars of the nobles. All the great feudal houses, gathered around the rival standards of York and Lancaster, were hurled against each other, in battle after battle, with frightful loss. Confiscations, executions, and exile, still further diminished their numbers and power, until, at the close of the contest, the ancient baronage of England was left a hopeless wreck. It is said that at one time and another, during these wars, the Crown held one-fifth of all the real estate in England as its share of the spoils. It is true, both lands and titles remained, some of them to return to their former owners or their kindred, but more went to enrich and ennoble the favorites of the king.

The nobility, thus re-created by royal clemency and royal bounty, was shorn of its traditional power and independence. It bore little resemblance to the grand feudal race that, coming down from the Conqueror, was as old as the throne and as proud; to the lordly race that, for centuries, had stood so firmly between the throne and the people, the support of the one against faction, and the defence of the other against tyranny.

We cannot help a feeling of admiration for the old-time baron of England, whether we recall him in time of peace, in the old ancestral castle, extending a rude but hearty hospitality, or in time of war, closing his gates and bidding defiance to all his foes. He feasted or he fought with equal relish, and was no respecter of persons, buckling on his armor as readily for a tilt with the forces of the king as with those of his quarrelsome neighbor. Said Earl Warrenne, as he flung his sword on the table before the commissioners of Edward I., sent to examine his title deed, "That, sirs, is my title deed." When Earl Bigod refused the demand of Henry III. for aid, said the latter, "I will send reapers and reap your fields for you." "And I will send you back the heads of your reapers," replied the fearless Earl.

We can but honor their patriotism as well as admire their fearlessness. Time and again did they come to the front in periods of national peril. The barons of England wrung from the tyrant John the great charter of freedom. Who that has read the story of Magna Charta has not longed to know which of the immortal twenty-four was the Jefferson who conceived and framed that wonderful instrument? But history is not silent as to the name of Simon de Montfort, the leader of that other immortal twenty-four that reared the House of Commons in the very face of the throne itself.

With the ancient baronage fell the Feudal System. Feudalism, as a power in England, expired, as it were, in a bright but lurid flame, when the House of Warwick, after towering for a brief period, high above the throne itself, suddenly went down on the field of Barnet. The regret of the reader will be but natural that Warwick, who has been fitly called the "Last of the Barons," could not have been the best as well as the last of his race.

— **The Loss of Constitutional Liberty.** From the Magna Charta to the Wars of the Roses, there was a slow but real progress in constitutional liberty, almost every reign bringing either a limitation of the royal prerogative or an enlargement of popular rights.

At the beginning of the Wars of the Roses, there had been established, so far as the intelligence of the people and the arbitrary dispositions of kings allowed, the following principles:—The king had lost the right to levy taxes, make or change the laws, and imprison or punish subjects arbitrarily. Parliament had gained, besides the control of laws and taxes, the right to impeach and remove the ministers of the crown, direct and investigate expenditures, depose the king, and settle questions of peace and war. During the Wars of the Roses, all these great principles and guarantees, won through centuries of toil and suffering, were rudely swept away, and it was a century more, before the nation had sufficiently recovered itself to re-assert and re-establish them. England may be said to have passed from an absolute to a limited monarchy, when, in the reign of Edward I., the king lost the right to levy taxes without the consent of Parliament. Edward IV. reduced England to an absolute monarchy again, that continued to grow more and more absolute, until, in the reign of Henry VIII., it had become a despotism as unmitigated as that of the Czar.

Nor is this strange. The nobility, shattered and dependent, had neither power nor prestige, and could no longer, if it would, stand between the people and oppression; the church that had so often stood side by side with the nobility in the contest with tyranny, was stricken with heresy, and paralyzed through fear of another reformation; the people were not yet sufficiently enlightened to understand or maintain their own rights; and so the crown was left with little or no restraint, and the descent towards absolutism was easy and rapid. Charters, statutes, and human rights were trodden under foot with perfect impunity. To use the language of Green, "The Crown which only fifty years before had been the sport of every faction, towered into solitary greatness."

Though constitutional liberty seemed, after the Wars of the Roses, to have departed from England, none of the great statutes advancing the cause of human rights were ever abrogated.

The Magna Charta was recognized as the supreme law of the land by kings and ministers, even while they trampled its provisions under their feet. The

Monarchy and the House of Lords were once abolished, but the House of Commons never. Though hated by tyrants, and so prorogued, dissolved, overawed, and ignored, it never for a moment ceased to exist.

The Decline of Civilization. The barbarous manner in which these wars were conducted was most debasing, not only to the soldiers who were actors, but also to the people who were spectators, in the horrible drama. "No quarter," was the savage order in many a battle. But more demoralizing than this were the cold-blooded executions that followed almost every victory. And most brutalizing of all was the hideous and sickening spectacle of ghastly heads and limbs of human bodies, impaled on stakes and walls in public places, and constantly staring the people in the face. What a school for the young were the Wars of the Roses! The nobler qualities of individual character were consumed in the fierceness of the hate which these wars engendered. There is hardly a chivalrous deed to be found in the whole gloomy record. War is not necessarily demoralizing to either individual or national character. When waged in the cause of truth and justice, it may be ennobling to both. A Washington or a Hampden may become great and good in the midst of conflict and carnage. But in the Wars of the Roses there was no principle at stake. The welfare of a nation was sacrificed to the interests of a house; the patriot was sunk in the partisan; the baser passions ruled, and civilization declined.

Edward V., April 9th to June 26th, 1483. York.

Usurpation of Richard, Duke of Gloucester. The people of England had settled down tolerably contented under Edward IV., in spite of the tyrannical character of his government. In fact, they were willing to accept almost any rule that could save them from the horrors of civil war, and give some promise of stability. At Edward's death, there was a general disposition to receive kindly his son Edward, as his successor. But there was one man in England who did not share this feeling, Richard, Duke of Gloucester, uncle to the young prince. With the subtle craft of which he was master, Richard concealed his ambition under a mask of loyalty, but at once put into operation a scheme of usurpation, that, for boldness of design and skill in execution, has few equals.

He first arrested on a trivial charge, Lords Grey and Rivers, Prince Edward's uncles on his mother's side, and threw them into castle Pontefract. He then possessed himself of the person of Edward, and afterwards, of Edward's younger brother, Richard, and lodged them for safe keeping, as he said, in the Tower. He next secured from Parliament his own appointment as Protector of England, and at the same time, with other peers, took the oath of fealty to Edward.

A few days after this, on the 13th of June, occurred a scene in the Tower, where the royal council were in session, marked in itself, but made forever classic by the genius of Shakspeare. Richard suddenly presented himself before this council, at the head of a file of soldiers, and charged its president, Lord Hastings, with sorcery and designs upon his life. "I will not dine," said he, at length, "till they have brought me your head." Hastings was quickly hurried into the courtyard by the waiting soldiers, and beheaded on a chance block of wood. The other members of the council were cast into prison. Having thus put out of the way all the immediate friends of the young princes, Richard's elevation to the throne became easy. He surrounded himself with soldiers, and was attended in public by a formidable array of prelates and nobles, many of whom were won to his side by the honors and offices he heaped upon them. The Thames is said to have been covered with the barges of his servants, while in London organized gatherings of the rabble were taught to shout, "Long live King Richard," and a shameless friar, in a sermon at Paul's Cross, pronounced the princes illegitimate, and declared the Duke of Gloucester to be the true heir to the kingdom. Finally, a deputation headed by the Duke of Buckingham, Richard's pliant minion from the beginning, invited him to take the crown, which, with a show of reluctance, he consented to do.

The next day, at an informal meeting of members of Parliament, the declarations of the friar received a shameless endorsement, and Richard, the following day, the 26th of June, occupied the royal seat at Westminster Hall, as King Richard III. The same day, Grey and Rivers were beheaded without a show of trial. The formal coronation took place on the 6th of July, and the well-planned tragedy, of which Gloucester and Buckingham were the authors and chief actors, the whole kingdom of England a stage, and all its people silent but interested spectators, was over.

Richard III., 1483 to 1485 — 2 years. York.

The Elements of Opposition to Richard. Although no open resistance was made to the usurpation of Richard, he had numerous enemies, including nearly all the adherents of the House of Lancaster and those of the House of York, who were, at heart, loyal to the rightful king, Edward V. There was, too, a general feeling of indignation at the harsh treatment of the young princes; for, at the accession of Richard, they had been removed from the palace of the Tower to its prison. There were whispers of a gathering storm. The Duke of Buckingham, now estranged from his old master, was getting ready for a rising to liberate the princes and restore Edward to his rights. Henry Tudor, Earl of Richmond, the last surviving member of the house of Lancaster, who had been saved at the fall of the Lancastrian cause, by flight to the continent, was busy enlisting English exiles and fugitives to return and assist in the rising.

The Smothered Princes. Richard had gone to the north on a "royal progress," and was at Warwick when vague rumors of Richmond's plans first reached his ears. A messenger of Richard's rode swiftly back to London on a secret mission, and soon it was noised abroad that the young princes were no more. How or when they had died no one knew; but that a foul murder had been committed, and that Richard was its instigator, all believed. The very mystery in which the fate of the princes was shrouded, as impenetrable as the gloomy walls that were its silent witnesses, served but to deepen the public horror of the crime, and the public abhorrence of the criminal.

After Richard's death, the hired assassins told how they smothered the little princes, sweetly sleeping in each other's arms, and buried them at the foot of the staircase that led to their apartment in the White Tower. In confirmation of this story, it is said that some workmen, sent by Charles II., in 1674, to make repairs, found buried in the ground at the foot of an old staircase, the bones of two youths.

— **Bosworth Field.** The rising that took place was unfortunate. Richmond, who had arrived with a fleet to aid the movement, was driven off the coast by a storm, and compelled to return to France. Buckingham, unable to cross the high waters of the Severn and join the confederates, was taken and executed. Richard now summoned his first and only Parliament, and attempted by wise legislation * to turn the current of public opinion, setting so strongly against him. It was too late. The death of the princes defeated the plans of the conspirators, but a new scheme was made to elevate Richmond himself to the throne, and to bring about his marriage with Elizabeth, eldest daughter of Edward IV., thus uniting the rival houses, and rallying to the support of Richmond the adherents of both. Richard tried to forestall a scheme so dangerous to his power, by one attempt to marry Elizabeth to his own

---

* Among others there were statutes making unlawful the exaction of "benevolences," — establishing a protective tariff, but allowing the free importation of books, — forbidding the seizure of the goods of persons suspected of crime before conviction, and allowing such persons to be liberated on bail, — giving freedom to all the serfs still left on the royal estates, — legalizing the sale of estates regardless of the entail, a statute that encouraged the breaking up of large estates, and the wider distribution of landed property among the middle and lower classes, usually accredited to the reign of Henry VII.

son, but the latter suddenly dying, by another, to espouse her himself, from which he was deterred by the force of public opinion.

In the meantime, Richmond was busy reorganizing his expedition, and word soon came that he had sailed from the mouth of the Seine. Richard took his stand at Nottingham, a central point, and, with horsemen on all the roads, awaited the beacon-lights on the distant hill-tops that were to signalize the time and place of Richmond's landing. August 7th 1485, the expedition entered Milford Haven, and a landing was effected. On the 22d, the opposing armies met on the Field of Bosworth. In the midst of the conflict, Lord Stanley went over to Richmond with all his forces. Northumberland followed, when Richard, with a cry of "treason, treason!" rushed into the thickest of the fight, with the desperate resolve to conquer or to die. Attempting to strike down his rival, Richmond, into whose very presence he had cut his way, he was surrounded and slain. His golden crown, that had rolled under a hawthorn-bush when he fell, was found and placed upon the head of Richmond, on the battle-field, and in the presence of the whole army. There was great rejoicing throughout England, when it was known that the hated king had paid with his life the penalty of his crimes. The Wars of the Roses and the reign of the House of York ended together on Bosworth Field.

Character of Richard. It is difficult to make a just estimate of the character of Richard III., good authorities differ so widely in their views of him. Until recently, he has been regarded as a monster of wickedness, and without a redeeming quality. But his apologists affirm, that the historians and dramatists, from whom we have derived our impressions, living in the Tudor period, and devoted to the interests of the Tudor sovereigns, painted Richard's character in colors altogether too dark. There is no doubt, that mere suspicions * of crime on the part of Richard have grown into a positive belief in his guilt, that his bad qualities and wicked deeds have been paraded in all their deformity, and his good qualities and worthy deeds passed lightly over. He showered benefits on those who served him, and performed many acts of kindness and justice. He restored to the family of Hastings the forfeited estates, secured her jointure to the widow of Rivers, and provided for the widow and daughters of Edward IV., who had taken sanctuary at Westminster, when Edward V. went to the Tower. He inspired more wise legislation in the single session of his Parliament, than can be found in the records of any previous reign since Edward I. — legislation that had the ring of liberty in it. As a ruler merely, he compares favorably with the kings of that period. But as to his character as a man, it seems difficult to reverse the verdict of history. The historians of the Tudor period, though partial, recorded

---

* The belief that Richard murdered Henry VI. with his own hand, and drowned the Duke of Clarence, his older brother, in a butt of Malmsey wine, seemed to rest in the fact that he was known to be in the Tower when they were reported to have died; and the belief that he was the one who stabbed the son of Henry VI. after the battle of Tewkesbury, rested on the fact that he was known to be present, but Hastings and Clarence were also present. The belief that he put out of the way Anna, his wife, to make room for Elizabeth, rested on the fact that she died very conveniently for his plans, although rather suspicious remarks are accredited to Elizabeth, in substance that "the better part of February had passed and she feared the Queen would never die." The Queen died about the middle of March.

and reflected the opinions of Richard's own contemporaries, the public sentiment of Richard's own times; and public sentiment, though not infallible, is, in the long run, a truthful mirror of the characters of men.

Richard began his public career about the year 1471, and continued for fourteen years to be actively engaged in public affairs, twelve in the service of his brother, Edward IV., and two as an actual sovereign. Almost his first recorded public act was one of heartless cruelty. A young man of less than twenty years, he was one of two judges that condemned to death so many Lancastrian nobles after the battle of Tewkesbury, when they had been induced to leave the sanctuary, to which they had fled, by a promise of pardon.

With the death of the princes the feeling against Richard became intense and universal. It was evident that personal ambition was his sole inspiring motive. Splendid talents and the most untiring energy were remorselessly devoted to one fixed purpose, to become King of England. As best suited his policy, he could assume the most daring effrontery and boldly strike down those who stood in his way; or, resorting to the arts of dissimulation, remove them by the hand of the secret assassin. Henry VIII. destroyed a hundred lives to Richard's one; but he did not inspire half the terror, for Henry's judicial murders were perpetrated under the color of law and in the light of day. Simply to secure his throne, Henry VII. put out of the way, with a form of trial, an unoffending royal prince, without exciting universal abhorrence.

There is nothing from which human nature so instinctively shrinks as a deed of darkness, no being it so abhors as an assassin or his employer; and it was the settled belief in Richard's almost Satanic capacity for deeds of darkness, that inspired all England with such a dread of him, and that has given to his character on the page of history a color of such unexampled blackness.

CHAPTER VIII.

Tudor Family, 1485 to 1603 — 118 years.

HENRY VII.	MARY.
HENRY VIII.	ELIZABETH.
EDWARD VI.	

Henry VII., 1485 to 1509 — 24 years. Tudor.

Union of York and Lancaster. That Henry was a descendant of John of Gaunt,* and an acknowledged usurper, would, under ordinary circumstances, have endangered his throne; but his opportune marriage with Elizabeth, a York princess, entirely appeased the jealousy of the House of York, while the satisfaction of the people at the overthrow of Richard fully reconciled them to the usurpation. This union of the Roses was a source of great strength, not only to Henry but to all the Tudor sovereigns.

Lambert Simnel. The only attempts worthy of note to disturb the new house were made by two impostors, Lambert Simnel, son of a joiner of Oxford, and Perkin Warbeck, son of a merchant of Tournay. Simnel claimed to be Edward, Earl of Warwick, escaped from prison, although at that very moment the real Warwick lay in a dungeon in the Tower, to which he had been

---

* It will be remembered that by the Treaty of Troyes, Henry V. received in marriage the hand of Catherine, daughter of Charles VI., the crazy king of France, and that after Henry's death, his widow married Owen Tudor, a Welsh chieftain, by whom she had a son. This son married a descendant of John of Gaunt, Duke of Lancaster. The issue of this marriage was Henry Tudor, Earl of Richmond, now Henry VII. Hence the name Tudor.

transferred by Henry. Landing in England with a force chiefly of Irish, he was beaten and taken captive in the battle of Stoke. As an expression of the king's contempt for the imposition he had practiced, Simnel was made a scullion in the royal kitchen, but was afterwards promoted to the office of falconer to the king.

Perkin Warbeck. Warbeck, a more dangerous but not less real impostor, personated Richard, the younger of the smothered princes, claiming that he too had escaped from the Tower, and had now come forward to assert his rights. He visited a number of foreign Courts, and had a variety of interesting adventures, being crowned as a real prince at Dublin, furnished with a royal body-guard at Paris, patronized as the "True White Rose" by the Duchess of Burgundy, and supplied with men and money, and wedded to a royal wife,* by James of Scotland. After two fruitless invasions, the one from Scotland under the lead of the Scottish king, and the other from the west, supported by the Cornishmen, Warbeck was deserted by all his followers and traced to the Sanctuary † of Beaulieu, in

---

* This was Lady Catherine Gordon, a member of the royal house of Stuart. She was famed for personal beauty and amiable traits of character. When Warbeck entered upon his dangerous career, he placed his wife for safe-keeping in the Castle of St. Michael's Mount. After his defeat, a body of horsemen surrounded the castle, and compelled its surrender. Even the cold, practical king was touched by Catherine's devotion to her husband, and gave her an honorable place near the person of the queen. The name, White Rose, by which she came to be known, though suggested by the false claims of her husband, was given as a tribute to her beauty.

† Sanctuaries were consecrated places, where criminals could, for a limited time, find shelter when pursued. They were analogous to the temples of refuge among the ancient Greeks, and the cities of refuge among the Jews. In England, as early as the seventh century, churches, and in some cases their grounds, were set apart for sanctuary purposes. Sometimes a stone seat was placed beside the altar, where the person of the fugitive was as sacred as the altar itself. Though the sanctuary might be surrounded, and the

the New Forest. Induced to surrender, he was thrown into the Tower, and afterwards hanged at Tyburn, on the charge of planning an insurrection with the young Earl of Warwick, his fellow-prisoner. Warwick was also executed, not because he was guilty of any offence worthy of death, but because he was the last male Plantagenet, and a source of possible danger to the throne of Henry.

The Statute of Allegiance. The attempts made on the throne, though not very grave, led Parliament to define by statute the allegiance of the subject. It was enacted that no one should be punished for allegiance to the reigning king, whether he be king "de jure" (by right), or king "de facto" (in fact). This was designed to guard against such wholesale executions, in case of a change in the dynasty, as followed the fluctuations of the Roses, when men were adjudged traitors one day for adhering to York, and beheaded the next for following Lancaster.

The Discovery of America. The reign of Henry VII. marks the era of discovery. When Columbus returned to Spain, under whose auspices he had sailed in 1492, and the startling news flew from port to port that a new world had been discovered far to the westward, it was like a bugle blast in the midst of a slumbering army. The maritime nations of Europe awoke to a

---

criminal forced by hunger to surrender himself, he had the right of " abjuration of the realm;" that is, he could go before the proper authority any time within forty days, confess his crime, and make oath to quit the realm and not return without the consent of the king. In that case he was protected until he could embark for some foreign country. Traitors were deprived of the right of sanctuary in 1534, criminals in the reign of Elizabeth, and insolvent debtors in 1697. But in Scotland, the Palace and Abbey of Holyrood still remain a sanctuary for poor debtors. Persons not criminals, whose lives were in danger, often took shelter in the sanctuaries.

spirit of enterprise and inquiry they had never known before. National pride and jealousy, and individual love of glory and adventure, sent expedition after expedition out into the broad and hitherto dreaded Atlantic, on its wonder-seeking mission. The printing press,* invented just before, aided in the general awaking. The story of the voyage of Amerigo Vespucci, published in Strasburg in 1505, was circulated throughout Europe, stimulating still more the thirst for discovery. When the first flush of wonder and excitement had passed away, and the public curiosity in regard to the new-found lands had been partially satisfied, dreams of empire, schemes of profitable trade, and a wild greed for gold, became permanent incentives to individual and national enterprise. In original discovery, England was second only to Spain, sending out an expedition under **John and Sebastian Cabot,** that reached, in 1497, the main land of North America. The same year an expedition, fitted out by the Portuguese, under **Vasco di Gama,** doubled the Cape of Good Hope, and opened a new way by water to the commerce of India.

The Revival of Letters. The Art of Printing had quickened the spirit of inquiry in other directions. There was in England a great revival of letters. On the taking of Constantinople by the Turks, in 1453,

---

* William Caxton learned the Art of Printing while in Holland, where, in 1471 he printed a book entitled "The Recuyell of the Historyes of **Troye.**" He brought his press to England in 1473, reign of Edward IV., and the next year published a work entitled "The Game and Playe of Chess." Long before the Christian Era the Chinese were familiar with block printing, and its use in Germany dates from the year 1138. Gutenberg invented cut metal types in 1414; Schœffer, types cast in hollow moulds in 1452.

many of the learned men of Greece found an asylum in Italy. Thither flocked students from all quarters, among whom, from England, were Grocyn, Linacre, Colet and Erasmus. On their return to England, fired with zeal, a new enthusiasm was awakened in the study of Grecian and Roman literature; and the Bible, that, in rare and costly manuscript, had been accessible to only a privileged few, reproduced in cheap editions, in print, was brought within the reach of many. Men began to think for themselves, not only in philosophy and science but in politics and religion. With the spread of knowledge, superstition began to lose its power. The minds of men were gradually enlarged and prepared for that second and greater reformation that ere long broke out in England with such irresistible power.

And we find here, too, the beginning of modern civilization, based not on the essential slavery of the Feudal System, as was the mediæval, but on the growing intelligence and increasing importance of the masses of the people.

The Character and Policy of Henry. With little love for learning himself, Henry had looked with an eye of cold suspicion on the signs of a new intellectual life brightening all around him. Even the discovery of America hardly disturbed the impassive king. He had been willing, indeed, that the Cabots should sail on a voyage of discovery, at their own expense, and he showed some appreciation of their grand achievement, by rewarding them with a present of ten pounds when they returned and laid a new world at his feet.

Henry was business-like and miserly. He kept two lawyers busy finding "cases" and exacting fines. Obsolete statutes, forgotten tenures, and petty violations of law, were so many drag-nets that swept into the courts multitudes of men, whose fines poured into the royal treasury a constant stream of wealth. He revived " benevolences," but improved upon the plan of Edward IV., who sought gifts only from the rich, by exacting them from the poor as well.* He omitted no opportunity to grasp the estates of those attainted, and made a large income from the rigid execution of the Statute of Liveries.

In feudal times the castles of the barons were like armed camps. Crowds of idle retainers, feeding on the bounty of their lordly masters, were ever ready, at their bidding, to storm a castle or menace a throne. The Statute of Liveries, enacted in a preceding reign, was designed to break up these great military establishments. Having fallen into disuse, it was revived and executed by Henry, with fine and forfeiture.† A new court, called the "Star Chamber," was appointed to

---

* By a cunning device, called from its author, "Morton's fork," he demanded money of those who made a display in their style of living, for display was evidence of wealth, and exacted gifts from those who made no display, on the ground that such must have grown rich by their economy.

† Bacon tells an amusing story highly illustrative of Henry's avaricious character:—" There remaineth to this day a report that the king was, on a time, entertained by the Earl of Oxford,—that was his principal servant, both for peace and war,—nobly and sumptuously, at his castle at Henningham. And at the king's going away, the earl's servants stood, in a seemly manner, in their livery coats, with cognisances, ranged on both sides, and made the king a lane. The king called the earl to him, and said: 'My lord, I have heard much of your hospitality, but I see it is greater than the speech. These handsome gentlemen and yeomen, which I see on both sides of me, are sure your menial servants.' The earl smiled, and said, 'It may please your grace, that were not for mine ease. They are most of them my retainers, that are come

have special reference to cases coming under this statute,—a court that, being solely under the control of the king, became, in later reigns, the instrument of great oppression. By sharp practice and rigid economy, Henry was able to amass an immense fortune (£10,-000,000 present value) for his son and successor to squander.

Though avaricious by nature, there was a policy in Henry's desire to be rich. He had one grand purpose ever in view,—the establishment of the Tudor throne on a safe and solid basis. He well knew that the great power of the Commons lay in their control of the public funds, and that the possession of abundant means on the part of the king was the royal road to independence. He exerted himself, therefore, to obtain money without appealing to Parliament, and was so successful that there was but one session of Parliament during the last thirteen years of his reign.

He tried still further to fortify his house, by connecting it, through marriage alliances, with the reigning families of Europe. His son Arthur was married to Catherine of Arragon, a Spanish princess, and his daughter Margaret to James Stuart, the King of Scotland. Henry died in 1509, and was buried at Westminster, in the magnificent chapel which he himself had built and which still bears his name. He was succeeded by his son Henry.

---

to do me service at such a time as this, and chiefly to see your grace.' The king started a little and said: 'By my faith, my lord, I thank you for your good cheer, but I may not endure to have my laws broken in my sight. My attorney must speak with you.' And it is part of the report, that the earl compounded for no less than fifteen thousand marks."

Henry VIII., 1509 to 1547 — 38 years. Tudor.

Character of Henry VIII. Henry VIII. came to the throne under circumstances peculiarly favorable. Representing in his own person the rival houses of York and Lancaster, he received their cordial and united support. Henry was eighteen years of age, a handsome, generous, and popular prince. But he changed much in disposition as he grew older. Naturally passionate and impulsive, and unused to self-control, he became, with opposition, malignant and unrelenting. He was as prodigal as his father had been penurious, and wasted in a few years the great fortune he inherited. One of the first official acts of the young king was designed to satisfy popular clamor. Empson and Dudley, the hated lawyers of Henry VII., were brought to the scaffold on a charge of treason.

Foreign Affairs. The foreign wars of this reign were comparatively unimportant. Henry has been called a good soldier, but a bad general. Both the king and his principal minister, Thomas Wolsey, were actuated more by personal than national considerations, in the foreign relations of the state. At one time Henry was ambitious to occupy the vacant German throne; at another, Wolsey aspired to fill the vacant papal chair; and each sought to shape the foreign policy of England to meet his own interests. In spite of the failures of his predecessors, Henry dared to dream of the conquest of France. His campaign in that country, in 1513, is chiefly celebrated for the battle of Guinegate, which the French themselves laughingly named the "Battle of the Spurs," from the amusing haste with which their cavalry, not whipt but well-scared, galloped off the battle-field. During Henry's absence in France, an event occurred in England of a far more serious character.

The Scots were in league with the French. Invading England under the command of their king, James IV., they were met at Flodden, the last of the Cheviot Hills, by an army under the Earl of Surrey. The bloody battle that followed left Scotland without a king, and almost without a nobility. Ten thousand gallant Scotch knights fell on Flodden Field. Being deserted by his allies, Henry made peace with the French king, Louis XII., giving the latter in marriage the hand of his eldest sister Mary.* In 1520 there was a meeting between Henry and the new king of France, Francis I., in English territory. The place of the meeting has been called the "Field of the Cloth of Gold," from the magnificence of the display. The most important of Henry's foreign relations was with the Pope of Rome.

The Divorce of Catherine of Arragon. Henry had married Catherine of Arragon, his brother Arthur's widow, soon after coming to the throne. He had been betrothed to her by his father years before, a special dispensation being obtained from the pope, as such a union was forbidden by the Levitical law and a canon of the church. Nearly twenty years after this marriage

---

*Louis XII. soon died, and Henry sent Charles Francis Brandon, Duke of Suffolk, to France, to bring his widowed sister back to England. Now it happened that Brandon was an old and accepted lover of Mary's, and her wishes had not been consulted by Henry when he gave her to the French king; princesses' wishes rarely were in those old times. Taking advantage of so favorable an opportunity, Brandon and Mary were married in France before they returned to England. Henry was, at first, very angry, but soon forgave them. They had a daughter, Lady Frances Brandon, who married Henry Grey, Marquis of Dorset. Lady Jane Grey, whose sad history we are soon to relate, was the offspring of this marriage.

had taken place, Henry began to have what he called conscientious scruples about its legality. He coupled these scruples with his "despair of having male issue by Catherine, to inherit the realm." He had but one living child, a daughter, Mary. Another dispensation was now required to dissolve his union with Catherine, before he could form a new alliance. Cardinal Wolsey was commissioned to secure it. Charles V., Emperor of Germany, was a nephew to Catherine. He had recently made war on the pope, taking Rome and making the pope his prisoner. For the pope to give the desired dispensation would offend the emperor; to refuse it would displease Henry, and so the pope temporized. Wolsey was as much puzzled as the pope to know what to do. To grant the divorce on his own responsibility would offend his superior at Rome; to refuse it would bring upon himself the wrath of the king, and so Wolsey temporized. For two years was the impatient king kept in suspense, his impatience made all the greater by the violence of his passion for Anne Boleyn, a pretty maid of honor to the queen. A court had been organized in 1529, under Wolsey and Campeggio, an Italian cardinal, to try the case in England. It sat nearly two months without result, when the case was ordered by the pope to be tried at Rome. This sealed the fate of Wolsey, and made a rupture with the pope inevitable. Wolsey, stripped of all his temporal honors and offices, was ordered into retirement at his See of York.

Cardinal Wolsey. Cardinal Wolsey was the son of a butcher, and was educated at Oxford. Brilliant talents had brought him to the notice of Henry VII., from whom he had received the appointment of royal chaplain. He afterwards attracted the attention of Henry VIII., who raised him from one position to another, until he became Lord Chancellor of the kingdom, and Cardinal in the church, and finally Papal Legate.

For twenty years he had stood at the head of church and state, the most powerful, if not the most able, subject England ever had. His genius was unequalled for breadth or versatility. He could play the courtier, and amuse the idle hours of the pleasure-loving king with ceaseless sallies of wit and mirth, or he could act the statesman, and guide with consummate skill the most intricate affairs of the government. It is interesting to follow him as he leaves the scenes of his former pomp and splendor, and devotes himself with simplicity and meekness to the ordinary duties of a parish priest, visiting the sick and dying, giving alms to the poor and needy, and ministering in countless ways to the temporal and spiritual wants of his grateful people. In about a year, the king ordered his arrest on a charge of high treason. He had committed no new offence, and had been pardoned for the old one; but he had an unforgiving enemy in Anne Boleyn.

In charge of the keeper of the Tower, Wolsey commenced his last journey towards London. He was taken ill on the road. On reaching Leicester Abbey, conscious that his end was drawing near, he said to the Father Abbot, as the latter gave him a kindly welcome, "I am come hither to leave my bones among you." This was Saturday night. The following Tuesday, November 29th, 1531, when at the point of death, he gave utterance to those ever memorable words, "If

I had served God as diligently as I have done the king, he would not have given me over in my gray hairs."*
The ingratitude of Henry VIII. was the basest of his many faults. He could crush long-tried and faithful servants, with as little feeling as he would tread upon the meanest reptile.

The Divorce of Catherine of Arragon Accomplished. The gordian knot of the divorce was finally cut by the ingenuity of Bishop Cranmer, who suggested to the delighted king the reference of the whole question to the universities of Europe. The pope forbade the divorce of Catherine and the marriage with Anne Boleyn, on pain of excommunication. But a majority of the universities, through bribery or menace, decided in Henry's favor, and Cranmer, now made Archbishop of Canterbury, pronounced, in 1533, Henry's union with Catherine null and void. Anne Boleyn, already married to the king, was publicly crowned Queen of England. The noble Queen Catherine, who had resisted to the utmost the disgrace and injustice heaped upon her, died in a few years, honored for her virtues and her piety.

The Oxford Reformers. We return once more to the beginning of Henry's reign. The young king, though fond of pleasure and display, was scholarly in his tastes and well educated, and carefully fostered the new spirit of enterprise and mental activity among his

---

* These words, addressed to Master Kingston, the Constable of the Tower, who had been sent by the king to convey Wolsey to prison, have been crystallized by the genius of Shakspeare:

"O Cromwell, Cromwell,
Had I but served my God with half the zeal
I served my king, He would not in mine age
Have left me naked to mine enemies."

people. Colet, who had been made Dean of St. Paul's by Henry VII., became, under the present king, head of a new school for the study of Latin and Greek literature; More was appointed to some civil office, and, later, at the fall of Wolsey, to the chancellorship; Erasmus received a professorship at Cambridge. These zealous pioneers in the new world of thought and conscience, vigorously applied themselves to the work of reform.

Erasmus. Erasmus, with a moral courage that reminds us of Wickliffe, wrote book after book, in which he aimed at reformation in politics and religion as well as learning, now holding up to ridicule the follies of the age, now to scorn and contempt the corruptions of the church, and now addressing the consciences of men in the most tender and affecting appeals. In his "Praise of Folly," he makes Folly, dressed in cap and bells, describe, in a speech to her associates, the religious teachers of the day, the old school men, as "men who knew all about things of which St. Paul was ignorant, could talk science as though they had been consulted when the world was made, could give you the dimensions of heaven as though they had been there and measured it with plumb and line, men who professed universal knowledge, and yet had not time to read the Gospels or the Epistles of St. Paul." But the work of Erasmus most potent in its influence, was his edition of the New Testament, in parallel columns, one in Greek and the other in Latin. Several editions were required to meet the popular demand. Said Erasmus, in speaking of the Scriptures, in his preface, "I wish that they were translated into all languages, so as to be read and understood not only by Scots and Irishmen, but even by Saracens and Turks. I long for the day when the husbandman shall sing portions of them to himself as he follows the plough, when the weaver shall hum them to the tune of his shuttle, when the traveller shall while away with their stories the weariness of his journey."

Thomas More. From the prophetic pen of More, appeared a work entitled "Utopia," or Nowhere, a satire on the times, especially the reign of Henry VII. Utopia was an ideal commonwealth, which an imaginary companion of Amerigo Vespucci, deserted on the American continent, found somewhere in the midst of the wilds. It had wide and cleanly streets, comfortable houses, a system of public schools in which every child received a good education, perfect religious toleration, and universal suffrage, though with a family, and not an individual ballot, and the sole object of the government was the good of the whole people, and not the pleasure of the king. Had More's pseudo voyager but wandered to the American continent a few centuries later, he would have found his model "Utopia" a real and not an ideal republic.

Opposition to the Oxford **Reformers.** This is but a slight glance at the work of the Oxford Reformers, extending through a period of forty years, in educating the people of England up to a higher plane of intelligence, and in preparing the way for that second and greater reformation that broke out in Germany under Luther one year after More wrote his "Utopia," and in England soon after. It must not be supposed that the old school men and theologians were silent, while the reformers were busy removing the very foundations of their mouldering temples. They bitterly opposed the reformation at every step. More once wrote to Colet, "No wonder your school raises a storm, for it is like the wooden horse filled with armed Greeks for the destruction of Troy." And such it proved. So popular did it become that others of a similar character followed; and it is said that, in the latter part of Henry's reign, more schools were founded than in three centuries before. Repeated attempts were made to destroy Colet; once, when, from the royal pulpit and in the very presence of the king, Colet had denounced the French wars, in which the king had enlisted so heartily; and again, when, at a convocation of bishops and clergy, being appointed to deliver the opening sermon, he boldly charged many of them with living worldly and immoral lives. The bishops of London, with others, lodged a charge of heresy against him. Said the bluff king to those who sought his help against Colet, "Let every man have his own doctor, but this man is the doctor for me." To Henry's protection did the Oxford Reformers owe their personal safety, and to his encouragement was the New Learning indebted for its rapid progress. And yet the very men he shielded from the most vindictive enemies he hesitated not to destroy at their slightest opposition to his own will.

Martin Luther and the Reformation. More than a century had passed away since Wickliffe inaugurated the First Reformation. We are now brought to the threshold of the second, under Luther, on whom Wickliffe's mantle seemed to have fallen. Martin

Luther was educated for the law, but in 1505, when twenty-two years of age, he became a monk in the monastery at Erfurt, and, in 1508, preacher at the University of Wittenburg, lately founded by the Elector of Saxony. An eye-witness to the corruptions of the church, and convinced, by a study of the Bible, of its errors in doctrine, he gradually came to accept "justification by faith" as the only way of salvation. Pope Leo X., ostensibly to raise money for the completion of the splendid temple of St. Peter, offered for sale, at a fixed price, indulgences or pardons for sin, and had sent his agents all over Europe to find purchasers. In 1517, when Wolsey was at the height of his power, and just after Erasmus had published his New Testament, Luther, learning that Tetzel, one of the pope's agents, was about to come to Wittenburg, nailed to the doors of his church his famous Propositions, denouncing the whole doctrine of indulgences, and the next day (day of All-Saints) read them to the assembled parish. Tetzel was forbidden by the Elector, Luther's friend and protector, to enter his dominions. There was a year or two of bitter controversy between Luther and the pope, during which the former boldly defied the latter, publicly burning the bull of excommunication issued against him. Luther was then summoned for trial before the Diet of Worms, held in 1521, over which the German Emperor himself presided. Luther boldly maintained all his declarations before that august assembly, refusing again and again to recant or abjure, and was condemned as a heretic. He had a safe pass to Wittenburg, to which place he returned, and henceforth devoted himself to the work he had undertaken, the reformation of the church. The emperor then issued his edict against Luther, consigning him to death at the stake; but before the sentence could be executed, all Germany was ablaze with the fires of reformation and revolt, and the emperor had little time to kindle that for the martyrdom of Luther.

Thus began the Great Reformation, but it did not end in Germany. We are soon to see it cross the English Channel, and separate England and Scotland from the Papal See. Nor does it cease, till, in the progress of time, it has brought within its resistless sweep the kingdoms of Denmark, Sweden, Switzerland, Norway and the Netherlands.

The Reformation in England. England was fully awake to the events occurring in Germany. King Henry, although a friend to reform in the church, still held to its principal tenets. While the Diet of Worms was in session, he had written a book against Luther, for which, in gratitude, the pope had called him "Defender of the Faith," a title still borne by the sovereigns of England. We have seen how, a little later, in 1529, a breach had occurred between the king and the pope, on account of the divorce of Catherine. This gradually widened into complete alienation, and Rome and England, bound together eight hundred years by that most sacred of ties, a common faith, were sundered forever. By a series of parliamentary enactments, beginning in 1531, annates (the first year's income of vacant bishoprics) to Rome were abolished, all appeals to the pope forbidden, papal jurisdiction over England extinguished, and finally, in 1534, the King of England was declared to be the Supreme Head of the Church of England. It was now that the bull of excommunication, long held over the head of Henry, was hurled against him. But the Rubicon had been crossed, and there was no alternative but a march on Rome.

Bishop Fisher and Thomas More Executed. Speech against the pope was no longer heresy; but denial of Henry's Supremacy was made high treason. For the latter offence perished on the scaffold, in 1535, Fisher, the good Bishop of Rochester, who came to the scene of his death with a copy of the New Testament in his hand, and read, as he knelt to lay his head upon the block, the words, "This is life eternal to know Thee, the only true God." For this, too, perished More, one of the most learned men in Christendom, who, believing the pope to be the divinely appointed head of the church, had resigned his office on Henry's assumption of Supremacy. He had been a life-long reformer; but he had labored for a reform of the church, and not separation from it. The Emperor Charles is said to have exclaimed, when told of the death of More, "I would rather have lost the best city in my dominions than so worthy a counselor."

Henry Supreme in Church and State. All the powers of pope and king were now concentrated in the person of Henry. He dictated the utterances of the pulpit as well as the enactments of parliament; he controlled the ecclesiastical as well as the civil courts; he declared what was truth and what heresy. Bishops and archbishops held their places only at his pleasure; and into his hand were poured the vast revenues that for centuries had flowed so steadily to the

Vatican. No priest could preach without a royal license, and no license was given without the Oath of Supremacy. Every priest was compelled to declare to his assembled parish their absolution from allegiance to the pope, and the duty of obedience to the new Head of the Church. Thus were the mute and bewildered people, constrained by respect for law on the one hand, and reverence for religion on the other, carried peacefully through the first and most critical step of a great religious revolution. In other nations the Reformation advanced only through a sea of blood. It is a pertinent inquiry, to what extent were the peace and order that marked the Reformation in England due to the overshadowing character of the throne, and the iron will of the despot that occupied it? As if to remove the last shadow of a limitation to the authority of the king, Parliament enacted that royal proclamations should have the force of statutes; and it is affirmed, that during the sessions of Parliament, if Henry's name were but mentioned, in his absence, the members would rise and bow before the vacant throne. Henry's next step was to reform the faith and practice of the church. He drew up with his own hand the articles of religion.* These showed that the king had

---

* They made the Bible the sole ground of faith; reduced the sacraments from seven to three, namely: Penance, Baptism and the Lord's Supper; retained transubstantiation and confession, but added justification by faith; and rejected pilgrimages, purgatory, indulgences, the worship of images and relics, and masses for the dead. The Ten Commandments and the Lord's Prayer were required to be taught in every school and family. A copy of Tyndal's Bible, the first ever translated into English, revised by Coverdale in 1535, was ordered to be chained to the pillar or desk of every church in England, and to be open to the reading of all. In 1539, a translation of the Bible was made by Cranmer.

taken the middle ground between Protestants * and Papists. They were essentially the views Erasmus had so long labored to impress upon the English people. The bishops and clergy gradually fell into the new order of things, but the monks remained unreconciled.

The Suppression of the Religious Houses. A commission was appointed to visit the religious houses. They reported a larger part of them as corrupt and immoral, and so, by statute, nunneries and monasteries were broken up, their inmates being turned out into the world, and their revenues poured into the royal treasury. Ten thousand nuns alone were made homeless by the cruel statute, which was probably inspired by no higher motive than the greed of the king for the wealth of the church. At the same time the tombs and shrines of the saints, many of them adorned with costly works of art and rich with the gifts of countless pilgrims, were robbed of their treasures and ruthlessly destroyed. The most famous of these was the tomb of Thomas à Becket, from which two great chests of gold and jewels were borne away to the royal coffers. This was followed by several risings, especially among the

* After the decision of the Diet of Worms, in 1521, Charles V., Emperor of Germany, issued an edict against Luther and the Lutheran heresy. A quarrel arose, in 1526, between Charles and the pope, and the former threw his influence against the latter in the Diet of Spires, then in session, and the following decree, entirely annulling the Edict of Worms, was issued: "Each state should, as regards the Edict of Worms, so live, rule, and bear itself as it thought it could answer it to God and the Emperor." The different German states thus became either Lutheran or Catholic, as they chose. But Charles soon settled his quarrel with the pope, and, as a result, the second Diet of Spires, held in 1529, re-enacted the Edict of Worms, and forbade further reform without the sanction of a regular council. Against this decision the Lutheran princes of Germany entered their "protest," and were therefore called "Protestants."

nobles in the north and west. These were readily put down, and the executions that followed remind us of the Wars of the Roses. Henry's principal minister, after the retirement of More, was Thomas Cromwell. He had taken service with Wolsey, and remained his friend to the last. When Wolsey retired in disgrace to his See of York, Cromwell went to London to "make or mar," as he expressed it. It was Cromwell who suggested to the king to solve the Papal problem, by declaring his own Supremacy. He became a member of Parliament, and was indefatigable in his efforts to protect and save Wolsey. He then became Henry's chief minister, and, when Supremacy had been achieved, Vice-gerent of the church.

The Bloody Statute. The Reformation had advanced with rapid strides, and was attended with many excesses on the part of extremists. A reaction was the result; and this led to the enactment, in 1539, at the dictation of the king, of a statute containing six articles, called by Fox "the whip with six strings," re-affirming the cardinal doctrines of the Catholic church. The penalty of death, by fire or the scaffold, hung over the heads of all who violated the terrible statute. The prisons were quickly crowded with offenders. Catholics were burned for not accepting the Protestant head of the church, and Protestants committed to the flames for rejecting the Catholic faith. The execution of this statute was relaxed after a few months, else it were difficult to see how there could have been a consistent Protestant or Catholic left in England.

Henry's Wives. Henry, in 1509, married Catherine of Arragon, who was divorced in 1533, having had a daughter, Mary. The same year he married Anne Boleyn, who was beheaded, in 1536, on a charge of being faithless to him, leaving a daughter, Elizabeth. The next day he married Jane Seymour, who died, in 1537, after giving birth to a son, Edward. In 1540, Cromwell arranged a match with Anne of Cleves, a German princess. But she was plain and awkward, and in a little over six months, Henry was divorced from her, and married to Catherine Howard. She, too, was beheaded, in about a year and a half, on a charge of unchastity before marriage, and the next year, 1543, he married Catherine Parr, who survived him. Cromwell was brought to the block when the king discarded Anne of Cleves.

Henry's Death. By an Act of Parliament, Henry was authorized to bestow the crown according to his own pleasure. He bequeathed it to his son Edward. The youth and old age of few persons present so great a contrast as those of Henry. A graceful and attractive youth, he became in old age so gross and offensive in his person that few could endure to remain near him. On account of his excessive corpulency, he was moved from chamber to chamber by mechanical aid. When his last sickness came upon him, and death drew near, at first no one dared tell him the terrible truth. Conscious at last of the coming change, he sent for Cranmer, who had retained his favor to the last, pressed his hand, and died.

Edward VI., 1547 to 1553 — 6 years. Tudor.

The Regency. The political history of the reign of Edward VI., which lasted only six years, is but an uninteresting record of the schemes of ambitious men, aiming at wealth and power. Henry VIII. had appointed a Council of sixteen members, at the head of which stood Cranmer, to govern the kingdom until Edward, who was now ten, reached the age of eighteen years. This Council, disregarding the will of Henry, appointed the Earl of Hertford, afterwards Duke of Somerset, one of its own members, Protector.

Edward and Mary, Queen of Scots. By a treaty with Scotland, made during the lifetime of Henry, Edward had been betrothed to Mary, the young Scottish queen. Somerset urged upon the Scots the execution of the treaty, but the combined French and Catholic influence prevailed to defeat it. Somerset raised an army and marched into Scotland to compel the observance of the treaty. At the battle of Pinkie, the last national contest between the two countries, the Scots were defeated with a loss of ten thousand men, but they became more bitterly opposed to the execution of the treaty than before. The Earl of Huntley expressed the prevailing sentiment among the Scotch nobles when he said, "He disliked not the match, but hated the manner of the wooing." Mary was then sent to France to render the marriage impossible. The Earl of Warwick, afterwards Duke of Northumberland, also a member of the Council, secured the overthrow of Somerset and his own appointment in his stead. Northumberland remained in office to the end of the reign.

Peasant Revolts. While Somerset was Protector, peasant revolts* broke out in different parts of the kingdom. The most important of these revolts occurred under one Robert Ket, at the head of twenty thousand men. Ket established himself at Norwich, as judge and law-giver for all the country around, making his headquarters under an oak tree, which he called the "Tree of Reformation." The revolts were quelled with the usual barbarities, the "Tree of Reformation" serving as a gallows.

Progress of the Reformation. But that which interests us most in this reign is the progress of the Reformation. Archbishop Cranmer, encouraged by the king, who was a zealous Protestant, vigorously carried forward the work begun by Henry VIII. The old

---

* It is not clear as to the exact causes in all cases. It will be remembered that after the ravages of the Black Death in the reign of Edward III., the scarcity of laborers caused high wages, and both together wrought a gradual change in the agricultural policy of the country. The farmers, abandoning crops that required much manual labor, turned their arable land into pastures for raising sheep. The suppression of the monasteries was followed by a like disposition of the church lands, the most of which went to satisfy the greed of favorite courtiers, and to found a new nobility, and were, by their new owners, turned into "enclosures" for sheep culture. The agricultural products were thus largely reduced in quantity, but enhanced in value. But the people, in the course of time, recovered from the depletions of the pestilence, and labor became abundant, and consequently cheap. Besides this, the monks had been good to the poor, and were generally beloved. There was a feeling of heartfelt sympathy for them, as homeless and penniless they wandered about the country, begging food and shelter. The monasteries were not all corrupt, and they had, in times past, served a useful purpose. They had afforded the means of education to the young, given shelter to the traveller, and been a refuge for the oppressed, in an age when there were no inns, few schools, and little protection for the weak and innocent against the lawless and brutal. The general dissatisfaction, especially in the rural districts, at their suppression, caused a reaction against the Reformation, and gave rise to plots for the return of Catholicism. All these things, therefore, "enclosures" for sheep culture, a surplus of labor and a falling scale of wages, small crops and the high price of food, the dissolution of the religious houses, together with a debasement of the coinage under Henry VIII., combined to produce idleness, destitution, and revolt.

statutes running back to the days of the Lollards, and those of a more recent origin on the subject of heresy, as well as the "new-fangled treasons" of Henry VIII., were all repealed. The Catholic clergy were removed from their livings, and their places filled with Protestants; the Latin mass was abolished; the churches were despoiled of their plate, the paintings on their walls, and the stained glass in the windows, were ruthlessly destroyed. The colleges connected with the religious houses and the chantries (places where mass was said for the dead) were broken up, their revenues being used, in part, by Edward, for the endowment of grammar schools and hospitals. Perhaps the most important step taken in promoting the Reformation was the preparation, chiefly by Archbishop Cranmer, of a "Book of Common Prayer." Cranmer took as a basis for his work the services that had been in use in the church since the primitive ages. Being printed in English, the people soon learned to love a form of worship which they could understand, and in which they could so intelligently participate. Its use was made obligatory in all the churches. Only two persons suffered at the stake during this reign, but many, who refused to conform to the Protestant worship, went to prison.

Edward's Will. Lady Jane Grey,* a member of the youngest branch of the Tudor family, had married Lord Dudley, son of Northumberland. As Edward was in consumption, and it was evident that he could not long survive, Northumberland prevailed upon him to alter the succession, and instead of leaving the crown

* See note on page 132.

to Mary, the rightful heir, to give it to Lady Jane Grey. Edward was no doubt chiefly concerned for the safety of the Protestant religion, and his last prayer is said to have been that England might be preserved from "Papistry." Lady Jane was a Protestant, Mary, a Catholic; and so zealous was the latter, that she continued to hold Catholic services at her own house in defiance of all the authorities. Northumberland was undoubtedly inspired by no higher motive than the aggrandizement of his own family. The failing king was placed by him under the care of a woman of reputed skill, but he declined more rapidly than before, and soon died, at the age of sixteen. Suspicions were not wanting that his end had been hastened to make more sure and speedy the accomplishment of Northumberland's plans. Edward was a youth of great promise, and his death was generally lamented. Northumberland at once hurried into the presence of Lady Jane Grey, with the intelligence that she was now Queen of England. This is said to have been her first knowledge that she was Edward's heir, and she assumed the crown only in obedience to the commands and entreaties of her husband's family.

Mary, 1553 to 1558 — 5 years. Tudor.

Lady Jane Grey. It had been the intention of the conspirators to seize the Princesses Mary and Elizabeth before the death of Edward became known; but Mary, being notified of its occurrence in season, took refuge in a castle on the coast, that she might escape to foreign parts, in case the fortunes of war went against her. She then prepared to assert her rights by force of arms.

The usurpation of Northumberland did not meet the approval of the people, who gathered rapidly to the support of Mary as their lawful sovereign. Lady Jane, convinced of her mistake, gladly laid aside the crown which she had so reluctantly assumed, and which she had worn but ten days, and disappeared entirely from the public sight. Her life had been passed in the delightful pursuits of learning. Though but sixteen years of age, she could speak fluently, Latin, Greek, French, and Italian, and had some acquaintance with Hebrew, Chaldee, and Arabic. Beautiful in person, sweet and guileless in disposition, and gifted in conversation, she was better fitted to shine in domestic and literary than in courtly circles. Mary speedily ascended the vacant throne. One of her first acts was to bring to the block the guilty Northumberland, and to cast into prison the innocent but unfortunate Lady Jane and her husband, Lord Dudley.

The next year a marriage was arranged between Mary and Philip of Spain, a bigoted Catholic. This match being odious to the English people, several risings occurred, implicating some of the friends of Lady Jane. The fate of the latter was sealed. From her window in the Tower, she saw the headless body of her husband borne away, and in a few hours followed him to the scaffold. John removed one who might be dangerous to his throne, when he put to death the little Arthur; Richard might have made the same poor plea when he destroyed the youthful princes in the Tower; but Mary had no excuse for putting to death this lovely girl, whose only crime was lending a too ready obedience to her husband's intriguing father.

Catholicism Restored to England. Mary was a zealous Catholic, and determined to restore England to friendly relations with the Papacy. Parliament was assembled, and proceeded, by statute after statute, to sweep away all the legislation of the preceding reigns establishing the Protestant religion. It refused, however, to re-establish the religious houses, and restore to them their lands; but Mary conscientiously yielded up all church property that remained in possession of the Crown. The Catholic bishops, who had been incarcerated in the Tower by Edward, were restored to their sees. Cardinal Pole, the legate of the pope, was received with great pomp, and, in presence of the sovereign and both Houses of Parliament, solemnly absolved the nation for its temporary departure from the Catholic faith. Under the guidance of Bishops Gardiner and Bonner, the queen inaugurated a system of the most terrible and unrelenting persecution.

The Martyrs at the Stake. During the four years of its continuance, multitudes perished by the axe, in prison, and at the stake, while thousands fled to foreign parts. At the stake alone, two hundred and eighty-eight suffered death, including fifty-five women and four children. Bishops Rogers, Hooper, Ridley, and Latimer, and Archbishop Cranmer, the foremost preachers of the preceding reign, were successively committed to the flames. Said the aged Latimer to his friend Ridley, as side by side they were chained to the iron stake, "Be of good comfort, Master Ridley, and play the man; we shall this day light such a candle, by God's grace, in England, as I trust shall never be put out." Latimer's prophetic words found a speedy fulfilment.

The fires of persecution enkindled anew the zeal and devotion of the Reformers. For every life that went out in martyrdom to the cause of religious liberty, there were a hundred converts to the Protestant faith.

Mary's Marriage with Philip of Spain. Mary's marriage with Philip took place in 1554, but it proved as unhappy for herself as it was unpopular with her subjects. On the part of Philip it had been a matter of mere State policy; on the part of Mary one of positive infatuation. Even before she had seen Philip, the representations which the Spanish Legate had made of his master inflamed her imagination, and excited her to an almost insane desire for the match. She was eleven years older than her husband, to whom she became devotedly attached, but by whom she was despised and studiously neglected. So unmanly was Philip, he even allowed her name to be made a subject of jest among the gallants of his court. Having received, by the abdication of his father, the sovereignty of Spain and the Netherlands, he spent most of his time on the continent, partly from his aversion to his wife, and partly from disgust at the insignificant position he occupied in the government of England. Though husband to the queen, and nominally king, he was refused by Parliament both the act of coronation and the right of succession.

Loss of Calais, A.D. 1558. Spain had engaged in a war with France. Philip came to England to secure the aid of Mary. A sudden descent of the French upon the English coast, and the desire of Mary to please her husband, led to a treaty with Spain and a declaration of war with France. Mary's cup of misery was filled to the brim when the news reached her that Calais, the boast and pride of England for two centuries, and its last possession on the continent, was wrested forever from English rule. Situated in the midst of marshes, it had been the practice to withdraw a portion of the garrison during the winter, and the defenses had been of late much neglected. Suddenly attacked by sea and land by the Duke of Guise, it was forced to surrender, after holding out eight days in the vain hope of relief. Said the wretched queen, "When I die Calais will be found written on my heart;" and she died, in less than a year, of a broken heart.

Extenuation of Mary's Cruelty. While the persecutions to which Mary was constantly spurring her lagging bishops, were atrocious, we can, at least, credit her with fidelity to her convictions. Brought up in a court as absolute as that of an eastern despot, and where a human life weighed little against a whim of the king, and reigning in an age not yet risen to even a faint conception of the perfect freedom of opinion, which is the crowning glory of that in which we live, there is some palliation for her bigotry and her cruelty. Mary conscientiously, and, in the only way she knew, by force, undertook to extirpate what she thought was heresy, and re-establish what she believed was truth. Nor should the facts of her personal history be forgotten. Disowned by her father just as she was entering womanhood, and branded as illegitimate by statute, and so cherishing for many years a bitter sense of wrong; despised and forsaken by a husband she adored; hated by a people whose welfare she sought to promote; crushed with a sense of shame at the loss of Calais, and worn and wasted with disease, it is no wonder she sank under an overwhelming load of woe. The title "Bloody," however justly prefixed to the name of Mary, could have been more appropriately given to her father, for much of whose cruelty there is no extenuation.

Elizabeth, 1558 to 1603 — 44 years. Tudor.

Protestantism Restored to England. The universal gloom that had settled over England during the last years of Mary's cruel reign, full of indications of a coming storm, passed quickly away amidst the pealing bells and blazing bon-fires that everywhere greeted Elizabeth's accession to power. The very day she entered London, the prison doors were opened wide to all confined for conscience' sake, still further heightening the universal joy. The first official act of the new queen was to restore the Protestant religion. The "Oath of Supremacy" required all bishops, priests, and civil officers to acknowledge Elizabeth as the Supreme Head of the Church, and to deny allegiance to all foreign authority. By foreign authority was meant the pope. All the bishops but one or two, refusing to take this oath, were removed from their sees, and Protestants put in their places. But the priests in the country parishes, almost without exception, took the required oath, and were not disturbed. As fast as their places, from any cause, became vacant, they were filled by Protestant clergymen, so that, in process of time, all the pulpits in the kingdom came to be in sympathy with the new religion. The "Act of Uniformity" required all the people to conform to the usages of the established Church. Even the neglect of public worship was punished with fine and imprisonment. The Book of Common Prayer, somewhat improved, returned to its old place in the religious service. Thirty-nine "Articles of Faith" became the standard of religious belief.

The Puritans. There appeared during this reign a new sect of Protestants called Puritans. The persecutions of Mary had driven into exile thousands of English Protestants. Many of them took refuge in Geneva, where, under Zwingle and Calvin, the Reformation had taken a more radical type than in England. By the Calvinists, as the Swiss Reformers were called, the surplice, liturgy, and bishops of Episcopacy, and every form and ceremony peculiar to Rome, were utterly discarded. Even that beautiful symbol, the Cross, was banished as an abomination, not only from religious worship, but from the church edifice itself; and "Merry Christmas," the joyful anniversary of the birth of our Lord, was metamorphosed into a solemn Fast, because both Cross and Christmas were so intimately associated with the Papacy. When Mary died, the English exiles returned to their homes, but brought with them the plainer worship and stricter mode of life they had learned to love abroad. The severe simplicity and purity of their religious faith, made the rule and compass of their daily life, produced character of the type of Sparta, of the mould of early Rome. Puritanism was a reform of Episcopacy, as the latter had been of Catholicism; so that Episcopacy occupied a middle ground between the two extremes. It retained many of the forms and ceremonies of the Papacy, while its system of faith was identical with that of the Puritans.

Despite its narrowness and bigotry—for its disciples did not rise entirely above the age in which they lived—there is nothing grander in all history than the developments of Puritanism during the sixteenth and seventeenth centuries. How it stirs the soul, how it ennobles our conceptions of humanity, deepens our faith in virtue and our trust in truth, to read the painful yet inspiring story of the Huguenots of France, the Covenanters of Scotland, and the Pilgrim Fathers—the story of their sublime fortitude, patience, suffering, as with unquestioning faith they obeyed the simple voice of conscience. Though shrinking from no sacrifice, their devotion to their religion was that of rational beings, and not blind devotees. Religion was to them an intensely personal matter. As nothing stood between their souls and their God, a consciousness of the Divine Presence was the one great fact of the Puritan life. Questions of individual responsibility and individual duty constantly occupied their thoughts. Life became to them an unceasing struggle. Inspired by constant meditation on the sublime realities with which they had to deal, but sobered in spirit by a sense of personal unworthiness, they exhibited unconscious heroism combined with the deepest humility, and achieved the grandest results without a thought of worldly fame.

The Dangers that Environed Elizabeth. Though the Puritans were a source of increasing embarrassment to Elizabeth, on account of the rapid increase in their numbers and their sturdy adherence to their principles, her chief danger lay in the hostility of the Catholics, both at home and abroad. Philip of Spain was the most bigoted as well as the most powerful sovereign in Europe, and the acknowledged champion of Rome. His empire embraced Spain, Portugal, the Netherlands, Italy, and the Indies, East and West. His armies had marched more than once to the gates of Paris, and his fleets commanded every sea. Philip, offended at Elizabeth's refusal of his hand, which he had offered her in a month after Mary's death, became her personal enemy.

France was as hostile as Spain to England, though not so dangerous, for her own soil was already the scene of a fearful religious struggle. Finally, the pope had early declared against Elizabeth, and had sought to unite the Catholic powers of Europe in behalf of Mary, Queen of Scots, her next of kin, and heir to the English throne. Pope Clement VII. had never recognized Anne Boleyn as the lawful wife of Henry VIII., and Pius V. now refused to recognize Elizabeth as their lawful issue. It will be remembered, too, that a statute of Parliament had also pronounced her illegitimate. Thus was Elizabeth environed by danger.

Elizabeth's Policy. With a title somewhat precarious, the ruler of a part of one small island whose population did not exceed six millions, without soldiers, ships, or allies, it would have been madness in Elizabeth, in the early part of her reign, to have courted conflict with any one of the hostile nations around her, especially with Spain. Her great want was time and peace, to enable her to establish her personal authority, to plant the Church of England on a solid basis, to develop the resources of the kingdom, and to build up a navy. To preserve peace and gain time taxed, constantly and to the utmost, the resources of Elizabeth and her ablest ministers. It was for this that she alternately raised and dashed the hopes of half a dozen royal suitors for her hand. It was for this that she engaged in endless negotiations and perpetual intrigues with foreign powers, holding Spain at bay by threatening alliance with France, and keeping France in check through fear of a treaty with Spain, deceiving neither, in fact, but outwitting and perplexing both. While accomplishing her object, the preservation of peace, she won for herself that reputation for duplicity and mendacity, in her public as well as her private relations, that has left so indelible a stain on her memory.

Whether deliberately planned or not, the moderate ground Elizabeth had taken in religion contributed to her personal power, and to the peace of her kingdom. While she required conformity to the usages of the established church, she punished no man for his opinions; and this was a step far in advance of her predecessors, as well as of the age in which she lived. Had she taken decided ground with either Catholic or Puritan extreme, she must, sooner or later, have faced a Puritan or a Catholic revolt. As it was, the great body of both religious sects remained staunch in their loyalty; and when at length the long-deferred crisis came, and Philip, towards the end of her reign, undertook the conquest of England, they rallied with fervent devotion around the royal standard. Side by side in the muster at Tilbury stood Catholic, Puritan, and Episcopalian, alike ready to die for their country and queen. Catholic gentry and Puritan traders alike offered their ships, all manned and equipped, for the struggle with the "Great Armada." When the threatened invasion had ended in disaster, and the galleons of Philip, beaten and broken, had straggled up the Tagus, a mere remnant of the mighty armament that had sailed out so proudly a few months before, and when England at once came to the front, undisputed mistress of the seas, the early peaceful policy of the great queen was amply vindicated. She might then have appropriated the proud boast of the great but patient Mazarin: "Time and I against any two."

This is a general view of the policy pursued by Elizabeth during the greater part of her reign, under the guidance of her able ministers, Burleigh and Walsingham. There remain to be noticed, briefly and connectedly, the relation of Mary, Queen of Scots to English history, and the well-matured but ill-starred expedition of Philip, just alluded to.

Mary, Queen of Scots. Mary, Queen of Scots,[*] though passed over in the will of Henry VIII., was the next heir to the throne after Elizabeth. She had been betrothed, when an infant, to Prince Edward, Henry's son and successor; but French and Catholic influence availed not only to break up the match with Edward, but to effect her marriage with the Dauphin, who, upon the death of his father, assumed the French Crown, under the title of Francis II. Mary, Queen of Scotland by inheritance, Queen of France by mar-

---

[*] Margaret, the eldest daughter of Henry VII., married James IV. of Scotland. Their son, James V., was the father of Mary, who inherited the kingdom under the title of Mary, Queen of Scots.

riage, now assumed the title of Queen of England, claiming, as did the Catholic world in general, that Elizabeth was not the rightful sovereign.

The Reformation, under the preaching of John Knox, had made great progress in Scotland. A French force had been sent to that country, for the double purpose of crushing out the Reformation and strengthening French interests. Elizabeth, conscious that her own throne, as well as the Protestant religion, was menaced by the action of France, hurried an army across the border to the help of the Scots. The French army was besieged in Leith and forced to sue for peace. By the treaty of Edinburgh, the French engaged to leave the country, and Mary to renounce her claims to the English throne during the life-time of Elizabeth. Mary refused to ratify her part of the treaty, and persisted in her refusal till near the end of her life. At the death of her husband, Francis II., she returned to her kingdom of Scotland and soon married Lord Darnley, the next heir to the Scottish throne.

Mary and Darnley were ardent Catholics, but their subjects were largely Protestant; and there naturally arose on the part of the latter great apprehension as to the future policy of the government in matters of religion. They sought to obtain from the queen a formal recognition of Potestantism as the national religion. This Mary would not give, but she expressed her readiness to assent to perfect religious toleration. The Protestants, believing that she designed the restoration of Catholicism, rose in arms. Putting herself at the head of her troops, with "pistols at her saddle-bow," the resolute queen soon quelled the revolt, and the banished lords took refuge in England.

Though Mary was but little over twenty-three years of age, she had reached the crisis period in her career. We are soon to see her fall, either innocent of serious offence, but hopelessly entangled in a net-work of misfortunes, or guilty of heinous crime and richly meriting the doom she speedily met. Since history has failed to furnish conclusive evidence of her guilt, let us remember her as the unfortunate Mary, Queen of Scots.

Mary's love and respect were changed to dislike and contempt, for a husband who treated her unkindly, and was addicted to many vices. Darnley, attributing the change in her feelings to the influence of her private secretary, Rizzio, of whom he was also jealous, entered the queen's apartments, at the head of a band of disaffected nobles, and slew Rizzio, almost in her very presence. The enraged queen vowed to have her revenge. Though apparently reconciled to her husband, the Earl of Bothwell became her confidential adviser, and, at last, the object of her affections. In less than a year after the murder of Rizzio, a house in Edinburgh, called the Kirk of Field, in which Darnley was lying sick, was, one night, blown up with gunpowder, and its unhappy inmate killed. That Bothwell was guilty of the crime is morally certain; but that Mary was accessory to it, there is no conclusive proof. Her speedy marriage with Bothwell, under circumstances peculiarly suspicious, created the most intense excitement. The Scotch lords flew to arms, and made the queen their prisoner. She was required to choose between war and the banishment of Bothwell. She chose the latter,* and was then hurried to Castle Lochleven, and forced to resign her crown in favor of her infant son.

Escaping in 1568, after nine months of captivity in the lonely island castle, she rallied her adherents, lost the battle of Langside, and was chased to the Solway, which she crossed in a boat, and took refuge in England. She demanded of Elizabeth a passage to France, or an army to recover her kingdom. Her demands were met by a royal order for her detention, and then her imprisonment. If she had been a cause of alarm to Elizabeth before, she became doubly so now. Her release and elevation to the English throne itself became the object of plot after plot among Romanists, both at home and abroad. Pope Pius V. issued a decree of deposition against Elizabeth. Jesuits poured into the kingdom in large numbers, to awaken discontent among the English Catholics.

The great Catholic houses of Neville and Percy rose in arms; but the Catholic masses, turning a deaf ear to pope, Jesuit, and noble, remained loyal to their queen, and the rising was easily quelled and its authors brought to the block. Finally a Catholic plot, under the leadership of one Babington, to assassinate Elizabeth and proclaim Mary, was brought to light, implicating Mary herself. Elizabeth was now compelled to act in defence of her life and throne. Mary, tried by a commission of Peers, in 1587, was found guilty and condemned to death, and the queen reluctantly signed the

* The banished Bothwell made his home among the Orkneys, and became the leader of a band of pirates. Being pursued, he found shelter, for awhile, among the Shetland Isles, whence he escaped to Denmark, where he died in a dungeon.

warrant for her execution. In the hall of Fotheringay Castle, her last prison house, this weary captive of nineteen long and dreary years, saddened by sorrow, but heroic still, calmly laid her head upon the block.

Her brilliant qualities of mind and person, the calm dignity with which she bore misfortune, and her affecting death-scene, have touched the cord of universal sympathy, and thrown a veil of charity over the frailties of her life and character. Both Council and Parliament considered Mary's death a State necessity. What would have been the result of her liberation we can only conjecture; but her execution was closely followed by the most imminent peril that ever menaced the throne of Elizabeth, if not the liberties of England. Of the disposition of Mary herself, we have the clearest expression in a letter to Elizabeth, written during the last of her captivity, when longings for liberty had overcome all worldly ambitions. "Let me go," she wrote, "let me retire from this island to some solitude, where I may prepare my soul to die. Grant this, and I will sign away every right which either I or mine can claim." Elizabeth turned a deaf ear to this touching appeal, and Mary then bequeathed all her rights to the English throne to Philip of Spain, — rights which Philip promptly claimed and began the most gigantic preparations to enforce.

The Maritime Growth of England. It seems necessary at this point to notice briefly the maritime growth of England. Elizabeth's moderate and pacific policy, persistently followed for thirty years, had produced the happiest results. The nation's advance in wealth and power had been rapid and healthful. Unexampled thrift characterized all its industries, while its commerce whitened every sea, pouring into London, then just becoming the great trade-mart of the civilized world, the wealth of every land and clime.

The thirst for adventure and discovery had sent daring spirits into every nook and corner of the earth, whose glowing reports of the wonders they had seen stimulated fresh expeditions, and opened to English enterprise new avenues of trade. It had led Chancellor to penetrate the Arctic ocean towards the east, and open a lucrative trade with Archangel. It had lured Davis and Frobisher into the same ocean towards the west, in search of a shorter passage to India. It had sent the famous Hawkins to the tropics, and opened an inexhaustible source of wealth in the ivory, gold-dust and slaves of Guinea. There was an extensive and growing trade with the ports of the North, Baltic, and Mediterranean seas. Every harbor on the coast had long sent out its fishing boats into the waters around, but now England began to rival France in the number of vessels sent to the cod-fisheries of Newfoundland and the whale-fisheries of the Polar seas.

There was another cause for the maritime development of England. The merciless slaughter of the Huguenots of France and the patriot Reformers of the Netherlands, had fired Protestant England with fierce resentment. But its politic queen coolly continued negotiations for marriage with a Catholic prince of France, even after the massacre of St. Bartholomew; and she long looked with apparent indifference at the butcheries of Alva in the Netherlands. The English people finally took the matter into their own hands, and made war on their own account. They flocked to the Netherlands by thousands and joined the Protestant army. English "sea-dogs," as they were called, commissioned as privateers by Condé of France and the Prince of Orange, or flying the French and Dutch flags without commissions, simply pirates, swarmed in all the waters frequented by French or Spanish traders. Aided by the English people all along the coast, and often by the royal officers themselves, prizes were constantly run into secret inlets and their cargoes discharged. Drake, the boldest spirit of them all, haunted the unguarded coasts of Spanish America, burning towns and intercepting Spanish galleons bound to Cadiz, laden with gold, silver, and diamonds for the Spanish king. In such schools were the brave and hardy mariners of England trained for the hot work which Philip was soon to furnish them.

Elizabeth's Defiance of Philip. Affairs were fast coming to an issue between Elizabeth and Philip. The former had long been embittered by Philip's secret efforts to awaken discontent among her Catholic subjects; the latter as long enraged at Elizabeth's duplicity in secretly aiding the Netherlanders, and shielding English pirates on Spanish commerce, while professing peace with Spain. Towards the last, Elizabeth threw off the mask. Under the pressure of public sentiment after the assassination of the Prince of Orange, and conscious that the Reformation in the Netherlands, unaided, must soon expire, she sent an army of eight thousand men to their assistance. It was under the command of the Earl of Leicester, one of Elizabeth's favorites, and accomplished little.

The campaign is chiefly memorable for the death of one of its most accomplished officers, Sir Philip Sidney. He received a mortal wound at the siege of Zutphen. When about to partake of a little water that had been procured with great difficulty, he saw a wounded soldier looking wistfully at it. "Take it," said the chivalric Sidney, who was himself burning with thirst, "thy necessities are greater than mine."

When Drake returned from one of his expeditions, enriched with the gold and jewels taken from Spanish galleons, and Philip demanded the surrender of the "pirate," Elizabeth publicly conferred on the latter the honor of knighthood, and wore the captured jewels in her hair. The death of Mary, Queen of Scots put an end to Philip's irresolution.

The Invincible Armada. Besides dethroning Elizabeth, it was Philip's aim to restore Romanism to England. To this double purpose, he now bent all his energies, and turned the vast resources of the whole Spanish empire. For three years, ships and stores were slowly coming into the Tagus, and forming what Philip boastfully called the "Invincible Armada." The English rovers were all called home. Drake, with a fleet of thirty sail, hovered about the Spanish coast, picking up Spanish traders and attacking unguarded points. Boldly entering the harbor of Cadiz, he destroyed the ships and stores collected there, delaying the sailing of the Armada for many months.

The great fleet left the Tagus the last of May, 1588. Overtaken by a storm, it put into Corunna to refit. The last of July, its approach to the English coast, under the command of the Duke of Medina

Sidonia, was signaled by blazing beacons on every hill-top. It swept slowly up the English channel, in the form of an extended crescent, seven miles from wing to wing. It was composed of one hundred and fifty ships, many of them of immense burthen. On its rear closely hung the English fleet of eighty sail, under the command of Lord Howard. Drake had command of the "sea-dogs," among whom were Hawkins and Frobisher. The huge and unwieldy galleons of Spain were captured or sunk, one by one, by the lighter and more active craft of the English. Still the mighty fleet held steadily on its way and dropped anchor in the roads of Calais. The Duke of Parma had been in camp at Dunkirk with thirty thousand men, ready to land on the English coast as soon as the Armada should arrive to protect their passage across the channel. Howard saw the necessity of decisive action to prevent the crossing of Parma's troops. The next night eight English ships, filled with combustibles and set on fire, were towed towards the Spanish vessels, and sent, with tide and wind, into their very midst, as they lay crowded together at anchor. The affrighted Spaniards cut their cables and fled to the open sea, stretching away in a broken line along the coast. At break of day, the fearless "sea-dogs," under the lead of Drake, fell upon the disordered line, and sunk, captured, or forced on shore, Spaniard after Spaniard, driving the still numerous but panic-stricken fleet northward. Medina no longer thought of the conquest of England, but of safety for his broken and scattered fleet. Not daring to return through the English Channel in the face of Drake, he sought to make the circuit of Scotland and Ireland, and reach Spain by way of the Atlantic. Drake, having exhausted his ammunition, gave up the pursuit, and the flying Spaniards disappeared in the waters of the North Sea. Overtaken by fierce storms, and unacquainted with the navigation of those dangerous seas, their unwieldy and disabled galleons were dashed upon the wild and rocky shores. The hapless crews escaped a watery grave, only to die at the hands of the savage natives. Eight thousand of the very chivalry of Spain are said to have perished on the western coast of Ireland. Nearly a hundred ships and fourteen thousand men were missing, when the shattered remains of the "Invincible Armada" once more dropped anchor in Spanish waters.

The Spanish king received the news of the destruction of the Armada "with his usual constancy," saying, with unchanged countenance, "I sent it against man and not against the billows." The English, too, recognized the fact that the elements, perhaps more than English valor, had won for them the victory. On an old English medal, commemorating the event, this inscription was written:—

"*Flavit Jehovah et dissipati sunt.*"
"Jehovah blew and they were scattered."

England's supremacy on the high seas was now achieved. Philip, indeed, with the energy of despair, gathered another Armada, but this only brought Drake and the English "sea-dogs" once more to the Spanish coast. Cadiz was taken and burned to the ground, and its ships and stores again destroyed. He once more became the scourge of Spanish America, taking treasure-laden galleons and destroying settlements; but all sense of danger from Spain passed away from Elizabeth and her people.

Great Names. The impulse given to learning in the preceding reigns, favored by the long peace of the present, began to bear fruit. Men of genius appeared in every department of intellectual labor. Raleigh, Spencer, Hooker, Bacon, Sidney, and Shakspeare are among the most illustrious names. There was a host of lesser lights. Though Elizabeth had the wisdom to be guided by statesmen in public affairs, in private life she admitted to favor men of little ability and still less virtue.

Death of Elizabeth. The closing years of her life were made sad and gloomy by the execution for treason of the last of her favorites, the Earl of Essex. In a moment of tenderness, years before, Elizabeth had given him a ring, requesting him to send it to her if he ever needed her help. Now that the earl lay under sentence of death, she looked, confidently, day after day, for the ring. But it never came; and the disappointed but resentful queen gave her signature to the fatal sentence; and the unfortunate earl was soon beyond the reach of mortal aid. Not long after this, the Countess of Nottingham, when on her death-bed, called the queen to her side, and confessed to her that Essex had sent the ring, and that she, out of enmity to him, had withheld it. Elizabeth's resentment at what she had believed to be the earl's contempt for her favor, changed to a paroxysm of rage and grief. Shaking the dying countess, who was praying for her pardon, Elizabeth cried, "God may forgive you but I never can." She became a prey to melancholy that deepened with her failing strength, until she died, like her sister, broken-hearted. On the night of her death she was asked to name her successor. At the mention of Lord Beauchamp, a member of the royal family, she said, with a touch of the old Tudor spirit, "I will have no rogue's son in my seat." James VI., king of Scotland was named, but she was speechless and could only signify her assent. The next morning, March 24th, 1603, she died, and James became king of England, with the title of James I.

Character of Elizabeth. In character, Elizabeth was a mass of contradictions. She had, in a marked degree, the iron will, imperious temper, and sound judgment of her father, the insincerity, vacillation and vanity of her mother. She was often coarse in her manners, and sometimes profane in her speech. Though arbitrary in her rule, like her father, she was never a tyrant like him, and she knew how to yield when the occasion required concession. Two years before her death she granted a large number of monopolies to favored persons. Seeing the dissatisfaction they had created, she sent a message to the House of Commons, announcing the reversal of all the grants. To a committee sent to express the gratitude of the House for the gracious act, she returned her thanks for reminding her of a mistake into which she had fallen through an error of judgment. From her supreme desire to win the love and promote the welfare of her subjects, despite her faults, she was known in her day, among the great mass of the English people, and is esteemed in ours, as "Good Queen Bess."

CHAPTER IX.

House of Stuart, 1603 to 1714 — 111 years.

JAMES I.
CHARLES I.
COMMONWEALTH.
CHARLES II.

JAMES II.
WILLIAM and MARY.
ANNE.

James I., 1603 to 1625 — 22 years. Stuart.

Union of Scotch and English Crowns. James I. was the representative of the royal families of both England and Scotland, and so united both their crowns. Although these countries now came under one king, their constitutional union, or union of **Parliaments**, did not take place till the reign of Queen Anne.

Persecution of Non-Conformists. The increasing severities towards non-conformists in the latter part of Elizabeth's reign, excited an intense anxiety in the public mind, to know what would be the policy of her successor. Before James reached London, he had been approached by both Catholics and Puritans; the former basing their hopes on his promise of toleration of Catholic worship, given to secure Catholic support, and the latter expecting much from his Puritan education. Both were doomed to disappointment. He avowed himself an Episcopalian; and although at first tolerant, he began ere long to execute the laws against non-conformists with more rigor than Elizabeth had done.

King James's Version of the Bible. In January, 1604, the king had called a convention of Episcopal and Puritan divines, to discuss the religious question. It accomplished but one thing of importance, the issue, in 1611, of a new translation of the Bible, called "King James's Version," the one still used by most Protestants. Fifty-four learned divines were occupied three years in its preparation. The hope that this convention would bring harmony among the clashing sects was not realized. King James, who had been the principal speaker in behalf of the Established Church, angry at the obstinacy of the Puritans, who failed to be convinced by his arguments, sought to convert them by a threat. "I will make them conform," said he, as the convention closed, "or I will harry them out of the land." The persecutions that followed forced multitudes to seek in foreign lands the safety and protection they could not have in their own.

The Gunpowder Plot. The discontent of some of the Catholics at the persecutions to which they were subjected, found expression in the "Gunpowder Plot," a scheme to blow up Parliament House, when king, lords, and commons were assembled. The conspirators hired the basement of the building, ostensibly for business purposes, and concealed therein thirty-six barrels of gunpowder. A warning sent to a Catholic lord, November 4th, 1605, the day before the meeting of Parliament, led to an investigation. The powder was found under a pile of wood and fagots, and Guy Fawkes, the keeper of the cellar, preparing slow matches for the explosion on the morrow. The conspirators dispersed in every direction, and sought places of concealment, but most of them were ferreted out and put to death. The abhorrence of Catholicism, excited among the English people by this diabolical plot, gave a death-blow to Catholic hopes of toleration. The laws against "Popish recusants" were made more severe and executed more rigorously than ever. They were required to take a new oath, renouncing the right of the pope to excommunicate princes, or absolve subjects from their allegiance.

The Pilgrim Fathers. One little Puritan band, after a brief stay in Holland, took passage in the Mayflower and sought, across the broad Atlantic, a refuge in the wilderness of the New World, content to sever the tender ties that bound them to home and country, and endure all possible hardships, that they might worship God as conscience directed them. The "Pilgrim Fathers," as we delight to call these first settlers in New England, landed at Plymouth, in the depth of winter, December 21st, 1620.

This was not the first permanent settlement made by the English on the continent. In 1606, three years after James's accession to power, two companies were chartered for the settlement of America. The territory of the London Company extended from the 34th to the 38th parallels of latitude, corresponding roughly with the mouths of the Cape Fear and Potomac rivers; that of the Plymouth Company from the 41st to the 45th parallels, corresponding with the mouths of the Hudson and St. Croix. The country between was open to settlement by either company. In 1607, under the auspices of the London Company, an expedition entered Chesapeake bay, and made a settlement at

Jamestown, on the James river, about fifty miles from its mouth. An attempt made by the Plymouth Company, the same year, to plant a colony near the mouth of the Kennebec, was not successful.

James's Assumption in Matters of Religion. James was a man of one idea, and that the inherited and absolute rights of kings. But this doctrine of the "divine right of kings" was not only a favorite theory, ever on the royal lips, but also the key-note to the royal policy, both in church and state. Parliament assembled in 1604. The House of Commons was largely Puritan, and its temper, in view of the absolutism set up by James, is clearly seen in its action. It petitioned for a redress of grievances in matters of religion The king's decided rejection of this petition was met by the equally decided protest on the part of the House: "Let your majesty be pleased to receive public information from your Commons in Parliament, as well of the abuses in the Church as in the civil State. Your majesty would be misinformed if any man should deliver that the kings of England have any absolute power in themselves, either to alter religion or to make any laws concerning the same, otherwise than as in temporal causes, by consent of Parliament."

James's Assumption in Matters of Government. James levied a tax on all exports and imports, and obtained a decision from the judges in favor of its legality. The House of Commons then petitioned for a redress of grievances in matters of state. His refusal to grant this petition brought another protest and prayer that a law be made to declare "that all impositions set upon your people, their goods, or merchandize, save only by common consent in Parliament, are and shall be void." Parliament was promptly dissolved, but the necessities of the king compelled its speedy reassembling. The questions dividing king and Parliament went to the people, and became the issue in the election of new members. The new House of Commons was more decidedly opposed to the policy of the king than the old one. It made a redress of grievances, especially that of illegal imposts, the condition of a grant of supplies. Its angry dissolution displayed the folly as well as obstinacy of the king.

Seven years of absolute rule, seven years of relentless extortion, only served to widen the breach between king and people. Illegal imposts continued; the odious "benevolences" were revived; the equally odious system of "purveyance"* was practiced without regard to the law; the sale of monopolies and the obsolete system of royal wardship, by which the incomes of the estates held under military tenure went to the king during the minority of the heir, were renewed; patents of nobility were so freely sold that, at the death of James, one-half the peers of England were those created by him. The shameless waste of the money thus obtained, on a corrupt court, excited the disgust as well as the indignation of the people.

* Purveyance was an ancient prerogative of the Crown, by which the king had the preference over all others in the purchase of supplies. He could take them at an appraised value, even without the owner's consent. The royal officers often practiced great injustice, purveyance becoming under some of the kings a system of royal robbery. An attempt was made to regulate it in Magna Charta, and by repeated enactments in succeeding reigns. It was finally surrendered by Charles II. for a compensation.

Personal favorites took the place of English statesmen, not only in the friendship of the king, but in stations of highest responsibility in the government. A mere adventurer, one George Villiers, became Duke of Buckingham and Minister of State. He was the Piers Gaveston of the infatuated king. Promotion to office, retention in office, and even access to the person of the king, on the part of men of the highest rank, depended on the pleasure or the bribery of this handsome but corrupt official.

Foreign Affairs. The foreign policy of James was almost as displeasing to the English people as his management of domestic affairs. Just as the life and death struggle between Catholics and Protestants was breaking out in Germany, warmly enlisting the sympathies of Protestant England in behalf of the latter, James was obsequiously courting the favor of Spain, and seeking to bring about a marriage between Prince Charles and the Spanish Infanta. The cry for another Parliament, coming from every quarter of the kingdom, forced the king to issue writs for an election.

The Parliament of 1621. The Parliament of 1621 is almost as famous as that of 1640, for the boldness with which it opposed the assumptions of the king. It demanded a war with Spain instead of a treaty of alliance, and a Protestant instead of a Catholic marriage for the Prince of Wales. "Bring stools for the ambassadors," was the ironical command of the king, as the committee, sent by the House of Commons to communicate their demands, was announced. He forbade further discussion by the Commons on affairs of State, asserting that all their rights were derived from himself and his ancestors. "Let us pray, and then consider of this great business," said a member of the Commons, as the king's commands were repeated by the committee. The resolution that followed, affirming freedom of speech as their ancient right, has the ring of the times of Henry III., when an armed baronage boldly confronted the tyrant at Westminster. The clanking of swords was then hardly more startling to the ears of Henry than the utterances of the Commons to James. With a purpose as aimless as it was impotent, he sent for the journals of the House, and with his own hand tore out the leaves containing the obnoxious resolution. James might indeed destroy the Parliament records; but the spirit of liberty, enkindled anew in the hearts of the patriot Commons, he could not extinguish. The sudden dissolution of Parliament ended the conflict, for the time being.

Prince Charles. Prince Charles, accompanied by Buckingham, visited Spain to complete the marriage contract with the Spanish Infanta. Mutual disgust broke off all negotiations, and Charles returned to England, and took sides with the people in demanding war. James, disappointed in his hopes of a Spanish alliance, was borne along by the popular current into another war with Spain. A new marriage was arranged for Charles with Henrietta, a princess of France. James died before its consummation.

Sir Walter Raleigh. The name of Sir Walter Raleigh had long been known in connection with public affairs. He began his public career in the reign of Elizabeth, and was prominent as a courtier, statesman and commander. Under the patronage of Elizabeth, he sent several expeditions to make settlements in the New World. His first colonists, at Roanoke Island, were ill-fitted for the hardships and privations of a new country, and took advantage of a chance visit of Drake, who was returning from one of his raids on Spanish America, to abandon their settlement. His second colony, when revisited after the expiration of three years, was found to have disappeared, leaving no trace behind. Early in the reign of James, Raleigh, being implicated (though on very slight testimony) in a conspiracy to overthrow the government and place Arabella Stuart, the king's cousin, on the throne, was sent to the Tower, under sentence of death. After twelve years of confinement, during which he occupied the dreary hours of prison life in writing a "History of the World," he was released on a promise to guide an expedition to a gold mine in Guiana. But the Spaniards, notified (some say by James himself) of the purpose of the expedition, made every preparation to defeat it. Raleigh, broken in spirit and fortune, returned to England, only to re-enter the Tower, and perish on the scaffold.

Character of James I. James was plain in person, awkward in manners, and intemperate even to drunkenness in his habits; but he had good natural ability and considerable learning, of which he was excessively vain. His pedantic display of his learning led Henry IV. of France, to characterize him as the "wisest fool in Christendom." The public contempt for his meanness was only surpassed by the public resentment at his usurpations. He was at once the most puerile and the most presumptuous of English kings.

As an index of the prevalent feeling towards this king, it is said that his peculiarities, both of person and character, were publicly caricatured in the theatres of London, to the infinite enjoyment of the people.

Charles I., 1625 to 1649 — 24 years. Stuart.

Constitutional Liberty at the Accession of Charles I. From the Wars of the Roses to the reign of James I., we hear little of constitutional liberty in England. Standing, as we now do, at the very threshold of a renewal of the constitutional struggle, a brief retrospect will make more intelligible the course of events upon which we are about to enter.

Mediæval civilization rested on the Feudal System, and fell with it, and both went down with the nobility in the Wars of the Roses. These wars reduced England to a state bordering on anarchy, and the only power that did save it, or that could save it, from utter anarchy, was a stable throne. To this all parties turned with the instinct of self-preservation.

The nobility, land owners, and moneyed classes, remembering the leveling doctrines of the socialists, looked to the throne to protect them from another peasant revolt.

The Catholic Church, conscious of the silent but vigorous growth of the ideas implanted by Wickliffe, turned to the throne to save it from another reformation.

The people, having suffered under the evils of a disputed succession, were ready to welcome any line of kings strong enough to shield them from the horrors of another civil war.

The House of Commons, that ancient hope of the nation, by a sweeping restriction of the elective franchise, and by wholesale corruption in the election of members, had sunk into a mere appendage of the crown, and, under some of the kings, into the great instrument of its oppressions.

Without marked violence or special opposition, the king deliberately gathered into his single hand all the powers of Church and State. That he should become arbitrary was natural; that he should grow despotic was not strange. Between the reigns of Edward IV. and Charles I., the government of England ranged through all shades and degrees of absolutism.

But even in the midst of absolute rule, silent forces were at work weakening its foundations, and destined, in the fulness of time, to accomplish its complete overthrow. The diffusion of knowledge and the elevation of the masses, had been rapid and general, especially after the invention of the printing press. There was noiselessly growing up an enlightened public sentiment on the relation of sovereign to subject that was far in advance of the theory and practice of the government. Faith in the doctrine of the "divine right of kings" became weak, as convictions of the sacredness of human rights grew strong.

During the reign of James I. it was evident that a collision between king and people was at hand. At the death of James, there was a lull in the gathering storm that was soon to break over the head of his son and successor. It will ever be a matter of wonder that Charles I. could so completely shut his eyes to the signs of the times, that he should take no warning from his father's mistakes, but should blindly and obstinately pursue his father's insane policy.

Renewal of the Constitutional Struggle. The struggle was clearly defined. It was constitutional liberty against the royal prerogative, an oppressed people against a tyrannical king. The English people, whom the crown alone could rescue from the robber barons in the reign of Henry II., whom the patriot barons alone could shield from the tyranny of the crown in Henry III., this great English people had at last outgrown dependence on king and baron, and proved in the end more than a match for them both.

Public feeling in England ran high against Romanism at the time of James's death. The "Thirty Years' War" in Germany, beginning in a contest between the Elector Palatine of the Rhine and Ferdinand, Emperor of Austria, for the Bohemian crown, had widened into a life and death struggle between Romanists and Protestants. Besides the sympathy English Protestants felt for their brethren in Germany, they were naturally interested in behalf of the Elector, who was son-in-law to King James. Spain had openly taken sides with the Emperor, and England had entered the lists against Spain, besides sending a small army to the help of the Elector. But the war with Spain lagged through the indifference of the government led by Buckingham, the chief minister of State. King Charles demanded a subsidy; but Parliament, suspicious of his intentions, and watchful of the liberties of England, limited the usual grant of certain life customs to a year. Resenting the limitation, Charles refused to accept the vote, and levied the customs on his own authority. Parliament then proceeded to discuss the public grievances, and was dissolved. A fruitless expedition against Cadiz, under Buckingham, leaving the king deeply in debt, compelled its re-assembling in 1626. Instead of relieving the king's necessities, the House of Commons, guided by that dauntless patriot, Sir John Eliot, proceeded to impeach the officers of the crown. Charges of corruption against Buckingham were carried in the House. Eliot, in a speech full of scathing invective, then arraigned the royal favorite before the House of Lords, and was sent by the angry king to the Tower. The refusal of the Commons to act on public affairs caused Eliot's release, but their request for the dismission of Buckingham brought another dissolution. Then followed more illegal taxation in the form of "benevolences" and "forced loans." Although many of the clergy preached the doctrine of passive obedience, men everywhere refused to give or lend to the king. Poor and friendless offenders were pressed into the army or navy; the rich and noble were thrown into prison or summoned before the Council.

Buckingham now had an opportunity to retrieve his falling fortunes. During the first year of his reign, Charles had married Henrietta Maria, a French princess. The marriage stipulation with reference to the toleration of Catholics having been broken by the king, Richelieu and Olivarez, the able ministers of France and Spain, planned a joint invasion of England. Buckingham sought to checkmate this scheme of invasion by an attack on France. He sailed with a large fleet to the relief of Rochelle, the stronghold of the Huguenots, which was besieged by French Catholics. Another disaster, more shameful than that at Cadiz, left the king still deeper in debt, and compelled the issue of writs for another Parliament.

Petition of Right, A.D. 1628. The people, now thoroughly aroused, returned a House more hostile to the king than the former one. Like that, it demanded redress before a grant of money. It proceeded to array its grievances and frame its demands into that second great charter of liberties, the "Petition of Right." This Petition forbade forced loans, benevolences, and every species of illegal taxation, imprisonment, and punishment; forbade martial law and the billeting of soldiers upon the people in time of peace, and imposed obedience to the laws on the ministers of the crown. The refusal of the king to sign this Petition was followed by a "Remonstrance on the State of the Kingdom." At the mention of Buckingham's name, against whom the Remonstrance was aimed, the speaker forbade further discussion, saying that he held a royal order to allow no member to speak against the ministers of the crown. The effect of this direct interference with free speech, one of the most unquestioned privileges of Parliament, beggars description. Eliot, who was addressing the House, sank stunned into his seat. There were a few moments of death-like silence, followed by sounds of suppressed excitement, and then exclamations of amazement, grief, anger, broke here and there from the seething assembly. Some wept and some prayed. Members rose to speak, but sat down overpowered with emotion. The venerable Sir Edward Coke at last took the floor, and in scathing language denounced Buckingham as the author of all the perils that menaced the liberties of England. Charles, alarmed at the dangers that threatened his favorite, sought to quell the storm by giving his signature to the Petition of Right. But it was too late. The House, bent on the destruction of Buckingham, pressed its Remonstrance, and was hastily prorogued.

But Buckingham soon ceased to be an object of anxiety to either the King or his Commons. While preparing to take charge of another expedition against France, he was killed at Portsmouth by one Felton, but whether for public or private ends is not clear. Felton had been discharged from the public service.

The King Can Do No Wrong. An explanation ought to be made of the persistency with which the House of Commons pursued Buckingham even after the king had assumed the responsibility of all the offences charged against him. It was then, as it is now, a settled principle of the English monarchy that " the king can do no wrong." In case of wrong doing by the government, the king's ministers are held responsible, and, aside from the removal or punishment of these, there is no way to coerce or punish the king himself except by revolution.

The Purpose of Charles to Rule Alone. At its next session, in 1629, the House summoned the collectors of the illegal taxes to its bar. They appeared but refused to answer, pleading the commands of the king. The speaker, being about to adjourn the House, in obedience to a royal order, was held down in his chair and the doors kept locked against the messenger of the king, until the resolutions offered by Eliot were passed.

These resolutions denounced "as a capital enemy of the kingdom any minister who should seek to change the established religion or advise the levying of taxes without consent of Parliament." The House then unlocked its doors and suffered the dissolution awaiting it.

Ringing bells and blazing bonfires had signified the public joy when the king signed the Petition of Right, for it was then thought there would be an end of royal oppression; but joy was changed to sorrow when the king, on the occasion of the last dissolution, announced that there would be no more Parliaments, that henceforth he should rule alone. Eleven years of personal government, during which Parliament was not once assembled, prove the earnestness of the royal threat, and form one of the gloomiest periods in the history of England. Nine of the more prominent opponents of the king were thrown into the Tower, one of them, the heroic Eliot, to die within its walls.

Laud, Strafford, and the Two Courts. There were two ministers upon whom Charles chiefly relied to carry out his policy of absolute rule, William Laud, who had been placed at the head of the church, and Thomas Wentworth, made Lord Strafford, once a bitter opponent, but now a devoted supporter of the king. There were two courts that were the chief instruments of the royal tyranny, the High Commission and Star Chamber, the former having jurisdiction over offences against the church, and the latter, those against the king. Besides these there was the "Council of the North," having almost absolute authority in the northern counties.

The High Commission and Puritan Emigration. Though not himself an avowed Catholic, Laud sought to make the Church of England Catholic in its spirit and practice. Through the court of High Commission he waged a pitiless warfare against Puritanism. Its ministers were everywhere driven from their livings, and its laymen subjected to tortures that rivalled those of the Spanish Inquisition. Patents were secured and companies organized for the settlement of New England. Eyes that looked longingly towards the distant refuge of the Pilgrims yet filled with tears, as, turning their backs upon scenes that were dear to them, the Puritans wended their way with unwilling feet to the place of embarkation. Hearts that swelled with grief as the shores of "dear old England" faded away from their sight, yet rose to a lofty purpose and a sublime resignation, as they laid home and country on the altar of their religious faith. They counted the peril, poverty, and hardship of their New England homes as naught beside the boon they sought and found,—"Freedom to worship God."

The Puritan exodus, once begun, continued until the New England coast was dotted with settlements. Lord Say-and-Seal and Lord Brooke obtained a charter for the settlement of the territory now embraced in the State of Connecticut. Several colonies were established under this charter within a few years. To furnish an asylum for persecuted Catholics, Lord Baltimore obtained a patent of the territory now known as Maryland. The first settlement was made in 1634. But the most interesting and important of these colonies, numbering eight hundred souls under John Winthrop, entered Massachusetts Bay, in 1630, and founded Boston. During the interval between the dissolution of the Parliament of 1629 and the assembling of that of 1640, twenty thousand Puritans had found homes in the New World. It is said that even Hampden and Cromwell once embarked for America, but were stopped by a royal order. The former had purchased a tract of land on Narraganset Bay.

The Star Chamber and Illegal Taxation. But while the High Commission was doing its wicked work in the name of religion, the Star Chamber was crushing out every vestige of civil liberty. Its officers surpassed even the lawyers of Henry VII. in the ingenuity with which they entrapped and mulcted the people. Laws and customs which had passed away with the feudal times in which they originated, but which had never been formally repealed, were brought to light and all offenders fined. Knighthood was forced on the gentry unless commuted with money. The forest laws were rigidly executed and poachers heavily fined.

James had attempted to check the growth of London by a royal order defining its corporate limits. Every house since erected beyond the specified line was ordered by Charles to be torn down unless its owner paid into the royal treasury a sum equal to three years' rent. Hundreds of the poor were made houseless by the execution of this relentless order. Monopolies prevailed more extensively than under Elizabeth or James, raising the necessaries of life to an exorbitant price.

Ship Money and John Hampden. But the climax to the national endurance was reached when the king ordered the levy of a tax called ship money. From the earliest times this had been a war tax levied on the maritime counties for the protection of the coast. Charles ordered the levy of ship money on all the people, inland as well as maritime, for general purposes, and in a time of peace. Eliot, the early champion of English liberty, was dead, but a worthy successor appeared in the person of John Hampden, a farmer of moderate means in the shire of Buckingham. Refusing to pay the tax assessed against him, he carried his case to the courts. Though defeated through royal influence, Hampden gained a great moral victory, for the injustice of the king was made apparent to all the nation, and the public mind was educated to resistance.

The Attempt to Force Episcopacy upon the Scots. The king had attempted to force Episcopacy upon the people of Scotland. A royal order enjoined the use of the Liturgy in all the Scotch churches. But those sturdy Presbyterians had imbibed the spirit as well as the faith of John Knox. A National Covenant, industriously circulated, received the signatures of nine-tenths of the Scotch people. The closing paragraph shows both the tenor of the Covenant, and the temper of the people.

"We promise and swear, by the name of the Lord our God, to continue in the profession and obedience of the said religion, and that we shall defend the same, and resist all the contrary errors and corruptions, according to our vocation and the utmost of that power which God has put into our hands, all the days of our life."

Charles at once hurried northward with all the troops at his command, to enforce obedience. But the

Scots quickly marshalled their clans under Leslie, a pupil of the great Gustavus, and, without waiting for the attack of the English king, pushed boldly across the border and offered battle. The astonished king feigned concession, and retired to await the levy of a larger force.

The Short Parliament. The crisis demanded the action of Parliament, and the king was forced to issue the usual writs for an election. The records of preceding Parliaments would answer for this. Instead of voting men and money for a Scotch war, it demanded redress, and, after a stormy session of three weeks, was angrily dissolved. "Things must go worse before they go better," said St. John, one of its members. They speedily went worse.

A Great Council of Peers, assembled at York as a last expedient, accomplished nothing but delay. The advancing Scots had reached New Castle and were on the march for York. Laud was mobbed in London, and the High Commission broken up at St. Paul's. All England was brought to the verge of revolt, when Charles once more, and for the last time, issued his summons for a meeting of Parliament.

The Long Parliament. Parliament assembled on the 3d of November, 1640. Having enacted that its dissolution could only take place by its own consent, it continued, with expulsions and intermissions, through a period of twenty years, and is known in history as the Long Parliament. All the accumulated grievances of the people since the advent of the Stuarts were poured into the House of Commons, in the shape of complaints and petitions, requiring the labors of forty committees for their examination. Then began the sharp work of reform. Patriots were released from prison; the Star Chamber and High Commission abolished; the judgment against Hampden annulled; ship money and arbitrary taxation once more forbidden, and royal officers impeached. Laud and Strafford, the two able but servile agents of the King, were thrown into the Tower, whence they came only to lay their heads upon the block.

The Attempt of Charles to Arrest the Five Members. The King looked bitterly but helplessly on, while the absolutism in which he had sought to entrench himself was roughly swept away. Conscious that his throne was crumbling beneath him, he attempted by one master-stroke to crush out all opposition and re-establish his lost authority. His blow was aimed directly at the House of Commons. With a company of soldiers at his back, he appeared at the door of the Commons Chamber, and demanded the surrender of five of its members on a charge of high treason. Pym and Hampden were of the number. "I see my birds have flown," said the king, after looking carefully over the silent assembly. With the expectation that "they would send the accused members to him," and a threat "to secure them for himself if they did not," the baffled king abruptly left the chamber.

Civil War Inevitable. The crisis had come. The occasion was too solemn for business, and the House adjourned. The next day a royal proclamation branded the five members as traitors and ordered their arrest. London rose as one man for their defence. Its trainbands held the city and guarded the House of Commons. They escorted the historical five back to their seats amidst the shouts of the excited people. Both parties began to prepare for the war that was now inevitable. The king raised his standard at Nottingham, August 22d, 1642. Parliament ordered the enrollment and muster of the militia.

Roundheads and Cavaliers. The great English people, farmers, traders, and artisans, mostly Puritans, with a sprinkling of peers, rallied around Parliament, and were called Roundheads, from the Puritan practice of wearing closely-cut hair. A majority of the nobles, gentry, and clergy, took sides with the king, and from their gallant bearing were called Cavaliers.

The two great parties into which England resolved itself, the one democratic and the other aristocratic, the one aiming at progress and reform, and the other clinging to the traditions of the past, have continued to this day, under the names of Whig and Tory, Liberal and Conservative, to struggle for the mastery.

Presbyterianism Made the National Religion. Parliament secured the aid of the Scots, by signing the Covenant, and adopting the Presbyterian as the national religion. As an offset Charles sought help from the Irish. In 1633, Strafford had been sent to Ireland, and for seven years had maintained in that country the iron despotism Charles struggled in vain to establish in Enggland. After Strafford's execution in 1641, and as a result of his severity, there broke out a wide-spread revolt of the Catholic Irish against the Protestant English. It was located chiefly in Ulster, that had been settled, thirty years before, in the reign of James I, by colonies of English Protestants. In a few days forty thousand people of English birth were slain. The plan of King Charles to bring over an Irish army to slaughter the English on their own soil caused the most intense excitement even among his own adherents. Officers in large numbers and of all grades threw up their commissions in the royal army and went over to the other side.

Edgehill, A.D. 1642. The first conflict, at Edgehill, was favorable to the king. Successive disasters in various quarters darkened the prospects of the patriot cause. Not the least among these was the death, in a skirmish, of Hampden, the Washington of England. The great want of the patriot army was cavalry. It was his strength in this arm that gave the king the advantage during the earlier stages of the war. A sturdy Puritan from the shire of Huntingdon, whose military genius we are soon to recognize, seeing the want, raised a regiment of horse, composed of men of like stamp with himself, and brought it into the field against the king.

Naseby, A.D. 1645. In the battles of Marston Moor and Naseby, Cromwell at the head of his invincible "Ironsides," scattered like chaff the horsemen of Prince Rupert, and then charging the close ranks of royal infantry, put them to utter rout. The king, conscious after the battle of Naseby that all was lost, rode into a camp of the Scots on the river Trent, and surrendered himself to Lord Leven, its commander.

Struggle Between Presbyterians and Independents. The Puritans of England were divided into two principal sects, Independents and Presbyterians. The former held that each individual church with its pastor should regulate its own affairs, independent of all others. The latter accepted the higher and ultimate authority of synods and bishops. The Independents were identical with the Separatists of the reign of James I., of whom the refugees at Leyden and the Pilgrim Fathers formed important bodies. But their original idea of church independence widened towards the close of the war into that of the complete separation of Church and State. The Presbyterian majority in Parliament proceeded to reorganize the Church of England on the Presbyterian plan.

The perils that environed civil liberty passed away with the surrender of the king to Lord Leven, but the religious intolerance that remained, and to which the Puritan majority still clung, became almost as dangerous to the State as the absolutism they had abolished. They had removed the civil, only to impose the religious, yoke upon the necks of their brethren.

Each party sought reconciliation and alliance with the king, as a means of success for itself; the Independents on the basis of religious toleration, the Presbyterians on the adoption of the Covenant. Charles rejected the offers of both parties, expecting to bring the one or the other to his own terms. "I am not without hope," wrote he, "that I shall be able to draw either the Presbyterians or the Independents to side with me for extirpating one another, so that I shall be really king again." "What will become of us," asked a Presbyterian, "now that the king has rejected our proposals?" "What would have become of us," replied an Independent, "had he accepted them?" Parliament bargained with the Scots for the possession of Charles's person, paying £400,000, the amount due them.

Struggle Between Parliament and the Army. The Presbyterians, now believing their victory assured, took a more decided stand. They established Presbyteries throughout the country, and voted to disband the old army which was Independent, and organize a new one with Presbyterians at the head. The quarrel between the religious sects in Parliament now changed to a struggle between Parliament and the army, ending, as we shall soon see, in the defeat of the former, and the establishment and continuance of military rule for a period of nearly twelve years. The army refused to disband, without an assurance of religious toleration. A body of its troopers surrounded the Holmby House in which the king was detained, and took him into custody. Parliament charged Cromwell with inciting the act. While denying the charge, he put himself at the head of his old soldiers and was soon on the road to London. Royal intrigue and treachery towards both parties,—the flight of the king to the Isle of Wight, his unsuccessful effort to reach the continent, and his detention in Carisbrook Castle,—a treaty with the Presbyterians, the principal terms of which were the assent of the king to the Covenant, and his re-instatement on the throne,— the mustering of the Cavaliers in various quarters, and the passage of the border by an army of Scots, to co-operate with the Royalists,—were events that transpired in rapid succession.

The Army Becomes Supreme. At the head of an army only too willing to follow where Cromwell led, with amazing rapidity he scattered the cavaliers mustering in the West, and then, turning northward, crushed the Scots at a blow and entered Edinburgh. Fresh concessions on the part of the king had given the latter an overwhelming majority in Parliament, and he was again seized by a body of troopers, and hurried away to Castle Hurst. A few weeks found Cromwell again in London. Surrounding the Parliament building with his soldiers, he excluded all the Presbyterian members. The Independents remaining were called the "Rump Parliament." They assumed, as representatives of the people, the supreme power of the State, and proceeded to the most radical legislation.

The High Court of Justice. They organized a "High Court of Justice," composed of seventy principal officers and members, for the trial of Charles Stuart on a charge of high treason. This Court met at Westminster on the 20th of January, 1649. Charles denied its legality and refused to plead. On the 27th, he was adjudged guilty and condemned to death. The death warrant was signed on the 29th, and on the 30th the unfortunate king was beheaded in front of Whitehall. The scaffold on which he suffered was covered with black and surrounded with soldiers. As the masked executioner, raising the head of the king streaming with blood, cried aloud, "This is the head of a traitor," a deep but audible groan burst from the assembled people, who fled horror-stricken from the awful scene. The people of England had never before witnessed the execution of their king, and Charles had borne himself, during the course of the trial, with such kingly dignity, and, after the fatal sentence, with such patience and resignation, as to win their reverence and sympathy. The anniversary of his death was observed with religious services, as the " Day of King Charles the Martyr," from the restoration in 1660, to the year 1859.

Three of Charles's children deserve notice; Charles, Prince of Wales; James, Duke of York; and Mary. The two former became Kings of England in turn. Mary married William, Prince of Nassau, and her son William became king after James.

The Commonwealth, 1649 to 1660 — 11 years.

The Commonwealth and its Perils. In less than a month after the execution of the king, the Monarchy was formally abolished and a Republic, under the name of Commonwealth, erected in its stead. The House of Lords shared the fate of the throne, and the Rump Commons were left the sole and supreme authority. They created a Council of State, composed of forty-one of their own members, as the executive branch of the government. Perils early thickened around the young Republic. The violent death of the king at the hands of his subjects caused an intense excitement among the monarchs of Europe. The ministers of England were driven from some of the capitals and murdered in others. Holland made haste to recognize Prince Charles, then a refugee at the Hague, as King of England.

The proud Cavaliers, though beaten into silence, looked with deadly hatred, as well as unspeakable disgust, upon the Puritan Republic, and they only waited for a favorable turn of events to attempt the restoration of the Monarchy. But the first movements of a royalist outbreak were crushed by the iron hand of Cromwell. A most dangerous spirit had crept into the army, which, if unchecked, would have led to the wildest excesses. The soldiers began to rise in mutiny against their officers. Mingled severity and mercy, promptly applied by the same vigorous hand, cured the discontent that was demoralizing the army.

The royalists in Ireland raised the standard of the Stuarts and speedily took every town but Dublin. Cromwell was dispatched with twelve thousand troops to reduce them to order. His campaign was short but terrible. He began with the capture of Drogheda and the merciless slaughter of its garrison of three thousand men. Town after town opened its gates, in panic, at his command, or quickly fell before his assaults. The memory of Ulster nerved every arm and steeled every heart in that dread army, for the work of vengeance. Not a man taken with arms in his hands was spared.

The proclamation of Prince Charles in Scotland, and the levy of an army for the invasion of England, called Cromwell back to London. With fifteen thousand men he pushed rapidly across the border, and, in a battle of an hour, annihilated the Scotch army at Dunbar and entered Edinburgh. The next year another army of Scots under Charles himself, finding the way open, pushed rapidly southward towards London.

Worcester, A. D. 1651. By forced marches, Cromwell placed his army directly in the path of Charles at Worcester. Cromwell characterized this battle as his "crowning mercy." Scarcely a Scot escaped.

Charles saved himself by flight; but left almost alone in the heart of England, with Cromwell's troopers occupying every road and scouring the country in search of the fugitive, his situation was perilous in the extreme. Threading his way, in one disguise and another, through innumerable dangers, hiding by day and journeying by night, in two months he safely reached the southern coast and took passage on a collier for France.

Parliament and the Army. Whatever may be said in defence of the extreme course of the Independents, both in Parliament and in the army, on the score of self-preservation, the Rump was but the fragment of a Parliament, and its long continuance was felt by all parties to be impolitic. Charges of greed and corruption against its members in appropriating the public spoils increased the odium attached to its name. Hateful from the outset to all denominations but its own, it was fast becoming hateful to that. Cromwell, impatient at the selfishness and uncertainty that characterized its action, urged a prompt "settlement of the nation," and an early dissolution. Parliament, in retaliation, resolved to disband the army. Failing in that, it sought to eclipse the splendor of its fame, by still more splendid achievements on the sea. The Dutch and English nations were maritime rivals, and their mutual jealousy was ready to break into open hostility on the slightest provocation. A statute, called the "Navigation Act," requiring all nations trading with England to bring their products to English ports in their own vessels, was aimed at the commerce of the Dutch, the common carriers of Europe. The English required the ships of other nations to lower their flags in British waters. An English fleet under Blake met a Dutch fleet under Van Tromp in the Downs. Blake's signal of three guns for the customary salute to the English flag was answered by Van Tromp with a broadside. The fight that followed led to a declaration of war with Holland. The first conflict sent the Dutch under De Ruyter into port to refit; the second forced the English, under Blake, to seek the shelter of the Thames, while Van Tromp exultingly swept the English Channel with a broom at his masthead; the third seriously crippled Van Tromp, and, for a time, gave Blake undisputed possession of the sea. Before this last victory of the English fleet, there was an understanding that Parliament should soon dissolve and the army disband; after it, the former evinced a disposition not to dissolve at all.

The Expulsion of the Rump Parliament. In 1653, a plan was made to call a new Parliament, in which all the members of the old Parliament should continue to hold seats, and also act as judges of the election of new members. Cromwell, who was a member of Parliament, was opposed to this scheme. A mutual council at Whitehall adjourned for one day, with the understanding that no action should be taken in the meantime. At the time appointed for the second meeting, but few of the friends and none of the leaders of the measure were present. A messenger soon arrived at Whitehall with the announcement that the bill was under discussion in Parliament and about to pass. Cromwell's hesitation vanished. Taking a file of soldiers and posting them in the lobby of the Parliament Chamber, he entered and took his accustomed seat. As he listened to the arguments of Vane who was speaking in behalf of the bill, he said to one who sat by his side, "I am come to do what grieves me to the heart." But he continued to listen. "The time has come," said he, at length, to another. "Think well, it is dangerous work," was the reply. Still he waited, but, just as the bill was evidently about to pass, he arose in his place and stepped out into the middle of the chamber. Pouring forth a torrent of abuse upon the members of the opposition, he stamped his foot as a signal for the soldiers to enter. "Your hour has come," were his words as the soldiers filed into the room, "the Lord hath done with you. It is not fit that you should sit here any longer. You should give place to better men. You are no Parliament." The Speaker was forced from his seat and the room quickly cleared by the soldiery. Lifting the mace from the table, "What," inquired he, "shall we do with this bauble? Take it away."

Cromwell Made Lord Protector. The Council of State, dismissed with as little ceremony as Parliament, was followed by another council, and that by a convention, composed of Independents selected from lists furnished by the churches, and called the Little Parliament, or Barebone's Parliament. It accomplished nothing, and voted its own dissolution after appointing still another council, composed of eight men with Cromwell at the head. This council summoned a Parliament to represent England, Scotland, and Ireland, the right to vote for members being granted to all having a property of two hundred pounds, except Catholics and those who had fought for the king. During the interim of nine months, for the preservation of order, Cromwell was induced by the council to assume the government with the title of Lord Protector.

The same body adopted an Instrument carefully defining the powers of the Protector, and organizing a strictly constitutional government. The advice of this council was made necessary in the management of foreign affairs, in questions of peace and war, and in the appointment of officers. Parliament was to meet once in three years, make the laws, subject for twenty days to the Protector's veto, and levy taxes.

Cromwell Usurps the Government. In the writs for an election of members, it had been expressly stated that Parliament should not have power to alter the government as settled in a single person and a Parliament. Its first step on assembling in 1654, was to take into consideration the organization of the government. The question of the Protector's veto power was debated for three days, when Cromwell, barring the way to the Parliament Chamber by a file of soldiers, turned back all who refused to sign an agreement not to alter the form of government. Three hundred signed and were allowed to enter. One hundred refused and were turned back. The signers adhered to their agreement, but fell back on the tactics of their predecessors, refusing to vote money for the army without a redress of grievances. This brought an angry dissolution, and the government relapsed into the absolutism from which the civil war had freed it. Taxes were levied and laws were made, on the sole authority of the Protector. The reaction in the public mind in favor of the monarchy was intense. Faith in the fundamental principles of the Commonwealth faded away, as its outward fabric crumbled under the usurpations of Cromwell. Royalist revolts broke out in various quarters, but they were easily crushed by the vigorous soldier who now had at his disposal all the powers of the State. England was divided into ten military districts, and each placed under martial law. Scotland and Ireland were reduced to order, but the severities practiced by English soldiers in the latter country have left to this day their bitter fruit of undying hatred of the English rule.

Prosperity Under Cromwell's Rule. In spite of the discontent and opposition of the royalists, the administration of public affairs under Cromwell was characterized by wisdom, moderation, and success almost beyond precedent in the history of England. Cromwell reformed the law and made its administration uniform. "To hang a man for sixpence and pardon murder," as he expressed it, did not accord with his idea of justice. He never swerved from the great principle on which he early took his stand, the principle of religious toleration. He allowed the Jews, who had been banished from the realm in the reign of Edward I., and who were still hated of all men, to return to England, and did his best to protect them. To a new sect of Puritans, called Quakers, the object of derision to all others, he extended the shield of his power. Cromwell's crude but effective statesmanship was best displayed in his management of foreign affairs. Kings, in whose capitals at the beginning of the Commonwealth, the lives of English ministers were not safe, earnestly solicited his alliance. A treaty favorable to England was made with Holland. The Mediterranean was cleared of the pirates that had long made their haunts on the African shore, and the liberation of the white slaves, held by the Barbary States, secured. Jamaica and Dunkirk were taken from Spain, and an entire fleet of merchant ships and galleon convoys was destroyed in the harbor of Santa Cruz. The Waldenses, occupying the valleys of Piedmont, among the Alps, were saved from massacre by his determined intercession. In 1656, Cromwell summoned another Parliament. It voted supplies, but it protested against the military despotism under which England continued. Cromwell at once withdrew the soldiers quartered in the ten military divisions. Although, on account of the opposition of the army, he refused the title of King, which this Parliament proposed to confer upon him, he accepted the power to name his own successor.

Cromwell's Death. Cromwell died September 3rd, 1658, of an attack of ague, but his end was hastened by anxiety. His last years were full of trouble. There was a growing discontent among the people at the strictness of his government. He was surrounded by conspiracies, and menaced with assassination. He became a prey to perpetual fear, wearing armor under his clothing, and arms about his person. His sleeping-room was constantly changed to lessen the danger of midnight attacks, and in going abroad, he returned by a different route to avoid an ambush of his enemies.

Cromwell's Character and Motives. Of Cromwell's character and motives there is a wide difference of opinion. Personally, he was one of nature's noblemen. Rising from the common walks of life to an estate and fame truly regal, he lost neither his simplicity nor his piety. That he felt some of the promptings of ambition, it is difficult to deny; that he possessed a great, earnest soul, chiefly animated by a desire to promote the welfare of his country, it is easy to believe. Had Cromwell been of royal blood, and the throne his birthright, his reign would have been the pride and boast of Englishmen through all time. Cromwell has been compelled to bear the odium of all the extreme measures that followed the civil war. Both when he was Captain General of the Puritan army and Lord Protector of England, did his moderate counsels avail to defeat the wild schemes that always spring up in times of revolution, and more than once did he endanger his influence with his own soldiers by his conservatism. Armies are rarely composed of men of such positive minds as the Puritan soldiers. Almost any one of them could preach to his fellows what was called a sermon, and he had, too, his own ideas of government as well as of religion. Even a Cromwell could not always mould such stiff-necked material entirely to his own will. It has been wisely said in regard to his policy with his army, that "to ordinarily govern, Cromwell was sometimes compelled to submit." In some respects he was far in advance of his age. England is to-day, in her treatment of the religious question, slowly plodding along in the path Cromwell marked out for her more than two hundred years ago. He had an intuitive sense of the nation's ills and the proper remedies to be applied. That his intuitions were, in the main, correct, finds its best proof in the marvelous success of his policy.

In his government, the personal and constitutional elements were strangely mingled. Ruling ordinarily in accordance with the laws, he did not hesitate, on occasion, to override or change them. When Parliament failed to meet his expectations, he dismissed it, and, like Charles, ruled alone. There the similarity ends. Charles ruled alone to maintain the royal prerogative; Cromwell to give peace and prosperity to England. But there was, while Cromwell lived, a universal feeling that the laws and the constitution were ever at the mercy of an individual will. Such a system as Cromwell's, however favorable to order and progress under a wise administration, was inconsistent with a free constitution. Under a weak head, it would inevitably result in anarchy; under an ambitious one, relapse into a despotism.

But Cromwell's enemies were unrelenting. It mattered little that he was the most tolerant man in England, to priest and churchman he was the very prince of fanatics, — that his rule was able and just, commanding the respect of all Christendom, to cavalier and noble he was only an upstart and an interloper, — that he made his country so great and powerful, that the very name of Englishman became a shield to the humblest citizen that bore it, in any part of the civilized world, to the royalist he was but a low-born usurper and a fit mark for every assassin's dagger. But it must be acknowledged, that, with all his patriotism, Cromwell was a usurper. The ruler who can, even once, manifestly set aside a settled constitution, or trample under foot established law, is a usurper. This Cromwell did at will. The people of England had just struggled through one revolution, that their traditional liberties might be preserved to them; but when the despotism, however violent, of the Stuarts, merely gave place to the despotism, however mild, of Cromwell, freedom was won only to be lost again. The legitimate result of Cromwell's usurpation in 1653, was the return of the Stuarts in 1660, and the disappearance of religious toleration and constitutional liberty for almost a generation.

Richard Cromwell. Cromwell named his son Richard as his successor. The father was both soldier and statesman, the son was neither; and so, after a few months of fruitless effort to control a mutinous army and govern an almost rebellious people, Richard resigned the Protectorship and retired to private life.

The Restoration. General Monk was in Scotland at the head of a well-appointed force. He commenced at once his march towards London, where his arrival was awaited with indescribable anxiety. Though long silent as to his intentions, he was favorable to the restoration of the monarchy, and was in secret correspondence with Prince Charles, who was at Breda. The famous "Long Parliament," once more coming together, issued writs for a new election, and voted its own dissolution, just twenty years from its first meeting. The new Parliament assembled on the 25th of April, 1660, and, agreeably to the wishes of all parties, invited Prince Charles to return to the home and throne of his father. He landed at Dover on the 25th of May, and was crowned King of England on the 29th. This is known in history as "The Restoration."

The Last Muster of the Puritan Army. One of the most suggestive pictures presented to us in the annals of the English nation, is that of the old Puritan army, thirty thousand strong, drawn up at Blackheath, to witness the return of Charles. It might be called "The Downfall of Puritanism." Those grim and stalwart men, who had been the arbiters of the fate of England for nearly twenty years, whose resistless charges had carried dismay into the ranks of the enemy at home and abroad, stood like lifeless statues, while the ringing bells and glad shouts of the people welcomed the returning Stuart to the throne of his ancestors. They had swept away the Throne, the House of Lords, and the Established Church, and had reorganized, or dismissed at will, the House of Commons. But in the presence of the people, re-inspired with their old reverence for royalty, they were beaten without a battle. Sadly and thoughtfully, but without a murmur, they laid down their arms and quietly returned to their former homes, henceforth to be distinguished from their neighbors only by greater industry and sobriety. Cromwell had been the representative of Puritanism, and his usurpation of power was regarded as a Puritan usurpation. When, therefore, he assumed all of royalty but the name, and ruled England through his army instead of his Parliament, Puritanism became a political force instead of a moral power, and its fall at the death of Cromwell was inevitable.

Charles II., 1660 to 1685 — 25 years. Stuart.

The Circumstances under Which Charles Became King. Charles II. ascended the throne in 1660, but

English history dates the beginning of his reign from the death of his father, in 1649. The circumstances under which he became an actual sovereign were auspicious. Perhaps no English king was ever welcomed to the throne with so wild a delight as he. A few words as to the circumstances may be proper.

That Cromwell was just in his rule and made England glorious, did not reconcile the people to the essential despotism he established. Even Republicans were unwilling to live under a government republican only in name. After the death of Cromwell, and during the administration of his son Richard, the government was fast relapsing into anarchy. With Richard's retirement, England was not only left without a head, but without a settled form of government. The monarchy had been abolished and the republic had proved a failure. What would follow none could tell; but it was plain to all, that the soldiers in arms were the sole arbiters of the fate of England. The one fate to be dreaded was a succession of irresponsible military rulers. Puritans and Churchmen, Republicans and Royalists, beheld the gulf that yawned before them, and, for a time, forgot their differences. For a peril that all could see but none could fathom, there was but one alternative, — the restoration of the monarchy and the return of the Stuarts. It was not then the fickleness of the English people, as is too often charged, but their conscious and narrow escape from nameless national woes, that caused such unbounded enthusiasm when Charles Stuart re-entered the capital of his ancestors.

The Social Revolution. The extreme legislation of the Puritans had made their rule irksome to the people. Innocent amusements had been strictly prohibited, and piety, or its profession, had been made an essential qualification for office. With the restoration of the monarchy and a repeal of Puritan legislation, there was an inevitable reaction. The dance around the May-pole on the village green was never so joyous as now, and Christmas festivities returned with more than their wonted hilarity. Had Charles possessed but ordinary wisdom, could the experience of his father and his own early misfortunes have taught him the one lesson to study and respect the wishes of the people, his reign would have been peaceful and popular. But he broke every promise he had made, and disappointed every expectation of the people.

Although they welcomed the removal of unnatural restraints, they were not prepared for the unbridled license that prevailed throughout the country after the restoration. Before long they were turning in disgust from the king they had welcomed so heartily, and wishing they had the great Oliver back again. Nothing more vividly illustrates the extent of this social revolution than the history of the stage. During the Puritan period, theatrical performances, however innocent, had been rigidly prohibited. With Charles returned the theatre, foul and revolting, without even a French refinement to its grossness. But the painted scenery and loose manners of the new stage only reflected real life in fashionable circles. The king himself led the shameless revels of the royal court; the court gave the standard of morality to the capital; and thence the deadly contagion spread, infecting fashionable society in all parts of the kingdom. Religion became a by-word and morality a mockery. It is but just to say that the great mass of the English people remained unaffected by this incoming tide of vice. Although Puritanism, as a political power, had fallen, and its very name had become a jest among the now dominant cavaliers, the sturdy virtues and the deep religious spirit that were its very essence, had been too deeply implanted in the minds and hearts of the English people to be easily removed. They still remained to mould English character, and modify English institutions, and they are, to-day, the richest inheritance of the English people.

The Convention Parliament. The Parliament that restored the monarchy is called the "Convention Parliament." It early passed an "Act of Oblivion and Indemnity" extending a general pardon to all offenders, except certain of the Regicides. Of these, thirteen were executed and many imprisoned for life, although Charles had virtually promised to pardon all who voluntarily came forward and surrendered themselves. Many fled to foreign parts, three of them, Goffe, Whalley, and Dixwell, finding refuge in America. This Act restored to the Royalists the estates taken from them by the Commonwealth, except when the transfer had been made by sale, but it gave them no redress for other losses. The dissatisfied cavaliers pronounced the "Act" one of oblivion to the king's friends and indemnity to his enemies, for they had been mulcted without mercy under the Commonwealth, and many had been forced to part with their estates to meet the demands of the government. This Parliament abolished the last relic of the Feudal System, the tenure of lands by knight service, including the wardship of minors and the marriage of heiresses, that had been fruitful sources of income to the king, in place of which he received a life-grant of £1,200,000.

The Restoration of the Episcopal Religion. The dissolution of this Parliament and a new election resulted in the return of the "Cavalier Parliament" of 1661. This body attempted by successive acts to reestablish Episcopacy as the national religion. "The Solemn League and Covenant" was ordered to be burned by the public hangman. Charles himself became an Episcopalian, declaring that "Presbyterianism was no religion for a gentleman." The "Corporation Act" required all public officers to worship in accordance with the usages of the established church, and to deny the right of the subject to bear arms against the king. The "Act of Uniformity" required all the clergy to adopt the prayer-book and assent to all its contents, on pain of expulsion. Two thousand Puritan clergymen were ejected from their livings in one day, the anniversary of St. Bartholomew, for non-compliance.

Attempt to Force Episcopacy upon the Scots. To gain the aid of the Scotch Presbyterians, Prince Charles, on New Year's Day, 1651, solemnly signed the Covenant at Scone, thus pledging himself to support the Presbyterian religion. But he now not only turned Episcopalian himself, but he resolved to force Episcopacy upon the Scots. The Earl of Lauderdale was sent to Scotland with unlimited powers to carry out the wishes of the king. Bishops were appointed, and soldiers posted at the various centres to compel attendance on the worship of the established church, and to collect fines from non-attendants. An impotent rising of the persecuted Covenanters in the neighborhood of Edinburgh became an excuse for the most barbarous legislation, and the most dreadful cruelty. The "thumbscrew" and "boot" became common instruments of torture. From this time, 1662, to the Revolution, in 1688, the Scotch Covenanters maintained their faith amidst persecutions and sufferings, from which the mind recoils with horror.

The "Conventicle Act" forbade all Puritan assemblies for public worship. The faithful Covenanters, armed for self-defence, held secret meetings, at midnight, in the depths of the woods. English soldiers sometimes burst upon them with merciless slaughter. The sea-girt prison on Bass Rock, and the gloomy walls of Dunbarton Castle, witnessed many an awful death by slow and cruel torture, many a sad and lingering one in dark and dreary dungeons. The "Five Mile Act" forbade non-conforming clergymen to appear within five miles of any town or the places of their former worship, and excluded them from the work of instructing the young, dooming them to penury and even starvation and death. An Act was passed for the suppression of Quakers, who were specially odious to the Cavaliers, from their refusal to bear arms. English as well as Scotch prisons were crowded with Puritan offenders.

Foreign Affairs. The history of the foreign affairs of this reign is but a humiliating record of royal intrigue and treachery. Charles is charged with involving the country in war for the simple purpose of obtaining a vote of money for its prosecution. The money once in his hands went to the support of shameless favorites, while English ships were left to decay, and their crews remained unpaid. The first of these wars was with Holland. It grew out of the rivalry of the Dutch and English merchants seeking a monopoly of the trade in gold-dust and ivory on the coast of Guinea. An English fleet, sent to America during the first year of this war, 1664, compelled the surrender of all the Dutch colonies to England. The government of these colonies was granted by the king to his brother, the Duke of York, from whom New York received its name.

The Plague in London. A signal victory, gained off the Suffolk coast, near Lowestoft, caused little exultation in London, for an enemy more dreaded than the Dutch was already in the suburbs of the great city. The worst fears were realized. That dread pestilence, the Plague, was soon in every house, bringing death and consternation to the crowded population. In six months one hundred thousand persons died. Grass grew in streets that were once the busy marts of trade. Scarcely a sound was heard but the rumbling of the carts, and the cries of the attendants echoing through the city and piercing the death-haunted houses, "Bring out your dead, bring out your dead."

The Great Fire of London. During the next year, 1666, called by Dryden the "Year of Wonders," the greater part of the city was laid in ashes by an extensive conflagration. In the end the fire proved a blessing, for it destroyed the filthy sections still infested by the Plague, and, in time, narrow lanes and wretched hovels gave place to wide, well-drained streets, and more commodious dwellings.

During the year following the fire, the Dutch, everywhere victorious by reason of the decay of the English navy, sailed up the Thames and threatened London itself. The war was ended by the Peace of Breda, in 1668. Clarendon, who had been at the head of affairs of state, becoming unpopular on account of the war, was compelled to resign to escape impeachment. He was succeeded by a Cabinet, or Cabal,* composed of five members.

Charles a Pensioner of Louis of France. But that which brands this administration with the deepest infamy, is a secret compact made with Louis XIV., king of France, in 1670. Louis coveted the possession of the Netherlands, and sent an army to invade its territory. To preserve the balance of power thus endangered, England, Holland, and Sweden formed the "Triple Alliance." While professing to enter heartily into this Alliance, Charles was busily negotiating a secret treaty with Louis. For an annual pension of £200,000, he agreed to withdraw from the Alliance, assist Louis' scheme of conquest in the Netherlands, and adopt the Catholic religion. It was stipulated that he should announce his change of religion as soon as it was prudent, and that Louis should lend him a French army in case of revolution. Charles did another thing especially humiliating to the nation. Dunkirk, that had been won from Spain by the valor of Cromwell, and had become almost as essential to English power, and quite as essential to English pride as

---

* These were Clifford, Arlington, Buckingham, Ashley, and Lauderdale, the initials of whose names form the word Cabal, a word known before, signifying a Cabinet. But so corrupt was the Cabal of Charles II., the word has ever since been applied to cliques of political tricksters.

Calais had been a century before, was sold to the French king for £400,000, merely to pander to the pleasures of a vicious court. Agreeably to the treaty made with Louis, Charles, in 1672, began the war with Holland. On the sea, the Dutch navy gained several victories over the combined fleets of England and France. The refusal of Parliament to vote supplies, and the unpopularity of the war, compelled Charles to make peace in two years. France continued hostilities till 1678, when, by the treaty of Nimeguen, she rose to the first rank among the powers of Europe. Though gaining many advantages during the war, she failed to conquer the brave little Republic.

Declaration of Indulgence. Just before the beginning of the war, Charles had issued a Declaration of Indulgence, establishing the principle of religious toleration to all sects. This Declaration gave instant liberty to thousands of Puritans, who, for many years, had pined in English dungeons. Bunyan left the cell he had occupied for twelve years in Bedford jail, and where he had composed that most wonderful allegory in the English tongue, Pilgrim's Progress. Twelve thousand Quakers alone were set at liberty by this edict. There was general distrust as to the motives of the king in issuing the Declaration of Indulgence. It was believed to be the initiative in a scheme to restore Catholics to office, and Catholicism to England. A persistent refusal of Parliament to vote supplies compelled the king to withdraw it.

The Test Act. Parliament quickly followed up its advantage by passing the Test Act, requiring all officers, civil and military, to take the Oath of Supremacy.

This Oath contained a denial of the peculiar tenets of Romanism, and an affirmation of those of the established church. The numerous resignations that followed showed to what an extent Catholics had already been brought into office, and confirmed previous suspicions of the Catholic tendencies of the king. James, Duke of York, the brother of the king and Lord High Admiral, an acknowledged Catholic, was forced to retire from the navy.

The Popish Plot. There were wide-spread fear and distrust. Whispers of Catholic plots filled the air. At this moment, when the public mind was excited with apprehension and ready to credit any tale however wild, one Titus Oates came forward, in 1678, with revelations of a Popish plot to murder the king and all the Protestants in England. It was like a spark in a powder-magazine. All England was thrown into a phrensy of excitement. The train-bands patrolled the streets of London. The Catholics, to the number of thirty thousand, were ordered to leave the city. They were excluded by statute from Parliament, and, for a century and a half, were debarred from membership in either house. Fresh testimony of the coming of a Catholic army caused a fresh panic, and every Catholic in the kingdom was disarmed. Trials, convictions, and executions followed each other with indecent haste. The most eminent victim was the venerable Lord Stafford, who was guilty of no offence, and was offered up to satisfy the maddened popular thirst for Catholic blood.

A bill to deprive James of the right of succession passed the House of Commons, but was defeated in the

House of Lords. The discovery of a letter to Louis, written by the Earl of Danby, who had become Prime Minister after the fall of the Cabal, soliciting money, and exposing the dependence of Charles on the French king, gave an air of reality to the revelations of Oates, and fanned still more the popular phrensy. Just at this moment it was discovered that the whole story of the "Popish Plot" was a pure fabrication.

The Rye House Plot. A real Protestant plot chiefly to secure the exclusion of James from the succession, came to light, later in the reign, implicating men of high rank, among whom were Lord Russell and Algernon Sidney. A few reckless men of the same party formed another scheme to assassinate the king and his brother as they rode past a place called the Rye House. The two plots were ingeniously made to appear as one, by the lawyers of the Crown, sealing the doom of the high-born conspirators, who speedily perished on the scaffold.

The Habeas Corpus Act, A.D. 1679. In this reign the Habeas Corpus Act, the third great statute advancing constitutional liberty, was passed. It was specially designed to secure the personal liberty of the subject, forbidding his detention in prison without cause duly shown before a legal tribunal. Although the principle established by this Act had been embodied in one of the leading sections of the Great Charter, the arbitrary wills of kings and the ingenuity of ministers had hitherto rendered it entirely inoperative. The freedom of the press was also secured in this reign. This was accomplished by a refusal of Parliament to renew the license law, by which a supervision of the press had been maintained. It was in this reign that Milton, deprived of the office he had held under Cromwell, poor, old, and blind, achieved that greatest triumph of his life, Paradise Lost.

The Merry Monarch. With all his faults, Charles was an easy, good-natured king, going quietly along in the path of his pleasures, even when the most exciting events were occurring around him. His excessive good nature has given him in history, the title of "Merry Monarch." The various plots, real and pretended, had brought a reaction in the public mind in favor of the king. While the latter avoided an open or defiant disregard of the laws, he went deliberately to work to make his government absolute, inaugurating what has been termed the second Stuart tyranny. The Test Act excluding Catholics from office was quietly ignored, and James was restored to his former position as Lord High Admiral. Although making no public avowal of his adoption of the Catholic faith, Charles desired the ministrations of a Catholic priest in his dying moments.

James II., 1685 to 1689 — 4 years. Stuart.

The Second Stuart Tyranny. During the preceding reign, James, Duke of York, had gained considerable credit as commander of the navy. All efforts to exclude him from the throne on account of his pronounced devotion to the Papacy had failed, and now, at the death of Charles without heirs, he assumed the crown without opposition, under the title of James II. Much was hoped from the supposed manliness of his character, and still more from the solemn avowal made in the presence of his council, at its first meeting after the death of Charles, to support and defend the established church, and execute the laws of the realm. But the high expectations that preceded the coronation were only equaled by the disappointment that followed it. Enthusiasm soon gave place to gloom, and gloom to horror. James was not a mere lover of ease and pleasure like Charles, but he soon showed that he was more indifferent to public sentiment, more defiant of the law, and more malignant towards men of other views. Within three days after his accession, and against the advice of his council, he levied customs without the consent of Parliament. The first elections were carried by fraud and violence in the interests of the king. Parliament, being subservient to his will, approved the levy, and voted the king a life income of £2,000,000. Its action on the subject of religion was moulded to suit the royal pleasure. Though silent on the subject in England, the laws against the Scotch Covenanters were made more severe and executed more rigorously than ever before. An ill-organized attempt of the Duke of Argyle to rouse the clans to resistance quickly ended in the death of the Duke and the scattering of the clans.

The Rebellion of the Duke of Monmouth. An attempt, equally rash, on the part of the Duke of Monmouth, in the west, having for its object the overthrow of James, and his own assumption of royal power, was even more disastrous in its results. The royal army defeated the rebels at Sedgemoor, July 6, 1685. The polished but cowardly Monmouth, when brought a prisoner into the presence of the angry king, prostrated himself at his feet, which he wet with his tears, while piteously begging for his life. He was quickly sent to the block, and his deluded followers were hunted down like wild beasts. These unfortunate attempts only strengthened the power of the king, for they enkindled a new feeling of loyalty in the hearts of the people. They furnished, too, a plausible excuse for a large increase of the army. The most severe measures were adopted against the rebels.

The English Reign of Terror. A Circuit Court was organized in the rebellious counties, whose action was better suited to the darkest of the Dark Ages, than to the enlightenment of the seventeenth century. Chief Justice Jeffries presided. We know not from which the mind recoils with deepest horror, the merciless judgments of this fiend in human form against the innocent and the guilty, or his heartless levity in the midst of the sufferings he inflicted. We search, in vain, the pages of history for a name that has descended to a more infamous immortality than has that of Jeffries. His Court has been variously characterized, in history, as "Jeffries' Campaign," the "Bloody Assize," and the "English Reign of Terror." Its first victim was a woman seventy years of age, Alice Lisle, widow of one of the members of the High Court of Justice. She was beheaded for giving food and lodging to a flying rebel. Another woman, Elizabeth Gaunt, was burned for the same offence, while others were scourged from town to town. One Captain Kirke, at the head of a company of troopers as inhuman as himself, and ironically called "Kirke's lambs," was charged with the apprehension and execution of the rebels. It is said that they were accustomed, for entertainment at their carousals, to have their prisoners hung on lofty gibbets in front of their windows, and the drums beat, to furnish music to the dance of the quivering bodies. To an American there is no parallel to this, except in the cruelties of the savage who dances in glee around his tortured victim. As in the Wars of the Roses, the heads and limbs of the dead were posted in public places to strike terror into the hearts of the inhabitants.*

It will hardly be credited that the queen herself, and her maids of honor, made merchandise of freeborn English subjects, begging the lives of the condemned that they might sell them into slavery in the West Indies. Even the innocent and thoughtless girls who had presented to Monmouth an embroidered banner, as he entered their native town of Taunton, were only saved from a like fate by the payment of £2,000, to the maids of honor. Jeffries returned to London, enriched with the pardons he had sold, and with the boast on his lips, that "he had hanged more for high treason than all the judges of England since William

---

* Knight, in his most interesting work, gives the following graphic picture of the barbarities practiced by a Chief Justice of England, and sanctioned by its king, less than two hundred years ago. "The pitchy cauldron was constantly boiling in the Assize towns to preserve the heads and limbs from corruption that were to be distributed through the beautiful Western Country. As the leaves were dropping in that Autumn of 1685, the great oak of many a village green was decorated with a mangled quarter. On every tower of the Somersetshire churches a ghastly head looked down upon those who gathered together for the worship of the God of love. The directing post for the traveller was elevated into a gibbet. The laborer, returning home beneath the harvest-moon, hurried past the body suspended in its creaking gimmaces (chains). The eloquent historian of this reign of terror has attested from his own childish recollections that 'within the last forty years, peasants in some districts well knew the accursed spots and passed them unwillingly after sunset.'"

the Conqueror," and was rewarded by his appreciating master with the Great Seal.

Attempt to Restore Catholicism to England. Flushed with success in crushing the rebellion, James next moved boldly towards the goal he had in view, the restoration of Catholicism to England. Catholics were put at the head of the army, now numbering 20,000 men, also of the navy, the council, and the courts. They filled the civil offices and swarmed about the court. Monks of all orders, dressed in their peculiar garb, ostentatiously paraded the streets, and even the Jesuits were allowed to establish a school in the Savoy. Parliament, hitherto the tool of the king, alarmed at his evident purpose, and at the boldness with which he moved to its execution, refused a vote of supplies, and was instantly prorogued. But the opposition of Parliament and the discontent of the people only increased the audacity of the king. He formed an Ecclesiastical Court of seven members with Jeffries at the head, commissioned to exercise complete control over matters of religion. It was the "High Commission" revived. The Earl of Perth, the inventor of the steel thumb-screw, one of James's favorite instruments of torture and conversion, was appointed to the government of Scotland, and the Earl of Tyrconnel, equally bigoted and intolerant, to that of Ireland. A royal proclamation, forbidding ministers to preach on disputed subjects, was answered by stirring appeals from almost every pulpit, while the public press teemed with the indignant protests of the people. James next sought to place the great institutions of learning under Catholic control. He tried to force upon one of the

Oxford Colleges a Catholic head. The Fellows had elected one of their own number, declining to accept the nominee of the king. James summoned them to his presence. "I am your king, I will be obeyed," said he! "Go to your chapel this instant, and elect the Bishop! Let those who refuse look to it, for they shall feel the whole weight of my hand!"

The Seven Bishops. All England was now in a ferment; but James, possessed with the insane obstinacy of his race, and deaf to the entreaties of his Catholic friends, and even of the pope who counseled moderation, pressed swiftly forward to his doom. He issued a "Declaration of Indulgence," similar to that of his brother, Charles II., abolishing all religious tests for office and all penal laws against non-conformists. This was ordered to be read to every congregation in the land. Only two hundred out of ten thousand clergymen obeyed. A protest signed by seven bishops was presented to the king. "It is a standard of rebellion," said James, as he sent the bishops to the Tower. They were speedily brought before the King's Bench on a charge of seditious libel. Being acquitted by the jury after a day's trial, they were released amidst the wildest acclamations of the people. That night, June 30th, 1688, was a memorable one in London. The whole city was illuminated in honor of the seven bishops, bonfires blazed in every street, and rockets lit up the heavens. To over-awe the city, James had established a camp at Hounslow, midway between Windsor and Whitehall. He was present with the army when the news of the acquittal arrived, but left at once for London. As he rode away he heard a great shouting behind him. "What is that?" asked the startled king. "It is nothing but the soldiers who are glad that the bishops are acquitted," was the reply. "Do you call that nothing?" rejoined the king, now bitterly conscious that he had lost the sympathy of the soldiers who were his only hope. Not daunted as yet, he dispatched the infected regiments to distant stations, replacing them with soldiers drawn chiefly from the garrisons of Scotland and Ireland. He assembled an army of forty thousand men, but he little dreamed that many of its officers were already in a league against him. Among these officers was Lord Churchill, afterwards, as Duke of Marlborough, to become the most famous general of his times.

William of Orange Invited to Take the English Crown. The very day the bishops were acquitted, seven leading nobles sent a secret invitation to William, Prince of Orange, who had married James's eldest daughter, to come to England with an army and take the crown, assuring him of abundant support. William had seen King James become the pensioner of Louis of France, his most inveterate enemy. He had watched his persistent efforts to restore Romanism to England. He had witnessed, with undisguised resentment, his evident purpose to transform Ireland into a Catholic state, to become (according to the French ambassador) an asylum for English Catholics, and a possible refuge for himself,—a scheme that threatened the integrity of the empire of which William's wife was the prospective heir. His counsels and his protests had been alike unheeded. Finally, when it was announced that the queen had given birth to a son, William shared the general belief, that it was a supposititious child, to be foisted upon England, in the interests of the Papacy. His purpose was formed, and the invitation of the English nobles accepted. James and Louis were in perfect accord. When William began to gather ships and soldiers for the English campaign, Louis schemed to detain him on the continent.

By the greatest mistake of his life, as some historians term it, Louis hurled his forces against Germany instead of Holland, and the latter country being, for the present, safe, William was free to pursue his English campaign. With a fleet of five hundred ships, and an army of fourteen thousand men, he sailed from the Scheldt, and landed at Torbay, on the southern coast, the 5th of November, 1688. His army took up its line of march for the interior, receiving at first but few additions. But soon powerful nobles began to arrive, and important towns to give in their adhesion.

The Flight of James to France. James struggled with the energy of despair to meet the crisis. He sought to turn the current of public opinion by correcting abuses and making concessions, and even went frantically about touching for the king's evil, but all to no purpose. The people were wholly alienated from their king. The army of forty thousand which he had gathered at Salisbury, retreated, in panic, before the banners of Orange, and began to break up. Its officers went over to William, or retired entirely from the contest. James was utterly deserted. " God help me, for my own children have forsaken me," said the wretched king, when he learned that his daughter Anne had gone over to his enemies. Tossing the Great Seal into the Thames, he quickly followed his wife and child in their flight to France, without striking a blow for his kingdom and crown.

The Glorious Revolution Peacefully Accomplished. The House of Peers held a session, and requested William to call a convention of the people and to assume, in the meantime, the provisional government of England. The convention assembled in January, 1689, and declared Mary, eldest daughter of James II., William's wife, to be the lawful heir to the vacant throne. But Mary declined to accept royal honors that were not shared by her husband, and the convention then invited William and Mary to become joint sovereigns of England, with the actual administration of the government vested in the former. This proposition was accepted. Having signed a Declaration of Rights, re-affirming the ancient liberties of the English people, William and Mary received their crowns, and "The Glorious Revolution" was accomplished. Well may a revolution be called glorious, that, without the shedding of a drop of blood, achieved results so grand. From that day to this we hear no more of punishment in England except for crime. Englishmen no longer pine in foul dungeons, or die in God's free air at the cruel stake, for their fidelity to their convictions. Instruments of torture now exist only in Museums, as relics of a by-gone age, exciting the wonder of the beholder, that any age, and above all, any Christian age, could have been so barbarous. The interval of two months between the flight of James and the coronation of the new sovereigns is known as the Interregnum.

William III., 1689 to 1702 — 13 Years. Nassau.

Mary II., 1689 to 1694 — 6 Years. Stuart.

The Grand Alliance. The elevation of William to the English throne was a serious blow to Louis, King of France. Besides enabling William to bring into the contest with Louis the fleets and armies of England, it largely increased his power and influence on the continent. He became at once the acknowledged head of the opposition to French aggression. The revocation of the Edict of Nantes,* in 1685, had enabled William to bring about a coalition of the Protestant princes of Germany. The recent and wanton ravages of the French armies in the Palatinate now enabled him to bring into the alliance the Catholic princes also.† France, single-handed, was compelled to face the combined power of England, Holland, Germany, and Spain. An English brigade was sent to the aid of the allies, but William himself was detained in England by the unsettled condition of the government,

---

* Louis XIV. had assumed to be the champion of the Papacy, and had defied the whole Protestant world by the revocation, in 1685, of the Edict of Nantes, under which, since the reign of Henry IV., the French Huguenots had enjoyed immunity from persecution. At once there was inaugurated perhaps the most dreadful persecution any people ever suffered for conscience' sake. A cry of anguish went up from every town and hamlet in France, as the helpless, tortured Protestants died in the maintenance of their faith. Huguenots crowded the prisons, and went in gangs to the galleys. Although thousands of fugitives were turned back from the frontiers of France, it is computed that half a million of the most peaceable and industrious of her population fled from her borders. Her work shops were closed, and her revenues reduced, while the arts and industries, that had been the chief source of her prosperity, were carried to foreign countries.

† The "Treaty of Westphalia," terminating the "Thirty Years' War," in 1648, had left Germany, already divided by the Reformation, a loose confederation of petty, independent states, united in times of common danger by a sense of individual weakness, but separated, in times of peace, by differences in religion.

and especially by the critical state of affairs in Ireland.

Rebellion in Ireland. Tyrconnel had accomplished his mission in that country. It had been brought completely under Catholic rule. The half-savage natives were everywhere let loose upon Englishmen and Protestants. In the south, the panic-stricken people, pursued with fire and sword, abandoned their homes and fled from the country. In the north, the hunted Protestants gathered within the walls of Enniskillen and Londonderry. Backed by fifty thousand Irish soldiers, Tyrconnel boldly raised the standard of the Stuarts. James himself arrived in Ireland with a fleet and army furnished by the French king. Londonderry sustained a siege of one hundred and five days, when an English ship broke through the boom stretched across the river Foyle, and brought relief to the starving inhabitants. The same day a sally was made by the garrison of Enniskillen and the besiegers beaten off.

Battle of the Boyne. Shortly after this, William landed at Carrickfergus with an ample force, and took up his line of march for Dublin. He found the army of James strongly posted behind the river Boyne. Crossing this river on the 12th of July, 1690, in the face of the foe, William gained a complete victory, destroying James's last hope of the recovery of his kingdom. The anniversary of this battle is still observed by the Orangemen, a society of Protestant Irish. James fled to Dublin and embarked for France. William, after an unsuccessful attempt to capture Limerick, leaving the further prosecution of the war to his deputies, returned to England, and soon joined his allies on the continent, over whom the French armies had gained victory after victory.

Peace of Ryswick. Flushed with success, Louis had been tempted, just after William left for Ireland, to prepare an expedition for the invasion of England. But his fleet was completely overthrown, off Cape La Hogue, by a Dutch and English squadron, and all danger of invasion passed away. The victory of La Hogue, and the presence of William on the continent, inspired the allied armies with fresh courage. Although the war lingered for several years with varying success, Louis, conscious, at last, that he had completely exhausted the resources of his people, and, in the language of Fenelon, "had made France a vast hospital," consented, in 1697, to the unfavorable Treaty of Ryswick. He surrendered all his conquests except Alsace, recognized William as king of England, and abandoned the cause of the Stuarts. This war, under the name of "King William's War," had spread to the English and French colonies in America. A feeble attempt on the part of the English to take Quebec, and murderous raids among the New England settlements by hostile Indians, were the only events worthy of mention.

The Bill of Rights, A. D. 1689. Although associated with William in the government, Mary had nothing to do with its administration. She died in 1694, universally esteemed for her many virtues. William survived her seven years. This reign was of great political importance to England. William's coming had been preceded by a declaration of his purpose to uphold the liberties of the country. During the first year he gave his signature to the Bill of Rights.

second, in importance, only to the Great Charter itself. This Bill made standing armies in times of peace, and levies of money without consent of Parliament, unlawful; guaranteed the right of petition, the frequent assembling of Parliament, and freedom of debate; and forbade interference with the laws on the part of king.

Other statutes, approved by William, established religious toleration and the freedom of the press; secured to persons accused of crime the right of counsel and a copy of the charges; and to those condemned, protection from excessive fines and cruel and unusual punishments. By the Triennial Bill, no Parliament could sit more than three years. The Act of Settlement excluded Catholics forever from the throne, making Anne, second daughter of James, the prospective heir, and, at her death without heirs, Princess Sophia, who had married the Elector of Hanover.

The Constitution of England. William's reign marks an era in constitutional government in England, not alone because it gave birth to new laws in the interests of liberty, but because it gave vitality to laws that were old. Before William's time there were charters and statutes enough, could they have been executed, to have made the English people free; but neither was public sentiment so educated and expressed, nor the royal prerogative so limited and defined, as to make it impossible for a tyrant still to rule. During William's reign the rights of the people and the prerogatives of the crown were clearly defined. Now sovereign and subject alike bow before the majesty of the law.

One principle was established in the reign of William that has made popular government in England secure, the principle that the ministers of the Crown must be in harmony with the House of Commons. If in any important matter, or one in which the opposing parties are at issue, the House refuses by its vote to sustain the policy of the ministers, these ministers at once retire, and their places are filled by men of the opposite party. The House of Commons can, therefore, dictate the policy to be pursued by the government, and is the chief ruling power.

There is a peculiar and interesting fact in connection with the English Constitution. It is comprehended in no single enactment, nor in the enactments of any single reign. It is composed of all the great charters and statutes that have been enacted from time to time since the reign of John, with such customs and precedents as have the sanction of long usage. Although it lacks the individuality of our own Constitution, yet as the slow and steady growth of ages, as the product of the wisdom and patriotism of the best English minds, standing as it does the tests of time and an advancing civilization, it commands our reverence and our admiration. Indeed, our own Constitution is but a collection and epitome of the various charters of freedom that lie scattered all along the pathway of English history.

To us the term "Mother Country" is significant, not alone as indicating the English origin of most of our people, and our early colonial governments, but also the English origin of our liberties and our laws. Nearly all those great principles of government which we hold so dear were conceived in English hearts and wrought out by English hands. The inalienable rights of man, life, liberty, and the pursuit of happiness, dawned in Magna Charta long before they shone full-orbed in the Declaration of Independence.

The Second Grand Alliance. The Peace of Ryswick had been hastened by the consciousness on the part of the principal actors, that the settlement of a new question of vital importance to the powers of Europe was soon to be forced upon them, the question of the succession to the Spanish throne. The death of the present king, Charles II., was near at hand. With him would end the Austrian line of Bourbon princes, that had ruled over Spain for two hundred years. The leading powers, including France, determined on a partition of the Spanish empire at the death of Charles, agreeing to recognize Archduke Charles of Austria, as heir presumptive to the Spanish throne. King Charles, indignant at the proposed partition, bequeathed his whole empire to Philip of Anjou, grandson of Louis XIV. Charles died in 1700, and Philip unopposed took possession of his inheritance. The exultant Louis, disregarding the treaty of partition of which he was one of the signers, accepted the will of Charles. Acting in the name of his grandson, he garrisoned the Spanish Netherlands with French troops, and returned a haughty refusal to William's demand for their withdrawal. England and Holland prepared for war. At this juncture, James II. died in France, and Louis publicly acknowledged the son of James as King of England, under the title of James III. England had never been in greater peril from a foreign power since the days of the Armada, for the elevation of

Philip had placed the Spanish empire on the side of England's foes. "The Pyrenees exist no longer", said Louis as his grandson went to take the Spanish crown. The soul of William rose with the emergency. With matchless skill and energy he brought to a successful issue the last great work of his life, the formation of a Grand Alliance embracing England, Holland, Germany, Sweden, and Denmark, pledged to oppose the ambitious schemes of the French monarch, and to support the claims of Archduke Charles of Austria to the Spanish throne.

Death and Character of William. But William did not live to prosecute the war he had planned. An accident, caused by the stumbling of his horse as he rode to Hampton Court, terminated fatally on the 8th of March, 1702. He had long been slowly sinking under the ravages of disease. Although his face was marked with the lines of suffering, and his frail form bowed with care, his eagle eye and firmly compressed lips showed to the last the fiery soul within. Trained in the school of adversity (for the House of Orange had lain prostrate during his early youth), he had learned to be watchful of public events, and reserved in the expression of his opinions. His family being restored to power just as he was entering manhood, William brought to the public service wisdom and prudence beyond his years. His genius was best displayed in great emergencies. He was never so cool as in the midst of the conflict, and never so dangerous as after a defeat. Owing to his silent, unsocial habits, and his manifest partiality for his own countrymen, he was personally unpopular during his lifetime. But his patience, constancy, and patriotism, and, above all, the wisdom of his far-seeing policy, securing to the English people prosperity at home, and an influence abroad unknown since the times of Cromwell, have made William of Orange an honored name in every English household. At William's death Anne was immediately proclaimed Queen of England, in accordance with the Act of Settlement.

Anne, 1702 to 1714 — 12 Years. Stuart.

The War of the Spanish Succession. The death of William created no little consternation among the nations composing the "Grand Alliance." And consequently, the announcement, made from the throne, shortly after Anne's accession, that the policy of William would be continued by the new government, was hailed with general delight. The Duke of Marlborough and Prince Eugene were placed at the head of the allied armies. The war, that now arose, called in Europe, the "War of the Spanish Succession," and in America, "Queen Anne's War," lasted till the year 1713. During its progress four great victories were gained over the French at Blenheim, Ramillies, Oudenarde, and Maplaquet. France, humbled and exhausted, was compelled to sue for peace. By a treaty signed at Utrecht, in 1713, while Philip was recognized as King of Spain, his possessions on the continent were divided among the allied powers. Louis consented to the formal cession of Nova Scotia, Newfoundland, and Gibraltar to England, recognized Anne as Queen of England, and again abandoned the cause of the Stuarts. This war had extended to the French and English colonies in America, being marked by the renewal of Indian barbarities, especially in Massachusetts. Plans were in progress for the sailing of a fleet against Quebec, but they were brought to a sudden termination by the announcement of peace.

Marlborough. For several years, party strife in England had been growing more and more bitter, the Whigs favoring, and the Tories opposing, the war. Its long continuance, the frightful losses attending its fiercely contested battles, and the rapid increase of the national debt, had made it, towards the last, exceedingly unpopular. The Whig ministers were compelled to yield their places to Tories. Marlborough, who had allied himself with the Whigs, lost favor with the queen, who was Tory at heart, and, at the close of the war, was dismissed from the public service, with charges of peculation and mismanagement. His wife, the famous Duchess of Marlborough, who had exercised almost unbounded influence over the queen from the day of her accession, also fell into disfavor, and was dismissed from all the offices which she held about the royal person. Marlborough retired from England in disgust. This remarkable man deserves a moment's notice. He was handsome in person and of polished address, skilled in diplomacy, and, confessedly, the first general of the age. It is said that he never lost a battle, nor failed in the attempt to take a town, during his whole military career. His serenity under all circumstances was something marvelous. He went as calmly into battle as to a parade, passed unmoved amidst the most terrible scenes of carnage and suffering, exhibited no fear at the presence of danger, and showed no elation even in the hour of victory. But there was another and a darker side to his character. He was guilty of habitual meanness and dishonesty, and bore exposure with little apparent shame. He had been a traitor to James, being among the first to join the league against him, and then a traitor to William, having enlisted warmly in a scheme for the restoration of the Stuarts, even after the accession of William. His master passion was love of money. He stooped to the most unscrupulous methods in acquiring it, and managed, while in office, to amass an immense fortune. Marlborough stands a marked example of mingled greatness and littleness.

Constitutional Union of England and Scotland. In the midst of the war, in the year 1707, England and Scotland were made, in all respects, one kingdom, their Parliaments being united, as their crowns had been a little more than a century before. By the Act of Union, Scotland was to be placed on a perfect equality with England in matters of trade, the courts of Justice were to remain unchanged, and the church of Scotland was to be maintained, as already established by law. Sixteen Scotch Peers were admitted to the House of Lords, and forty-five members to the House of Commons. Although this union was bitterly opposed by the Scotch people, it has contributed immensely to their prosperity. Little fishing hamlets have grown into great commercial cities, manufactures have sprung up and thrived, and to-day, in some departments of industry, Scotland stands among the foremost nations. The reign of Anne was distinguished for its intellectual greatness, contesting with that of Elizabeth the right to be called the "Augustan Age." It is radiant with the genius of such men as Pope, Steele, Swift, and Addison.

Death of Good Queen Anne. Queen Anne died, in 1714, of an attack of apoplexy. Her people kindly remembered her as "Good Queen Anne." She was not attractive in person, and possessed but moderate ability. If, like Elizabeth, she made an unwise choice of personal favorites, and weakly surrendered herself to their influence, like Elizabeth, too, she had the good sense to put able men at the head of the government. After the Duchess of Marlborough (who was a whig) had lost favor with the queen, the latter fell under the influence of Mrs. Masham, one of her attendants. By her husband, Prince George of Denmark, she had nineteen children, all of whom died in infancy, or early youth. Domestic cares and sorrows make up the burden of her twelve years of rule. Prince George, though husband to the queen, had little to do with the government of England. That his abilities were limited may be gathered from the following sarcasm of the Merry Monarch: "I have tried him drunk and sober, and can find nothing in him." In accordance with the "Act of Settlement," Anne was succeeded by George, Elector of Hanover, son of Sophia, who was a granddaughter of James I.

CHAPTER X.

House of Brunswick or Hanover.

GEORGE I.	GEORGE IV.
GEORGE II.	WILLIAM IV.
GEORGE III.	VICTORIA.

George I., 1714 to 1727 — 13 years. Brunswick.

The Jacobites. George I. was thoroughly German in his tastes and habits, as well as birth and speech. He manifested little interest in English affairs, passing most of his time in his German kingdom, which Thackeray has pronounced as fortunate for the English people, since they were left the more free to confirm their newly acquired liberties. The adherents of the exiled Stuarts, called Jacobites, from Jacobus, Latin for James, had been very busy all through the reign of William, plotting his overthrow, usually in league with Louis XIV. of France. Anne, being a Stuart and a Tory, was undisturbed by them, but during the latter part of her reign, there was a deep laid plot to place on the throne, at her death, the son of James II. This plot was defeated through the vigilance of the Whigs, and its leaders were forced into exile, or brought to trial and punishment. The Jacobites were sufficiently active during the reign of George I., to keep the latter in a state of perpetual alarm, but the decease of Louis, their most powerful friend, was a death blow to their prospects.

The Pretender. In 1715, James Francis Stuart, son of James II., and called the Pretender, caused his standard to be raised in Scotland, under the Earl of Mar. Nothing came of the attempt but sorrow and suffering to the deluded Highlanders who had rallied to his support. Mar escaped to France in company with the Pretender.

Two years later, Charles XII. of Sweden, having a personal quarrel with King George about the ownership of certain German territory, planned an invasion of Scotland in the interests of the Pretender, but the sudden death of the warlike Swede, while besieging a castle in Norway, brought this scheme to a sudden termination.

Another attempt was made in 1719, when Spain, attempting to recover the territory of which she had been despoiled, provoked a quadruple alliance of England, France, Germany, and Holland, pledged to oppose her scheme of recovery. Her fleet being almost annihilated by an English squadron, off the coast of Sicily, King Philip, in retaliation, planned an invasion of England and a rising of the Jacobites, in favor of the Pretender. The Spanish fleet was dispersed by a storm, and this scheme, too, came to nought.

The South Sea Scheme. But one thing of interest remains to be noticed, the South Sea Scheme. The expensive wars of William had made necessary a national debt, amounting, at this time, to fifty-three million pounds. The offer of the South Sea Company to assume the entire debt, and lend money to the government at the low rate of four per cent., besides paying a bonus of seven million pounds, in consideration of the sole right of trade to the South Seas, was accepted by the government. The plans of the company required an immense outlay. Not having sufficient capital for so gigantic an enterprise, the company issued an indefinite amount of South Sea stock, promising large dividends to all who would invest. The well-known annual return of the galleons of Spain laden with the gold, silver, and precious stones of South America, and the glowing accounts of voyagers to the distant Pacific, concerning the tropical wealth of its myriad islands, led to the most extravagant notions of the value of the South Sea trade.

In addition to this, the South Sea Company had the virtual endorsement of the government. Its stock sold readily, and the price went up until shares worth a hundred pounds sold for a thousand. The excitement became intense and increased to a phrensy. All day long, eager throngs crowded around the counters of the company. The hard-earned savings of the poor, as well as the superfluous wealth of the rich, were swallowed up in the all-devouring Maelstrom. Other companies* sprang up for absurd, and even impossible objects, finding eager victims, so prevalent was the insane spirit of speculation. It is estimated that their entire stock would amount to five hundred million

---

* There were companies "to fish for wrecks on the Irish coast," " to extract silver from lead," " to import asses from Spain," " for a wheel for perpetual motion," "for an undertaking that shall in due time be revealed," &c., &c.

* All these companies found willing victims. As if the companies just mentioned were not a sufficiently palpable burlesque on the prevailing mania for speculation, a company was announced " for the invention of melting down saw-dust and chips, and casting them into clean deal boards without cracks or knots."

pounds sterling, twice the value, at that time, of all the land in England. The South Sea Company, by an Act of Parliament, secured the suppression of all its unlicensed rivals. Public confidence in speculative schemes was shaken. South Sea stock shared in the general distrust, and came into the market in increasing quantities; the price went down; a panic ensued; and the bubble burst, causing wide-spread ruin and dismay.

The Septennial Act. A single constitutional change was made during this reign. The Triennial Act had limited the sitting of Parliament to three years, but the frequent occurrence of elections kept the country in a state of constant turmoil, and the Septennial Act was passed, lengthening the sitting to seven years. George I. was stricken with apoplexy while travelling in Hanover, and died in his carriage. He left one son, who succeeded him with the title George II.

George II., 1727 to 1760 — 33 Years. Brunswick.

Robert Walpole. Robert Walpole was Prime Minister of England during the last six years of the reign of George I., and he continued, during the first fifteen years of the reign of George II., to guide the affairs of State. He first came into prominence at the time of the South Sea excitement, having, from the first, warned his countrymen against the delusive "dream." But it was in the midst of the dismay that followed the awaking, that Walpole displayed his matchless skill as a financier, suggesting plans to equalize the losses, and so to alleviate the general distress. The chief merits of his policy were its firm adherence to peace, and the encouragement it gave to industry. Its grand results were an unprecedented development of the national resources, and the re-establishment of the public credit. The English people, being no longer distracted by questions of religion and liberty at home, or war abroad, directed their energies, as never before, to the arts of peace. A new interest was awakened in commerce, and English merchant ships increased in every sea. A new impulse was given to manufactures, and great busy towns grew up, as if by magic. But Walpole's administration, though favorable to the production of material wealth, was destructive to public virtue. He retained power only through the indiscriminate practice of bribery. Honors, offices, titles, and gold, were unsparingly distributed to carry borough elections, and control parliamentary votes. "Every man has his price," was Walpole's pernicious estimate of human virtue, and the key-note to his policy.

War with Spain. The Treaty of Utrecht, in 1713, limited the commerce of England with Spanish America to slaves and the use of a single ship. The treaty restriction had never been enforced by the Spanish officials, and a lucrative trade had gradually grown up. Sometime after Philip had mounted the Spanish throne, the two countries of France and Spain had made a secret treaty, afterwards called the "Family Compact," France engaging to restore Gibraltar to Spain, and Spain engaging to break up English trade with South America. Almost every ship that arrived from South American waters had some tale to tell of search and outrage by Spanish cruisers, raising the war feeling, among the English people, to fever height. Walpole long struggled to maintain peace, but, in 1739, he yielded to the pressure and declared war with Spain. Hearing the bells that proclaimed the popular joy, Walpole is said, with a wise foresight, to have remarked, "They may ring their bells now; before long they will be wringing their hands." The war was unfortunate, and, as often happens, the man who was least responsible was most generally blamed. Walpole had to bear the odium of the now unpopular war. But its area soon widened.

War of the Austrian Succession. At the death of Charles VI., Emperor of Germany, his daughter Maria Theresa inherited his dominions. The Elector of Bavaria also claimed the German crown. France and Spain supported the cause of the Elector; England and Holland that of Maria Theresa. This war began in 1741, and was called, in Europe, the "War of the Austrian Succession," in America, "King George's War." Its feeble conduct on the part of England, charged to the apathy of the great "peace minister," made him so unpopular, that his majority in the House of Commons dwindled to a single vote, forcing him to resign in 1742. King George joined the army on the continent, and won, at its head, the battle of Dettingen. The war continued till 1748, when, by the Treaty of Aix-la-Chapelle, the claims of Maria Theresa were allowed by all the powers.

The only event of importance that occurred in America during this war, was the capture of Louisburg, on Cape Breton Island, called from its great strength the Gibraltar of America. It was taken by an expedition that sailed from Boston, in 1745, under the command of Sir William Pepperell. Much to the disappointment of the colonists, the Treaty of Aix-la-Chapelle compelled the restoration of Louisburg to the French.

The Young Pretender. While the war was in progress, and the very year that Louisburg was taken, another and a last attempt was made by the Stuarts to recover the English crown. A grandson of James II., Charles Edward Stuart, called the young Pretender, landed on the western coast of Scotland with but seven followers. The Highland clans were easily roused at the call of a Stuart, and the Pretender, gaining a victory at Preston Pans over the troops sent to oppose him, soon found himself at the head of six thousand men, and marched rapidly on London, causing, for a time, the greatest consternation. English soldiers were hastily withdrawn from the continent, and an ample force soon stood between the Pretender and the capital. Scarcely a Jacobite had joined him, nor were there any signs of a Jacobite rising, and the disappointed Prince, after reaching Derby, was forced by the Highland chiefs to retreat.

Culloden. He was overtaken, in 1746, at Culloden Moor, near Inverness, and his army was defeated with great slaughter. The Pretender escaped from the battle-field, only to wander a hunted fugitive amidst the wilds of Scotland. His romantic adventures and hair-breadth escapes remind us of the perilous wanderings of Charles II. after the battle of Worcester. With English dragoons patrolling all the roads, and guarding every pass, and English cruisers closely watching the Scottish coast, it seemed impossible for the unfortunate prince to escape. For five months he found shelter among the rough but devoted Highlanders. At one time he was thrown upon the mercy of a band of robbers, living with them in a cave near the coast. But neither Highlander nor robber was tempted to betray him by the reward of thirty thousand pounds, which the king had placed upon his head.

The Last of the Stuarts. With the departure of the Pretender from the shores of Scotland, the Stuarts disappear forever from the pages of English history. Forced from the soil of France by the Treaty of Aix-la-Chapelle, the Pretender went to Rome, where he eked out a wretched existence, and died, in 1788, a miserable death. His younger brother Henry, Cardinal of York, the last of the Stuarts, died at Rome, some twenty years later. A monument, erected by Canova, in St. Peter's at Rome, in 1816, bears three empty titles, James III., Charles III., and Henry IX.

The French and Indian War. The French owned Canada and Louisiana, and laid claim to the Ohio and Mississippi valleys, by virtue of early explorations by Jesuit missionaries. The English occupied the Atlantic sea-board from New Brunswick to Florida, and claimed the country westward to the Pacific, basing their title on the discoveries of the Cabots. Both parties therefore claimed the great Mississippi basin, stretching from the Alleghanies to the Rocky Mountains. In 1749, George II. had granted a charter to a company to settle the Ohio valley.

To forestall and prevent its occupation by the English, the French planned a chain of forts, running along the line of the Ohio and Mississippi rivers, purposing thus to connect their settlements in Canada and Louisiana. They had already built three of these forts, beginning with Presque Isle, on Lake Erie, when the Governor of Virginia, in 1753, sent George Washington on a mission of inspection and remonstrance. He reported the French as firm in their purpose to occupy the disputed territory. Washington was sent, the next year, with a military force to protect the laborers of the Ohio Company, who were engaged in building a fort at the junction of the Alleghany and Monongahela rivers. Before his arrival, this fort was captured and completed by the French, who named it Fort Du Quesne. Washington, attacked by overwhelming numbers, was forced to retreat beyond the Alleghanies. France and England, realizing that the time had now come for the struggle for dominion in America, hurried forces to their respective colonies; and thus began, in 1754, the French and Indian War.

The Five Important Points. The French, at the outset, occupied five important points, against which the efforts of the English were mainly directed. Fort Du Quesne, standing at the head-waters of the Ohio, commanded the Ohio Valley; Fort Niagara controlled the fur trade and the navigation of the Great Lakes; Forts Ticonderoga and Crown Point stood right in the great natural highway between Canada and New York; Quebec was the key to the possession of Canada, while Louisburg controlled the fisheries, and the gulf and river of St. Lawrence. The earlier conflicts were favorable to the French, but the appointment of William Pitt at the head of the English ministry caused a more vigorous prosecution of the war, and the tide soon turned in favor of English arms. Louisburg and Du Quesne surrendered in 1758, the latter being named Fort Pitt, in honor of the great minister. Ticonderoga, Niagara, and Quebec, yielded in 1759.

The Battle of Quebec. The capture of Quebec decided the war. It was taken by the English under Wolfe, who scaled the heights of Abraham, and defeated the French under Montcalm, on the plains above. Wolfe and Montcalm both fell mortally wounded, while fighting bravely at the head of their forces, and each died willingly, the one rejoicing in his country's success, and the other unwilling to survive his country's defeat. As Wolfe lay on the ground, with his life blood fast ebbing away, an officer near him exclaimed, "They run, they run!" Wolfe raised himself on his elbow, and asked "Who run?" "The enemy, the enemy," was the reply. "God be praised, I die happy" murmured the noble patriot, as his great soul passed away from earth. Montcalm, when conscious that his wound was mortal, asked the surgeon how long he could survive. "Perhaps a day, perhaps less," was the reply. "So much the better," said the suffering hero," I shall not live to see the surrender of Quebec." On an obelisk, erected in the gardens of the government house at Quebec, the name of Wolfe was placed upon one side, and that of Montcalm upon the other, — a noble tribute of a nation, grateful to a patriot son, and generous to a manly foe.

A Proud Year in English Warfare. The year 1759 is one of the proudest in the annals of English warfare. The battle of Quebec, fought on the 13th of September, settled the question of dominion in America.

Five days after this battle, Quebec opened its gates to the English army, and the following year, all Canada came under English rule. In the old world — where the war was known as the "Seven Years' War"— the French had planned two campaigns, the one for the seizure of Hanover, and the other for the invasion of England itself. The victory of Minden, won August 1st, chiefly through the valor of the six English regiments in the army of Ferdinand of Brunswick, forced the French back to the Rhine, and Hanover was safe.

The French fleet, designed to aid in the invasion of England, was blockaded in the harbor of Brest by Admiral Hawke. The latter being driven by a storm from the coast, the French ventured out, but his sudden return forced them to take shelter among the rocks and shoals in Quiberon Bay. The pilot on board Hawke's flag-ship remonstrated against the latter's decision to attack the French on so dangerous a coast, and in the midst of a gale. "You have done your duty in this remonstrance," said the brave commander. "Now lay me alongside the French Admiral." And there, amid rocks and shoals, in the darkness and tempest, the brave mariners of England won imperishable honor. The French fleet was destroyed or dispersed, and England was saved from all danger of invasion.

The Struggle for Dominion in India. Hardly less important was the struggle between France and England for dominion in India. In 1600, during the reign of Elizabeth, a company was chartered for purposes of trade with the East Indies. In 1662, Bombay was acquired by the marriage of Charles II. with Catherine of Braganza. By successive Acts of Parliament, the

East India company was vested with the sole government of the English East India possessions. It organized and maintained its own army, and established its own courts of justice. Its principal stations, at the time of the accession of George II., were Madras, Bombay, and Calcutta. The French, also, had trading stations on the coast, the principal one being at Pondicherry. During the "War of the Austrian Succession," the French governor conceived the idea of expelling the English altogether from the Indian peninsula. Allying himself with the native princes, the authority of France was soon established throughout most of the Carnatic. Only a single native prince held out against the French, and he was closely besieged in his last stronghold. In 1751, Robert Clive, a poor clerk in the employ of the English Company, having obtained a commission, raised a small force of two hundred English, and three hundred native soldiers, and suddenly surprised Arcot, the capital of the Carnatic. With the aid of the Mahrattas, warlike tribes inhabiting the mountains, Clive defeated the French and their native allies in battle after battle, and established the supremacy of the English.

Plassey. In 1756, Surajah Dowlah, the Viceroy of Bengal, fell suddenly upon Calcutta, making captive its entire population. One hundred and forty-six prisoners were crowded into a dungeon belonging to the fort, called the Black Hole of Calcutta, eighteen feet long by fourteen wide, and having only two small windows. All but twenty-three were dead when the door was opened the next morning. When the news reached Madras, Clive raised a force of one thousand Englishmen and two thousand natives, and pushed rapidly northward towards the Viceroy's capital. He was met at Plassey, in 1757, by the Viceroy himself, at the head of sixty thousand savage natives, fifteen thousand of whom were cavalry. But this great host was completely overthrown by the brave little army under Clive, and the rich and populous district of Bengal was added to British India. The war against the French was prosecuted with vigor, and, in six months after the accession of George III., the English dominion in India was firmly established.

George III., 1760 to 1820 — 60 Years. Brunswick.

The Peace of Paris. The first two kings of the House of Hanover were German to the last in taste and feeling, and there was little in common between them and their English subjects. But George the Third used to boast that "he was Briton born," and it was then something to be proud of, for England, under the guidance of the "Great Commoner," had taken the foremost rank among the nations of Europe. In 1763, the "Seven Years' War" was formally terminated by the "Peace of Paris." Few treaties have made such sweeping changes as this. France relinquished to Great Britain not only the disputed territory in America, but all Canada besides. She surrendered to Spain the island and the town of New Orleans, and all her territory west of the Mississippi. Of her vast possessions in North America, she retained, as fishing stations, only two small islands, St. Pierre and Miquelon, lying south of Newfoundland. By the same treaty, Spain gave Florida to England, in exchange for Havana and the

Philippine Islands, which England had taken from her during the war.

Causes of the American Revolution.

The Repressive Policy of England. The policy of the mother country towards her American colonies had always been a repressive one. Both commerce and manufactures had been discouraged by laws confining their trade to English ports, and to the use of English ships. This policy was inspired, in part, by a purpose to protect home industries, and, in part, by a desire to keep the colonies in a state of dependence.

Search Warrants. With the increase of colonial wealth, came schemes for a colonial revenue. Duties were laid on certain imports, and, as a result, the colonists, without calling in question the propriety of such duties, resorted to an organized system of smuggling. To correct this evil, captains of English cruisers were empowered to search, and, in case of suspicion, to seize, every merchant ship entering a colonial port; and, on the land, officers, provided with "search warrants," were authorized to break into stores, and even private houses, if suspected of containing smuggled goods, violating a principle long dear to the English people, that "Every man's house is his castle."

The Stamp Act. No direct tax had ever been laid on America. Such a tax had been suggested as early as the ministry of Walpole, but a consciousness of its injustice had hitherto deterred English ministers from attempting to levy it. In 1765, during the ministry of Lord Grenville, a tax was laid on stamps, whose use on papers, pamphlets, and legal documents, was made obligatory by Act of Parliament. This direct tax was held to be justifiable, on the ground of the expenses incurred by the home government in prosecuting the French and Indian war. But this was a mere pretext, for the English ministry could not have been ignorant that the colonies had borne more than their share of the burdens of the war. The spirit of opposition in the colonies was so intense and universal, that the Stamp Act was repealed the next year; but the repeal was coupled with an affirmation of the right of Parliament "to bind the colonies in all cases whatsoever."

Boston Port Bill. After resorting to various devices to secure submission on the part of the colonies, even sending regiments of soldiers, as a menace to the people of Boston, the British government, in 1773, laid a trivial tax of three pence per pound on tea. But this too failed, for with the colonies, it was not a question of money, but of principle. They had no voice in the deliberations of the body that taxed them. "Taxation without representation is tyranny," was the principle on which they took their stand. New York and Philadelphia sent the unbroken chests of tea back to England. In Charleston, they were stored in damp cellars, until their contents became worthless. At Boston, the cargoes of three ships were poured into the bay by men disguised as Mohawks. In retaliation, the port of Boston was closed to commerce, and the charter of Massachusetts annulled, by Act of Parliament.

Battle of Lexington, April 19th, 1775. From this moment, the colonies were a unit in the purpose to oppose the oppressions of the English government. The public mind was rapidly educated to resistance by such dauntless patriots as John Hancock, John Adams, Samuel Adams, Patrick Henry, and Benjamin Franklin. Delegates from twelve colonies met at Philadelphia in September, 1774, forming what is known as the First Continental Congress. While expressing their loyalty to the mother country, they boldly asserted their rights as colonies. Their petitions and protests were slighted by Parliament and spurned by the king. The breach rapidly widened, and war became inevitable. General Gage, commander of the British troops in Boston, having learned that military stores were being collected at Concord for the use of a colonial army, sent a detachment of eight hundred soldiers to destroy them. But its march had been preceded by a swift messenger, the gallant Paul Revere, who gave notice of the coming of the British. The whole country on the line of march was aroused, and " minute men" began to muster. A company was drawn up on the village green at Lexington when the British force came up. Refusing to disperse at the order of the commanding officer, seven men fell dead at the first volley of the British soldiers. The latter then marched on to Concord, and succeeded in destroying some of the stores, when the gathering of "minute men" from all quarters compelled them to retreat. But retreat was more dangerous than battle. All along its line, rocks, and trees, and walls, concealed the undisciplined but now determined colonists, whose unerring bullets constantly thinned the British ranks. Reinforcements alone saved the latter from annihilation.

The battle of Lexington, fought on the 19th of April, 1775, was the signal to all the colonies that the war had actually begun. Volunteers came pouring in from all parts of New England. In a few days after this battle sixteen thousand "minute men" were gathered in the environs of Boston.

The Declaration of Independence. The Second Continental Congress assembled at Philadelphia in May, 1775. Measures were taken to raise and maintain an army, of which George Washington was elected Commander-in-chief. But the most important work of this Congress was the passage, on the 4th of July, 1776, of a Declaration of Independence. Hitherto, the colonies had petitioned, respectfully but earnestly, for a redress of grievances ; now, as a sovereign people, they boldly declared, and prepared to maintain, complete independence.

It was an unequal contest. A few weak and scattered colonies were opposed to the most powerful empire in the world. In the field, an untaught militia, scantily supplied with munitions of war, and often destitute of food and clothing, were pitted against well-trained and well-furnished veterans. But inspired by the example of Washington, their noble commander, the patriot soldiers endured privations without complaint, suffered defeat without despair, and patiently learned the art of war from its practice.

The earlier events of the war were unfavorable to the Americans. Their gallant stand at Bunker Hill, and the successful siege of Boston, while giving them confidence in themselves, weighed little on the issue, compared with the defeats at Long Island and

White Plains, and the forced retreat of Washington through New Jersey and across the Delaware. The prospect that had looked so gloomy during the year 1776, brightened a little, at its close, with a brilliant success at Trenton, and with another, in the early part of 1777, at Princeton. The crisis of the war was reached in the latter part of the year 1777.

Surrender of Burgoyne and Alliance with France. The British had planned two campaigns, which, if successful, they confidently believed, would bring the colonies to terms. One of these had for its object the capture of Philadelphia, then the colonial capital, and the other, the isolation of New England from the rest of the country. The first, though successful, proved to be of no advantage to the British. Washington, beaten at Brandywine and Germantown, was compelled to yield the capital to Howe. Congress removed to York. The second was disastrous to the British. General Burgoyne had organized, in Canada, a grand expedition composed of ten thousand well-armed and well-trained men. He moved up Lake Champlain and along the line of the Hudson, capturing forts and driving the Americans before him. Checked at Bemis's Heights, he was surrounded and beaten at Saratoga, and compelled, on the 17th of October, to surrender his whole force to General Gates. The effect of this signal success was marked both at home and abroad. It was, in fact, the turning point in the war. The Americans took new courage. Foreign nations were inspired with increased respect for a people struggling so bravely against such fearful odds. France had watched the course of the contest with keenest interest. Though animated by the bitterest hatred of England, and anxious for the success of the colonies, she had been unwilling to ally herself with an uncertain cause. After Saratoga, she hastened to acknowledge the independence of the colonies, and to make with them a treaty of alliance. She sent a fleet and an army, at once, to their assistance. Spain and Holland acknowledged their independence a little later.

William Pitt, Earl of Chatham. Not less marked was the effect of the surrender of Burgoyne on the English people. Public sentiment grew strong against the war. Some of the ablest English statesmen urged an immediate peace. A motion was made in Parliament by the Duke of Richmond, to acknowledge the independence of America and withdraw British soldiers from American soil. This brought William Pitt, Earl of Chatham, once more and for the last time, into the House of Lords. Leaning on his crutches, with his limbs swathed in bandages, pale and emaciated, but with faculties apparently undimmed, the great orator denounced, with the impassioned eloquence of which he was still master, the proposition to yield up one of the fairest possessions of the British empire, as he said, at the dictation of France. Attempting to speak again in reply to the Duke, he fell back in a swoon, and was borne away to die. Pitt had opposed the scheme of taxation from the outset, and he had resisted, step by step, the policy of coercion which had been adopted. Illness had forced him to retire from office in 1768, but he had not ceased, in his retirement, to utter his solemn warnings to the government and to the nation. On occasions of importance, though ill, he had been brought into the House of Lords, in which his Earldom entitled him to a seat, to participate in its deliberations. Pitt was the friend of America because he was the friend of justice, but he was an Englishman and a patriot, and his soul revolted at the thought of the dismemberment of his country.

Yorktown, A. D. 1781. It was owing to the obstinacy of King George, that the motion of Richmond did not prevail. Though the war lingered for several years, chiefly in the South, the final issue was never doubtful after the success at Saratoga. Its closing scene was laid at Yorktown, in Virginia. Lord Cornwallis, hemmed in, on one side, by an ample force of French and Americans under Washington, and, on the other, by a French fleet under Count de Grasse, was compelled, on the 19th of October, 1781, to surrender.

Peace of Paris. Though virtually ended in America, the war still continued among the European combatants. England gained repeated victories on the sea. The most interesting event was the heroic defence of Gibraltar by General Elliot, against the combined forces and fleets of France and Spain, through a siege of three years and seven months. September 3rd, 1783, articles of peace were formally signed at Paris, and the United States of America took her place, unchallenged, in the great family of nations.

Causes of the French Revolution.

The Despotic Rule of Louis XIV. Louis XIV. was a superb monarch. His court was as magnificent and his rule as absolute as those of an Eastern despot. Louis uttered no idle boast when he once said, "I am the

State," for all the powers of the State were centered in his single person. The French nobles, though slaves to the king, were tyrants to their tenants, grinding them with taxation, from which they were themselves almost wholly exempt. Louis' system of government was a Feudalism as oppressive to the poor as that of the Middle Ages. With him passed away much of the regal splendor that had dazzled, and the personal power that had awed, the people of France. But the worst features of his system, its despotism, extortion, and extravagance, remained under his successor.

The Corrupt Rule of Louis XV. Louis XV. surpassed all his predecessors in the vileness of his private life, and in his wanton waste of the public money. Evidences of discontent among the suffering people became more and more apparent. The king plainly foresaw a coming storm, but he took no means to avert its calamities from his people, or from his successors on the throne. He was only solicitous for his own safety. "Things will last my day," was his monstrous speech on one occasion. "After us the deluge," replied the royal favorite, Madame Pompadour, and the reckless pair only plunged the deeper into every species of excess.

The Inefficient Rule of Louis XVI. Louis XVI. was a mild and pious king, but he had neither the ability, nor the vigor, to cope with the perils that gathered darkly around the throne which he inherited.

The French Sceptics. The popular discontent had been intensified by a class of literary men, who had flourished in the preceding reign, among whom Voltaire and Rosseau had stood foremost. With the fiery eloquence peculiar to French genius, they had disseminated the most extreme views on subjects that profoundly agitated the public mind, such as class privileges, unequal taxation, and popular rights, kindling in the excitable bosoms of the French people a burning love of liberty, and a bitter hatred of oppression. But they also taught infidelity to religion, and contempt for established order, striking at the very foundations of society itself. The seed sown by French sceptics, at this period, took deep root, and ripened, before long, into bitter fruit.

The Influence of the American Revolution. One other influence, operating on the French mind, remains to be mentioned, and one of no light import at this period. The French soldiers had returned from America, at the close of the revolutionary war, full of the republican spirit, which they readily communicated to their friends and neighbors, making them familiar with the idea of revolution, and especially, with the merits of a democratic form of government.

The States-General. Louis XVI., conscious that the public credit was gone, and that a crisis in the finances of the government was at hand, in 1789 summoned the States-General, a body composed of nobles, clergy and commons, that met only in times of national peril. Its last session was in 1614, in the time of Richelieu. But the meeting of the States-General only precipitated the storm which it was designed to avert. The commons, or Third Estate, as they were called, ignoring nobles and clergy, declared themselves to be the supreme authority of the State.

The Revolution Sweeps away Church and State. This action of the commons was revolution, whose bloodless beginning in legislative halls was but the first breath of the coming storm, that was soon to rock, to their very base, all the institutions of Church and State, and, finally, to involve them in complete and indiscriminate ruin.

A Paris mob destroyed the Bastile, the hated prison, in whose dungeons had been silenced, for so many generations, the murmurs of the people. The blameless king and his accomplished queen, Maria Antoinette, subjected to one indignity after another, at last perished under the guillotine. The Monarchy was overthrown, and a Republic was erected in its stead. The Christian Sabbath was abolished, and every tenth day was made a day of secular rest. A solemn vote decreed that there was no God, and Reason was enthroned as the object of supreme worship. Over the entrance to every cemetery in the land was written, "Death is an eternal sleep."

The Reign of Terror. One political party followed another in power, each more violent than the other, until, under the National Convention, with Robespierre at the head, the climax was reached in the inauguration of a "Reign of Terror." The guillotine was glutted with victims, and the best blood of France flowed like water. It is computed that a million persons perished during this mad carnival of blood. The excesses of the Republic at home, and its efforts to arouse the revolutionary spirit abroad, soon raised against it a coalition of the most powerful nations of Europe.

Napoleon Bonaparte. The stirring events of the times brought to the surface, about the year 1795, the most extraordinary man of modern times. Napoleon Bonaparte was born on the island of Corsica, a French dependency in the Mediterranean. He was educated at a military school in Brienne, a town in France, showing, even in youth, the germs of that genius which afterwards made him so distinguished. His skill and courage at the siege of Toulon, and his bold defence of the Directory, the successor to the National Convention, against the National Guards, in 1795, placed him, at once, at the head of the armies of the Republic. He returned from his first campaign in Italy, the idol of the French people. His second in Egypt and Syria, in 1797, designed to establish a French empire, and undermine that of England, in the East, was a complete failure. Napoleon won the battle of the Pyramids, but was repulsed at Acre, while his fleet was annihilated by Nelson, in the battle of the Nile.

Leaving his generals to complete the hopeless campaign, Napoleon returned to France to overthrow the Directory, and to become First Consul in 1799, Consul for life in 1802, and Emperor in 1804. From the time of his election as First Consul in 1799, to his fall in 1814, the history of France, and almost of Europe, is the history of Napoleon. Coalition after coalition of the powers of Europe sprang into existence, only to be dissolved by his diplomacy, or crushed by his power. These coalitions were no longer formed for the destruction of the Republic, or the restoration of the Monarchy, for Napoleon had overthrown the one, and restored the other, but they were formed against Napoleon himself, who had inspired more terror in the hearts of the kings, than had even the dread spectre of Democracy itself.

Admiral Nelson. England alone, of all the powers of Europe, remained, through Napoleon's whole career, undaunted and unconquered. England alone, deserted at times, by all her allies, stood between Napoleon and universal conquest. Said the great soldier, when, in 1802, he had gathered one hundred thousand trained soldiers at Boulogne, and a vast fleet of transports to land them on the shores of England, "Let us be masters of the Channel for six hours, and we are masters of the world." But the fleet, designed to protect the crossing of the transports, was swept from the Channel, and blockaded in the harbor of Cadiz by the gallant Nelson, and the invasion was not even attempted.

The French and Spanish fleets, venturing forth from Cadiz, were met and annihilated, off Cape Trafalgar, in 1805. It was on this occasion that Nelson gave the famous order, "England expects every man to do his duty," — the grandest sentiment ever signaled from the mast-head of a flag-ship, on the eve of battle. It was Nelson's last order. He was struck, in the very heat of the contest, by a musket ball, while standing on the deck of his ship, the Victory. Covering his face with his handkerchief, that the crew might not see who was wounded, he was carried below, and died just after victory was assured.

The Struggle on the Spanish Peninsula. In 1808, began the struggle between England and France for the mastery in Spain, the army of the former being under the command of Arthur Wellesley, distinguished for his services in India, that of the latter, under Soult, one of the most illustrious of Napoleon's marshals. Victory long wavered in the balance, but finally, in the early part of the year 1814, the scale turned in favor of English arms, and the last French soldier was driven across the Pyrenees into France. For his success in Spain, especially at Talavera, in 1809, Wellesley was rewarded with the title of Duke of Wellington. In other parts of the continent, Napoleon had generally been victorious, carrying the eagles of France into almost every capital. Ulm and Austerlitz, Jena and Wagram, were witnesses of his amazing success.

The Invasion of Russia. In 1812, when at the summit of his power, Napoleon undertook the invasion of Russia. This has been regarded as the turning point in his career. After advancing for a period of three months, during which several bloody battles were fought, he reached Moscow, the ancient capital of the empire, only to see it speedily laid in ashes. The rich and beautiful city was sacrificed, that the invader might find no shelter. The food in all the country around had been destroyed, and winter was fast approaching. After waiting more than a month, in the vain hope of peace, there was no alternative for Napoleon but retreat. The story is a sad one. Thousands of brave men died at the hands of the wild Cossacks, clouds of whom hovered around the devoted army, day and night, ever on the alert to attack the helpless masses, or cut off straggling soldiers. Thousands more perished with cold, hunger, and exhaustion, amid the drifting snows which cover that vast region of pine and plain. Nearly half a million gallant and stalwart men began the proud march that was to add Russia to the list of Napoleon's conquests. Only thirty thousand wan and haggard spectres lived to recross the Niemen.

The Battle of the Nations. To any but Napoleon, the Russian disaster would have been overwhelming. But with an energy almost superhuman he gathered up the fragments of his armies, made fresh conscriptions, and boldly faced a new, and still more powerful coalition of his foes. The decisive conflict, the "Battle of the Nations," occurred at Leipsic, in 1814, lasting three days, and ending in the complete discomfiture of the French. A desperate but hopeless struggle on the soil of France deferred, but could not prevent, the fall of Paris.

Napoleon at Elba. Napoleon was deposed and banished to the island of Elba, over which he was allowed to rule with the title of Emperor, and Louis XVIII. was placed upon the throne of his ancestors. While a congress of sovereigns and ministers of the leading powers was in session at Vienna, to re-adjust the disordered affairs of Europe, Napoleon, secretly leaving his little empire in the Mediterranean, landed on the shores of France, and began a triumphant march on the capital. Thousands of the old soldiers of the empire flocked to his standard, and he soon entered Paris, surrounded by an excited populace, whose old, familiar cry, "Long live the Emperor," rent the air on every side. Louis XVIII. fled in dismay to the frontiers.

Waterloo, A. D. 1815. The astonished kings at Vienna, suddenly startled from their dream of fancied security, and conscious that their crowns and kingdoms were once more at stake, quickly formed a new coalition. The council chamber was forsaken for the camp, and half a million of men, coming from every quarter of the continent of Europe, were soon on the march for France. The armies of England and Prussia were first in the field. Napoleon, hoping to crush them in detail, before their junction with the rest, hastened to Belgium, the great battle ground of Europe, where he found himself confronted by the English under Wellington. On the field of Waterloo,* at the close of a Sabbath day in June, Napoleon's sun once more set, never to rise again. His last devoted army, after dash-

---

* The battle of Waterloo — called by the French St. Jean — was fought on a Sunday. All night before, the rain had fallen in torrents; and when the troops rose from their cheerless bivouac among the crushed and muddy rye, a drizzling rain still fell. The armies faced each other upon two gentle slopes, near which ran the high road to Brussels. The army of Wellington numbered more than 70,000, — that of Napoleon about 80,000 men. Between, in a slight hollow, lay the farm-houses of Hougomont and La Haye Sainte, round which the bloodiest combats of the day took place. The battle began at ten o'clock. Napoleon knew that he was a ruined man unless he could pierce and break the red masses that lay between him and Brussels. He kept closely to one plan of action, — a **storm of shot and** shell upon the British ranks, and then a rapid rush of lancers and steel-clad cuirassiers. **But the British infantry, formed** into solid squares, met every charge like **the rocks that encircle their native** shore. Again, and again, and again the baffled cavalry of France recoiled with many an empty saddle. This was a terrible game to play; and well might Wellington, when he looked on the squares, growing every moment smaller, as soldier after soldier stepped silently into the place of his fallen comrade, pray that either night or Blucher would come. It was seven o'clock in the evening before the distant sound of the **Prussian cannon was heard. Blucher** had outmarched Grouchy, and was hastening to **Waterloo.** Napoleon then made the grandest effort of the day. The Old Guard **of France,** unconquered veterans of Austerlitz and Jena, burst in a furious onset **upon** the shattered ranks of Britain; but, at one magic word, the British squares dissolved into 'thin red lines,' glittering with bayonets, and, with a cheer that rent the smoke-cloud hovering above the field, swept on to meet the foe. The French columns wavered — broke — fled; and Waterloo was won.—[Collier.

ing again and again, like ocean billows, against the red English squares that stood "like the rocks that encircle their native shore," poured, bleeding, back to France.

Napoleon at St. Helena. In 1815, about twenty years after his first appearance on the stage of European politics, Napoleon Bonaparte was consigned to perpetual captivity on the island of St. Helena, in the heart of the Atlantic. His career constitutes one of the most thrilling episodes in all history. Reverses of fortune are among the most common events of human life, but the annals of the past furnish few instances to compare with that of Napoleon. Since few can rise to so dizzy a height of power and glory, few can experience so great a fall. What a contrast! Napoleon the Emperor, and Napoleon the Exile! Napoleon conquering states and dispensing thrones, at once the terror and admiration of a continent, and Napoleon, sad, solitary, and forgotten, looking hopelessly out from the lonely, barren rock, upon the silent, shoreless sea, the mighty soul within stirred only with the melancholy memory of vanished grandeur! On the 5th of May, 1821, while a hurricane swept with unusual violence across the unprotected isle, and the surging billows beat with a mournful and monotonous sound upon the shore, the fettered, restless spirit of the great soldier passed away from earth. What a commentary does the career of Napoleon furnish, on the instability of worldly things, and the evanescent character of worldly glory. Resting on any other foundation than that of everlasting truth and right, the grandest conceptions of the genius of man often prove as fleeting and unreal as the "baseless fabric of a dream." His gilded creations, however stable they may seem, will flash for a few brief hours in the sunlight of hope, and then fade with the gathering twilight, and vanish utterly away in the quick coming night.

Causes of England's Second War with the United States.

Right of Search and Impressment of Seamen. In the midst of the wars with Napoleon, and just as the latter was getting ready to invade Russia, England engaged in her second war with the United States, in defence of the "right of search" and of the "impressment of seamen." So exhausting were the wars with Napoleon, that England could with difficulty find seamen for her navy. It was a settled principle of her government, that a person born a British subject could never surrender his allegiance to his country, no matter in what part of the world he might take up his abode. Acting on this principle, her captains boldly searched American ships on the high seas, and impressed all British-born seamen found therein.

This course was unqualifiedly condemned by the United States, whose policy it has always been, to regard all persons of foreign birth living under the protection of its flag, who had either been naturalized, or had taken any of the legal steps necessary to that end, as American citizens, and as such, entitled to the protection of the government. The case against Great Britain was aggravated by the fact, that, in many instances, the impressed seamen were of American birth. Above six thousand seamen were forcibly taken from American ships and compelled to serve on British men-of-war, within the period of a few years.

"**Decrees**" **of Napoleon and** "**Orders**" **of the English Council.** The war feeling in the United States was increased by the "decrees" of Napoleon and the "orders" of the English Council, declaring, respectively, the ports of England and France to be in a state of blockade. This was particularly injurious to the United States, since, being a neutral power, she was, to a considerable extent, engaged to do the carrying trade of Europe. Between French and English cruisers, the commerce of the United States was well-nigh swept from the seas. Napoleon, in 1811, withdrew the application of the "decrees" from the United States, making the war feeling against England all the more intense. Between the year 1807, and the declaration of war in 1812, it has been computed that one thousand American merchant ships were taken by British cruisers.

Declaration of War by the United States. War was declared by the United States, June 19th, 1812. It was fought chiefly on the sea, the United States gaining many signal victories. Privateers, being commissioned in large numbers, frequented all the routes of English commerce, and gained a rich harvest in the capture of English merchant ships. Operations on the land were limited to the Canadian frontier, and to descents on exposed points along the coast. General Ross, sailing up the Chesapeake, made a sudden raid on the capital, and, with a vandalism that belonged to a by-gone age, burned to the ground most of the public buildings.

Battle of New Orleans. The last battle of the war was fought at New Orleans on the 8th of January, 1815. The British under Sir Edward Packenham were completely repulsed by the Americans under General Jackson, Packenham himself being slain.

Peace of Ghent. It was, of course, unknown to both commanders, that fifteen days before, on the 24th of December, 1814, peace had been made at Ghent. Although the treaty of peace left unsettled the questions at issue between the two countries, English captains never afterwards searched American vessels to find British subjects, and a few years ago, the English government formally abandoned the whole doctrine of the "right of search." During the greater part of this reign, William Pitt, second son of the Earl of Chatham, was at the head of the government.

The Regency. During the last nine years of his life, King George was blind and insane, and the Prince of Wales ruled as Prince Regent. Though obstinate and conservative, George III. was much better than the other kings of his name. The simple, homely, familiar ways of "Farmer George," as he was called, gained him the good will of the people, and the great misfortune that clouded his later years, won their heartfelt sympathy.

George IV., 1820 to 1830 — 10 years. Brunswick.

England after the Napoleonic Wars. England emerged from the wars with Napoleon the most powerful nation in Europe. During this long and desperate struggle, nearly all the European nations had, at one time and another, been drawn or forced to the side of England's foes, and, in consequence, their fleets had, one after another, been swept away by the superior navy of England, so that her supremacy on the sea, first achieved in the reign of Elizabeth, was now universally conceded. Isolated from the nations of the continent, her own soil had known nothing of the desolations that war had brought to theirs. Her industries had not only remained undisturbed, while theirs had been paralyzed, but they had been forced to an unnatural expansion, bringing unexampled prosperity to her capitalists. On the other hand, the return of peace caused a re-action, that was followed by a crisis in both the national finances and the national industries. Manufacturing establishments, stimulated to an over-production during the war, could not at once adapt themselves to the new conditions of a state of peace, and they were compelled to contract, and, in many cases, to close, operations altogether. Thousands of operatives in all the manufacturing districts were thus thrown out of employment, who, having laid up nothing during the time of prosperity, were now suddenly reduced to want.

The disbandment of the army and navy forces had released multitudes of men, many of whom could not find the employment they sought, while more were restless in spirit and had little taste for the quiet pursuits of life. Although the rates for the poor were everywhere largely increased, destitution and suffering were everywhere inevitable. The Napoleonic wars had greatly increased the public debt, which at their close amounted to £800,000,000, and the people were heavily burdened with taxation. The necessaries of life had reached exorbitant figures during these wars, enriching land owners and large dealers, but bearing heavily on the poor.

The Corn Law. During the year after the close of the Napoleonic wars, the land owners, with a policy as short-sighted as it was selfish, secured the passage of a law placing such a duty on corn as virtually to prohibit its importation. High prices were thus maintained, especially on the bread of the poor, after their income had greatly diminished or had ceased altogether. Idleness, poverty, and suffering produced discontent and incipient rebellion, but this only brought upon the unhappy people the strong arm of the law, and aggravated the miseries of their condition.

Agitation on the Subject of Reform. The people attributed their distress to bad legislation, and not wholly without cause, and the remedy, in their minds, was increased political power on the part of the masses. Then began an agitation on the subject of reform in the laws, never known before in England. The active English mind, no longer engrossed with the excitements of foreign war, employed itself in questions of domestic policy, and the resources of the ministry and statesmen of England were taxed to the utmost, to meet the social and political problems that constantly presented themselves for solution. From the passage of the Corn law, in 1815, to the present time, England has been the arena of an unintermitting strife on the subject of reform. Reform has been the all-engrossing theme at the fireside and in the cabinet, at the hustings and in legislative halls. Reform and Anti-Reform have been inscribed on party banners, and have been the issues of party politics. The period embraced in the last three reigns, those of George IV., William IV., and Victoria, might be called the Era of Reform. We can here notice only the most important matters that have successively agitated the public mind, and the leading measures that have been enacted, tending to the removal of class and religious distinctions, to the equalization of civil and political rights, and especially, to the amelioration of the condition of the poor, and their advancement in the scale of being. If the progress of reform has been slow, on account of the bitter resistance of powerful conservative elements, it has also been sure. No essential step in this grand march of the English people towards the ideal of all just government, the greatest good to the greatest number, has been retraced. Temporary checks and defeats have made their ultimate triumphs all the more complete.

The Repeal of the Corporation and Test Acts. The Corporation Act, passed in the reign of Charles II., required the officers of corporations or boroughs to conform to the rites of the restored Episcopal Church, and was specially designed to effect the removal of Puritans, who occupied most of the borough offices.

The Test Act, passed later in the reign of Charles II., made the same requirements of civil and military officers, with the addition of the Oath of Supremacy, and was enacted at a time when it was supposed Charles was scheming to restore Romanism to England. But the perils against which these statutes were designed to guard, had, at the time of George IV., long since passed away. The State church was firmly established, and proscriptive laws on account of religion had not only become needless, but they were a source of perpetual discontent. After much agitation, in 1828, both these Acts were repealed in their most odious features.

The Catholic Emancipation Bill. But the Catholics had disabilities more irksome than those just mentioned. At the time of the "Popish plot" excitement, in the reign of Charles II., Catholics were made ineligible to Parliament, and although this plot was proved at the time to be a pure fabrication, they were not restored to their former right to membership. For a century and a half they continued to have no voice in the counsels of the nation. The Irish people labored under peculiar hardships. To conciliate them at the time of the Napoleonic wars, the constitutional union of Great Britain and Ireland had been effected. In 1801, thirty Irish lords, and one hundred commoners were admitted to the English Parliament. But this very union drew in its train a new grievance, that became in time as fruitful of discontent as the old one. Only Protestants could sit as members in the Parliament chambers. It is difficult to say which was felt to be the greater grievance to Catholic Ireland, *no* representation or a *Protestant* representation. There were other things scarcely less trying to the Irish people, to be noticed later. Their discontent rose to fever height, and produced repeated outbreaks, which were trodden out in blood. Bill after bill for the relief of the Irish was brought up in Parliament only to be voted down.

Daniel O'Connell. Associations, in which almost every Catholic and many Protestants became enrolled, were formed throughout Ireland to secure the repeal of laws excluding Catholics from Parliament. Daniel

O'Connell, an eloquent Irish barrister, the acknowledged head of these associations, was at this time all but supreme in his power over the Irish people. In 1827, he was elected to Parliament from the County of Clare, but was ineligible on account of his religion. The climax to Irish endurance was reached, when O'Connell was refused the seat to which he had been elected, and Parliament soon came to see that there was but a choice of alternatives, justice to Ireland, or war with a united and a determined people. A bill was accordingly introduced to admit Catholics to Parliament. Even Wellington, long the opponent of reform, who had looked calmly on death in many a bloody battle-field, shrank from the horrors of a religious war in Ireland. Said the Iron Duke, on moving the second reading of the bill, "If I could avoid, by any sacrifice whatever, even one month of civil war in the country to which I am attached, I would sacrifice my life to do it."

In a little more than a month, April 13th, 1829, the bill, having passed both houses, received the royal signature and became law. Roman Catholics were placed on an equality with Protestants, except that they remained ineligible to the throne, the chancellorship, the lord-lieutenancy of Ireland, and to offices in Protestant Universities. O'Connell at once took his seat in the House of Commons.

Navarino, A.D. 1827. In the early part of the reign of George IV., the Greeks, who had suffered under Moslem rule for more than three centuries, rose in rebellion. The sailing of an expedition from Egypt to lay waste the Morea, and to carry away its inhabitants into slavery, caused a coalition of England, France, and Russia in behalf of the helpless Greeks. The allied fleets, entering the harbor of Navarino in the latter part of 1827, annihilated the entire Turkish and Egyptian navies. Greece was made an independent kingdom, and Otho, a Bavarian prince, was placed upon the throne. A touching and romantic interest is connected with the struggle of the Greeks for independence, on account of its association with Lord Byron. The unhappy poet devoted his fortune and the last efforts of his genius to the cause of Greece. On its classic soil, and in its service, he breathed his last.

Character of George IV. George the Fourth is one of the most uninteresting, as well as despicable, sovereigns that ever sat on the English throne. The time had gone by when an English king could override the laws, else George IV. would have been a tyrant. He threw what little influence he possessed against the cause of reform, retarding, but not defeating, its progress. He was profligate in the extreme, and spent most of his time in the company of the worthless. His flatterers called him "the first gentleman in Europe," a title that rested solely on his possession of a well-shaped figure, polished manners, and exquisite taste in matters of dress. Through his licentious habits he had lost the respect of his people, while his relentless persecution of his wife had excited their intense and lasting dislike. He had married, when Prince of Wales, his own cousin, the Princess Caroline of Brunswick. After submitting to every species of indignity from her husband, Caroline returned to her home on the continent. After the elevation of George to the throne, a bill was introduced into Parliament for the divorce of the crownless queen, but so intense was public feeling against the king, it was finally allowed to drop. Queen Caroline died in about a year, broken down with shame and grief. George IV. died in 1830, leaving no heirs, and the throne descended to his brother William.

William IV., 1830 to 1837 — 7 years. Brunswick.

State of Feeling in England at the Accession of William. The brief period of William's reign was one of unprecedented political excitement. The question of reform, fairly launched upon the sea of English politics during the preceding reign, became the exclusive object of public attention. During the first year of William's reign a revolution broke out in France, that excited grave apprehensions in England as well as on the continent. The French people had caught the spirit that animated the English masses, and were calling loudly for reform. The French ministry sought to crush this spirit by ordinances, subverting the constitution of the country, and destroying the freedom of the press. The exasperated Parisians rose at once in arms. For three days were the streets of the capital the scene of indescribable confusion and carnage, when the government troops were driven from the city, and the king, Charles X., was compelled to abdicate the throne. Louis Philippe, Duke of Orleans, was appointed Lieutenant-General of the kingdom. For awhile, the tricolor, the symbol of French republicanism, floated over the city of Paris in place of the white flag of royalty, but, in the end Louis was made king under a liberal constitution. A feverish and almost revolutionary spirit was kindled among the masses throughout Europe by the revolution in France. In Brussels, a rising of the people terminated in a separation from Holland, and the founding of the new kingdom of Belgium. The excitement in England, created by this revolution, happily found vent in the election that was near at hand, which resulted in returning a House of Commons overwhelmingly liberal. The conservative Duke of Wellington was forced to yield his place as Prime Minister to Earl Grey, who was in sympathy with the new House. We are now brought to the consideration of another of those great statutes, that stand like mile-stones in the pathway of English progress, the Reform Bill of 1832.

The Reform Bill of 1832. One of the crying grievances of the English people was the inequality of representation in Parliament. In early times the kings had designated the towns that were to be represented in the lower house. They usually selected those most important. Towns were occasionally added to the list, sometimes as a matter of justice, and sometimes as a matter of favoritism. There was no law or basis of representation. In the course of time a great change came over the face of England. The growth of manufactures had made new centres of population. Thriving towns and cities, such as Birmingham, Leeds, and Sheffield, had sprung up in the wilderness. On the other hand, flourishing towns had dwindled into mere hamlets, and in some cases had disappeared altogether. But through all this shifting of the population, there had been comparatively few changes in the representation in Parliament. Old Sarum, without a house within its limits, continued to send two representatives to every Parliament, while Birmingham, a great busy hive of industry, remained entirely unrepresented. These "rotten" or "pocket" boroughs, as the towns were called, that had representation, but little or no constituency, were under the control of noblemen, who either selected the persons to represent them, or offered the places for sale. A Reform Bill was introduced into Parliament early in 1831, designed to readjust and equalize the system of representation. It passed the House of Commons after a prolonged discussion, but was defeated in the House of Lords. The excitement in England became intense. Riots and conflagrations constantly disturbed the peace of the kingdom. The conservative Lords becoming alarmed at the temper of the people, which threatened the most serious results, followed the example of the liberal Commons, and passed the Reform Bill at their next session in 1832. Fifty-six "pocket" boroughs, having one hundred and twelve representatives, were disfranchised, while thirty more were allowed each a single representative, making a total reduction of one hundred and forty-two members. The vacant seats were distributed among forty-two large and flourishing towns, that had previously no representation.

Results of Reform Legislation. Besides leading to immense material benefit to the people, the Reform Bill of 1832 conferred on the liberal element a power it had never known before. The cause of reform gained a prestige that made other progressive movements easy and rapid. For the first time, the manufacturing and general business interests had able and adequate representation in Parliament.

Hitherto, the land-holders had moulded legislation to meet their peculiar wants. Now, measures began to be devised and framed into statutes, for the development of commerce and manufactures, making them, in time, the leading interests of the British people. As an illustration of the progress made, it may be stated, that, at the beginning of the reign of William IV., Great Britain had three hundred and fifteen steam-vessels with a tonnage of 33,441. At its close she had six hundred steam-vessels with a tonnage of 67,969. At its beginning there was but a single railway line of importance on the island. At its close all the great manufacturing centres and mining districts had railroad facilities for the transportation of goods and passengers to the metropolis and leading seaports.

Abolition of Slavery in the Colonies. The abolition of slavery in the colonies was one of the subjects that had agitated the public mind. Wilberforce and other philanthropists had labored for nearly forty years in the cause of emancipation. In 1833, a bill was introduced into Parliament, giving freedom to all the slaves in the British colonies, and appropriating £20,000,000 as compensation to the planters. It passed without serious opposition, removing one of the foulest stains that ever disgraced a civilized nation.

Character of William IV. William IV. was called the "Sailor King," from his early connection with the English navy. He was a worthy man and a just and able ruler. He was in hearty sympathy with the reform movements of the day, and for this reason was held in high esteem among the people. The careless, easy, open manners of the sailor clung to him to the last, increasing still more his popularity among the English masses. He had long been afflicted with hay fever. In 1837, his disease assumed a more aggravated form, and he sank rapidly under its attacks, and died on the 18th of June, in the seventy-second year of his age.

Victoria, 1837. Brunswick.

Reform Legislation in the Reign of Victoria. William IV. died without heirs, leaving the crown to his niece, Alexandrina Victoria. As the Salic law prevailed in Hanover, forbidding female succession, that kingdom reverted, at once, to Ernest, Duke of Cumberland, the nearest male heir of the House of Brunswick. Hanover had been a useless and an expensive appendage of the British empire since the accession of George I., and its return to the condition of an independent state was not regretted by the English people. The legislation of this reign has been characterized even more than that of its predecessors by the spirit of progress. We shall not undertake so much as to name all the unequal and oppressive statutes and practices, the relics of less civilized ages, which have been swept away forever, nor all the measures that have been devised to perfect the liberties and enlarge the opportunities of the English people. "Reform Bills," the matured products of an enlightened statesmanship, have followed each other in rapid succession. Under the inspiration and guidance of such men as Wilberforce, Brougham, Cobden, and Bright, the reform movements have advanced with rapid strides. The English government, at first following somewhat slowly and reluctantly in the footsteps of an advancing public sentiment, now leads the van in the grand march of improvement. Not only has it secured to the English people, in a broad and general sense, the enjoyment of civil and religious liberty, but it has brought within the scope of its inquiry the minutest details of their condition. And not alone at home, but to the remotest limits of an empire "upon which the sun never sets," has a beneficent legislation extended a hand of helpfulness to British subjects.

Repeal of the Corn Laws. Although the Corn laws, passed in 1815, had undergone repeated changes, they still fettered English commerce and remained an oppressive burden to the poor. The discontent of the people found expression, in 1839, in an organization, called "The Anti-Corn-Law League," designed to secure the repeal of all duties on breadstuffs.

At the head of this League stood Richard Cobden and John Bright, two of England's noblest sons. The difficulties in the way of a repeal of the Corn laws seemed almost insuperable. Notwithstanding the increased representation of the manufacturing and commercial classes in Parliament, nine-tenths of the members still represented the landed interests, and held firmly to a high tariff on imported grain. They argued that the repeal of the Corn laws would destroy the profits of agriculture, at that time the leading interest; that the land would cease to be cultivated and return to a state of wilderness, and that the condition of the rural population, dependent, as they were, on the cultivation of the soil, would become deplorable.

The Reform League directed its efforts not so much to the conversion of members of Parliament, as to the creation of a public sentiment in favor of free trade, and so to a gradual change in the complexion of the House of Commons. Public speakers were sent into all the rural districts, where they addressed vast assemblies of the working people in behalf of their favorite doctrine. Papers and pamphlets, advocating the same views, were scattered all over England. The result of efforts so persistent and systematic may easily be anticipated. The great change that took place even among the people of the agricultural districts, was soon perceptible in the increasing number of free traders elected to Parliament. But the Corn League met unexpected opposition from another and an older organization, also devoted to the interests of reform.

The Chartists. No sooner had the excitement attending the reform movement of 1832 subsided, than a new agitation began to occupy public attention. It finally culminated, in 1838, in an organization bearing the name of "The Chartists." Its principles and objects were embodied in a document called "The People's Charter," under six distinct heads: — 1st. Universal suffrage. 2d. Vote by ballot. 3d. Annual Parliaments. 4th. Payment of members of Parliament. 5th. Abolition of the property qualification. 6th. Equal electoral districts. At the rise of the "Anti-Corn-Law League," the Chartists sought to unite the forces of the two movements, but the leaders of the League refused to adopt the six articles of the Chartists, thinking it wiser to direct their efforts to the

accomplishment of the single end they had in view —
the repeal of the Corn laws. The Chartists, under the
lead of Daniel O'Connell, then threw their influence
against the cause of the League. In spite of all obstacles the latter organization carried its point. Sir
Robert Peel, who was at the head of a conservative
ministry, became a convert to the doctrine of free
trade, and a bill for the repeal of the Corn laws passed
through both Houses in 1846. But the complete extinction of duties on breadstuffs did not take place till
1849. The same year the famous Navigation laws,
originally passed during the Commonwealth, in 1651,
and amended from time to time, were entirely repealed,
and thus the last obstacle to trade with England was
removed. The predictions of disaster to the agricultural interests and to the rural population, so freely
made during the progress of the campaign, were not
realized. Since that day "free trade" — the right to
buy in the cheapest, and to sell in the dearest, market
— has been the watchword in England.

The Chartists had divided into two wings, the radical and the conservative. The excesses of the radical
wing, and its threats to overthrow the government and
to establish a Republic, unless "The People's Charter"
were adopted, had brought the whole movement into
disrepute. Little was heard of it again until the year
1848, when another French revolution disturbed the
peace of Europe. Its effect in England was an immense
revival of Chartism. Petitions were industriously
circulated for the adoption of "The People's Charter"
by parliament. These petitions, claiming to have
5,700,000 signatures, were to be carried to the House

of Commons, at the head of a procession of half a million persons. The possibility that a revolution might be attempted, similar to that which had just taken place in France, led the government to make the most gigantic preparations to meet it. The procession was declared to be illegal and forbidden to take place. Special constables, to the number of one hundred and seventy thousand, were sworn in, among whom was Prince Louis Napoleon Bonaparte, who was soon to accomplish another revolution in France, and to place himself at the head of the restored Empire. All available troops were brought to the capital and placed under the command of the Duke of Wellington. The preparations of the government terrified the Chartists, and on the day appointed for their grand demonstration only thirty thousand assembled at the rendezvous on Kennington Common. No procession was attempted and the monstrous petition was wheeled to the House of Commons and respectfully presented by Feargus O'Connor, the Chartist leader. A careful examination of its contents discovered that there were less than two, instead of more than five, million signatures, and a large number of these were found to be spurious. From this moment Chartism, convicted of fraud, and branded as revolutionary, fell into public contempt, and the whole Chartist organization speedily dissolved. But its elements, re-organized, and carrying forward the work of reform in a less odious manner, have partially accomplished the objects of "The People's Charter." The property qualifications have been nearly abolished, the right of suffrage made almost universal, and the secret ballot substituted for open voting. A bill, passed in 1858, modified the oath required of Jews, making them eligible to Parliament.

The Disestablishment of the Irish Church. The Catholic Emancipation Bill had done much towards the pacification of Ireland. Of the grievances still remaining, the requirements of the law in regard to the established, or Anglican, church, were perhaps the most exasperating to the Irish people. The communicants of this church numbered about one-eighth of the population, those of the various dissenting bodies somewhat less, while the Roman Catholic church embraced within its pale the rest, somewhat more than six-eighths of the entire population. Besides supporting their own worship, the Catholics were compelled to pay certain specific tithes, to support the worship of the Anglican church. Although all the temporalities of the church, amounting to £16,000,000, with an income of nearly £1,000,000, were in the hands of the Anglican clergy, the very bread was often taken from the poverty-stricken hovel of the delinquent Irish Catholic, or his solitary cow driven away, and "the wolf left at his door," that God might be worshiped in Ireland after the established manner. We cannot wonder that the Irishman, as he saw his hungry children gather about the scanty board, sometimes turned, in rage or despair, with a murderous purpose, upon the exacting tax-gatherer, or that violence and misery filled the beautiful, but misgoverned, land.

In 1869, during the Gladstone ministry, a bill was introduced into Parliament to disestablish the Irish church. This bill placed all the religious sects on the same level, making them alike dependent on the voluntary contributions of the people for their support. It passed the House of Commons by a large majority. In the House of Lords, though denounced as "the most revolutionary measure ever submitted to Parliament since the Reformation," it also received a majority of the votes cast and became law.

The Irish Land Bill. But the measure best calculated to give peace and prosperity to Ireland was termed the "Irish Land Bill." The rebellions and confiscations of times past had placed most of the land in the hands of a few proprietors. The great estates were divided into small farms and rented to the Irish people, the greater part of whom were dependent on the cultivation of the soil for a livelihood. Being mere tenants at will of the great proprietors, and so, liable, at any moment, to be turned out of their homes, the Irish had neither pride nor interest in making permanent improvements, such as the erection of new buildings, or the reclamation of waste lands. The Irish Land Bill gave the tenant a virtual ownership of the farm which he occupied. If compelled to vacate, he was allowed, as damages, the value of all the permanent improvements which he had made. Under the operations of this bill the Irish people will, in time, return to the full ownership of the lands, of which they were so unjustly deprived.

The Education Bill. The same Parliament passed a measure, establishing a national system of public schools. It resembled, in many respects, the New England system, having local school boards, and furnishing all needed help to indigent children. The necessity of legislative action on a subject so vital to the welfare of the nation was made apparent during the consideration of the bill. An investigation showed that two-thirds of the children of England were utterly destitute of school privileges. Of 83,000 children in Birmingham, only 26,000 attended school. Of 90,000 in Liverpool, but 30,000 had school advantages. The Education Bill was warmly supported by men of both parties, and became law on the 22d of July, 1870. Under the direction of boards of education, schools were speedily established in all parts of England, and to-day, except in some of the more sparsely settled districts, every child in England can receive the rudiments of an English education.

The Foreign Policy. The foreign policy of this reign has, on the whole, been peaceful. Its wars have been distant, and, for the most part, unimportant. They have been waged chiefly in Asia and Africa. A useless war with Affghanistan, in 1839, grew out of jealousy of the designs of Russia in Asia. A war was waged with Abyssinia in 1867 to effect the release of English subjects, held in captivity by Emperor Theodore.

War with Egypt. In 1840, the Pasha of Egypt threw off the Turkish yoke. He entered Asia at the head of a large army, for the purpose of detaching Syria from the Ottoman empire. The Sultan, unable to rescue his Asiatic dominions from the grasp of the warlike Pasha, appealed to Russia, England, and France for help. France, though inclined to aid the Pasha, remained neutral, while Russia and England united to preserve the integrity of the Ottoman empire. Their combined fleets, under the command of

Commodore Napier, bombarded the strongly fortified town of Acre, the key of all Syria, and compelled its surrender in three hours. The appearance of the allied fleet before Alexandria forced the rebellious Pasha to sue for peace. But the treaty that followed was more favorable to Egypt than to Turkey, for it left the Pasha only a nominal subject of the Ottoman Porte, and the Pashalic of Egypt was made the inheritance of his family. Syria, that under the brief but enlightened rule of the Pasha had entered upon a new career of peace and prosperity, was left to groan under the iron heel of the Moslem power.

Wars with China. A shameful war was waged with China to force upon her the trade in opium. The Emperor of China, seeing the deadly effects of the poisonous drug upon his people, forbade its importation. The English merchants, unwilling to give up the profitable trade, and having resorted to smuggling, were imprisoned by the Chinese government, and whole cargoes of opium were seized and destroyed. War was declared by the British government in 1840. The surrender of Canton to a British army, and the siege of Nankin, forced the Emperor to submit. The cession of Hong Kong to the British, and the opening of five principal ports to commerce, were the results. The renewal of war in 1856, on account of an outrage to a vessel sailing under British colors, resulted in a treaty, opening all China both to merchants and to missionaries.

The Balance of Power. In his "Law of Nations," Vattel thus defines the expression "balance of power": " By this balance is to be understood such a disposition of things, as that no one potentate or state shall be able absolutely to predominate and to prescribe to the others." The mere principle of an alliance among states exposed to a common danger is as old as the existence of states themselves; but the use of this principle in ancient times was only occasional or accidental. Its adoption by any number of states as a definite and permanent principle of action is comparatively modern. The states of Greece often combined against some one of their number, that seemed to be attaining to a power dangerous to the rest. The coalitions against the occupation of Italy by the French under Charles VIII., and against the ambitious schemes of Ferdinand II. of Germany, the repeated alliances to repel the aggressions of Louis XIV. of France, and the wars inspired by the vaulting ambition of Napoleon, are all illustrations of its use in modern Europe.

After the close of the Napoleonic wars, the idea of a permanent organization of powers to maintain the established equilibrium in Europe took definite shape. The five great powers of Great Britain, France, Russia, Prussia, and Austria, constituted themselves a standing tribunal to preserve the balance of power in Europe. From that time to the present, this colossal tribunal has dominated over the entire continent, and, as a result, comparatively few changes have taken place in territorial lines. It has operated not only to prevent the undue expansion of any one state, but also to break up empires whose overshadowing power made them dangerous to the rest. The partition of the Spanish empire, after the death of Charles II., is an illustration of its practical application in this direction. An attempt was made in a congress at Vienna, in 1853, to obtain a vote to restore the kingdom of Poland, on the plea, that its dismemberment had disturbed the balance of power in Europe. The opposition of Prussia and Austria, each of whom possessed a portion of the dismembered kingdom, defeated the project. But the chief value of this principle lies in the security which it gives to the smaller and weaker states, preventing their absorption by their more powerful neighbors. It shielded the little Dutch Republic from the ambitious designs of the most powerful monarch of his time, Louis XIV. It has availed thus far to preserve the integrity of the Turkish empire against the aggressions of Russia, whose chief ambition is the possession of Constantinople.

The Crimean War. In 1853, Russia invaded Moldavia and Wallachia, the upper Danubian provinces of Turkey. This was declared by a congress of nations at Vienna, to be a violation of the balance of power in Europe. Upon the refusal of Russia to withdraw from the invaded territory, England and France sent their combined fleets to the Black and Baltic Seas. The effort to reach St. Petersburg being defeated by the strength of the fortifications at Cronstadt, the allies concentrated their forces on the Crimea, and laid siege to Sebastopol, the great stronghold of Russia on the Black Sea. The allied armies landed near the town of Eupatoria, the 14th of September, 1854, but it was not until the 9th of September, 1855, that they occupied the deserted fortifications of Sebastopol. We cannot dwell on the painful and protracted siege. To the sufferings of the soldiers, insufficiently provided with food, clothing, and shelter, for a Russian winter, were added the horrors of a wasting pestilence rendered all the more fatal by a lack of medical stores. About eighteen thousand British soldiers died of disease during the siege, while only four thousand perished through the casualties of war. But the gloomy picture is illumined by a heroism more lofty than that of arms. A band of noble women, under the charge of Florence Nightingale, left the comforts of their English homes, to minister to the wants of their sick and wounded countrymen in the plague-stricken camp on the Crimea.

The passage of the Alma,— the "Charge of the Light Brigade" at Balaklava, — the repulse of the Russians at Inkermann,—and the capture of the Malakoff Tower,— were the most interesting events of the war. The occupation of the Malakoff led to the fall of Sebastopol, and forced the Czar of all the Russias to sue for peace. By the treaty that followed, Russia consented to abandon all control over Moldavia, Wallachia, and Servia, to relinquish her claims to control the mouths of the Danube, to dismantle the fortifications of Sebastopol, and to maintain no fleet and no naval station in the Black Sea. A few small armed vessels were allowed the principal nations, in the Black Sea, for the protection of commerce, which was made free to all nations.

The Sepoy Rebellion. British India had gradually extended its boundaries to the Himalayas on the north, and to the Indus on the west. There was but a handful of English soldiers in the whole of this vast empire, the garrisons in the different departments being composed chiefly of native soldiers, called Sepoys, with English officers.

The government had decided to supply their Indian troops with an improved rifle using a greased cartridge whose end required to be bitten off in loading. The fat of cows or swine is an abomination to a Mahometan or a Hindoo, and the Sepoys, imagining that the government was seeking to entrap them into Christianity by requiring them to use a greased cartridge, began to revolt. But there was another cause of revolt, a deep-seated disaffection on the part of the natives, growing out of the extortion practised by English officials. From the time of Warren Hastings * to the breaking out of the revolt, the English had made office in India an avenue to wealth, and the long smothered resentment of the natives was ready to burst forth on the first occasion. The first movement of the revolt occurred at Meerut, in Bengal, May 10, 1857. The garrisons in the different districts following the example of that at Meerut, all India was soon in a state of insurrection. Over the atrocities perpetrated on English residents, and especially on helpless women and children, we must draw the veil. Indian soldiers, hitherto their trusted and faithful protectors, were suddenly transformed into merciless fiends.

Havelock and the Relief of Lucknow. Cawnpore on the borders, and Lucknow in the interior, of Oude, garrisoned by a small number of British soldiers, were

---

* Warren Hastings was a man of marked ability. Originally a clerk in the employ of the East India Company, he rose in 1774 to the position of Governor General. He came to the government of India at a time of great danger. The French in alliance with native chiefs renewed the struggle for the possession of the Carnatic. With a skill and vigor that remind us of Robert Clive, Hastings not only re-established the English authority, but he also greatly extended the English dominion. His administration was as unscrupulous as it was able, and on his return to England he was impeached for cruelty and extortion. His trial lasted from 1788 to 1795, and is one of the most remarkable on record.

besieged by a great multitude of savage natives. General Havelock, with a small force, of whom only fourteen hundred were English, pressed bravely forward to relieve the beleaguered towns. He encountered the Indian hordes under Nana Sahib (an enlightened and hitherto friendly chief, but now the most fierce and bloodthirsty of the rebels) in battle after battle. Though victorious, he was every day getting deeper into the enemy's country, and his little force was slowly melting away. At last he reached Cawnpore only to learn that its entire English population had been massacred. He started at once for Lucknow, fearing lest he should be too late to save its inhabitants from a like fate. Constantly assailed on every side by a host of fierce, swarthy foes, and exposed to the burning rays of a tropical sun, the heroic little band pressed bravely on and finally reached their destination. They found the English shut up in the Residency, which had been hastily fortified at the beginning of the revolt. Havelock unable to fight his way out, encumbered with women and children, could only maintain himself within the poor defences of the Residency, and wait for help.

Campbell and the Second **Relief of Lucknow.** The English Government hurried re-enforcements, as fast as possible, to the theatre of war. Sir Colin Campbell was placed at the head of the army. Taking an ample force, the gallant Scotchman rapidly advanced to the second relief of Lucknow. He had need to hurry. Exposed to the incessant fire of the enemy, whose shot pierced every part of their retreat except the cellars, where the women and children found shelter, the English soldiers at Lucknow were falling fast. If we can but feebly imagine the sufferings and the horrors of the siege, as month after month rolled away without a sign of succor, still less can we realize what must have been their emotions, when they heard, beyond the circle of their yelling, blood-thirsty foes, the distant sound of the Highland music, and, as it came nearer, they caught the notes of that old familiar air, "The Campbells are coming!" Lucknow was relieved on the 17th of November, 1857. Though far inferior to the rebels in number, Campbell conducted the survivers of the terrible siege to a place of safety. But the noble Havelock, who had borne up under incessant toil and exposure so long as danger threatened the helpless people under his charge, quickly sickened and died, when the crisis had passed; and another name was added to the British roll of honor. The prompt and efficient measures of the government were crowned with abundant success. The English authority was re-established more firmly than ever in all the revolted districts. An important and needed change was made in the transfer of the government of India, from the Company, to the Crown. The Queen has since been made Empress of India, which she governs through a Viceroy aided by a Council of five members.

The Affair of the Trent. In 1861, a civil war broke out in the United States, that early threatened to involve that country in another war with Great Britain. The revolted states organized a separate republic, under the name of "The Confederate States of America." Two commissioners, Mason and Slidell, were appointed to advance the Confederate interests at London and Paris. They succeeded in running the blockade, and reaching

Havana, where they took passage on the Trent, a British mail steamer bound for Liverpool. This vessel was overhauled by the United States frigate San Jacinto, under the command of Captain Wilkes, and the Confederate commissioners and their secretaries were forcibly removed to the latter vessel, and brought to the United States. The excitement in England, created by this illegal act, was intense. The British government demanded the instant surrender of the captured commissioners, and, without waiting for the reply of the United States, began vigorous preparations for war. Her army and navy were speedily put on a war footing, and regiments were dispatched to Canada to secure the frontier. But the excitement subsided as quickly as it had risen, for the United States promptly disavowed the act of her rash captain, and gracefully restored the Confederate commissioners to the protection of the British flag.

The Alabama Claims. But the United States had a grievance against Great Britain, growing out of the war, which the latter country was not so ready to disavow and settle. Several vessels, the most noted of which was the Alabama, had been built and equipped in an English dock-yard on the Clyde, for the use of the Confederate States. Though notified by the American minister of the destination of the vessels, the English government took no measures to detain them, and they sailed away to prey upon Northern commerce. The United States could not afford, during the continuance of civil strife, to press claims that might lead to war, and so these claims were allowed to remain in abeyance. At the close of the war, they became the subject of diplomacy between the two nations. Finally, in 1871, a Joint High Commission, composed of five members on each side, met at Washington and arranged the basis of a treaty. By this treaty all the questions at issue between the two countries were referred to a tribunal, composed of five arbitrators, to be selected, one each by the United States, Great Britain, Italy, Switzerland, and Brazil. This tribunal met on the 15th of June, 1872, at Geneva, Switzerland. It rejected the claims of the United States for indirect damages, but awarded as direct damages, on account of the depredations of the Alabama and other English-built privateers, the sum of $15,500,000, in gold. This award was promptly paid by Great Britain, and the relations of the two countries became once more harmonious.

Queen Victoria. Victoria was but eighteen years of age when she assumed the sovereignty of the vast empire of Great Britain. She was possessed of refined and unpretending manners, a cultivated mind, and a deeply religious spirit. Almost forty years have elapsed since the memorable morning of the 20th of June, 1837, when as an acknowledged queen she took her seat, for the first time, at the head of the Council table, and, in low but melodious tones, made the Declaration, of which the following is the opening clause: —

"The severe and afflicting loss which the nation has sustained by the death of his majesty, my beloved uncle, has devolved upon me the duty of administering the government of this empire. This awful responsibility is imposed upon me so suddenly, and at so early a period of my life, that I should feel myself utterly oppressed by the burden, were I not sustained by the hope that Divine Providence, which has called me to this work, will give me strength for the performance of it, and that I shall find in the purity of my intentions, and in my zeal for the public welfare, that support and those resources which usually belong to a more mature age and to long experience."

The rare fidelity with which, during a period already longer than that of most English reigns, the principles of this Declaration have been carried out, demonstrate that it was not the hollow utterance too common on such occasions. Few English sovereigns have been actuated by a more profound desire to promote the best interests of the English people than the reigning queen. Moderately liberal, never partizan, and always conscientious, she has followed, amidst the strife and excitement of party politics, the strict line of constitutional duty. When, in addition to this, we recall the virtues of her private life, her faithfulness as a wife, and her devotion as a mother, we can understand the love as well as the loyalty which she has inspired, so deeply and so generally, in the hearts of her people.

Prince Albert. In 1840, Victoria married Prince Albert of Saxe-Coburg-Gotha. In 1861, the Prince died, deeply lamented by the English people. Although a German by birth, he came to feel all the deep solicitude for the welfare of the nation, that animated the queen herself. Possessed of marked ability, superior judgment, and liberal views, he was an unostentatious, but an invaluable, counselor to the queen and to her ministry. To him is due the inception of that series of International Exhibitions, that have apparently become a permanent institution in the world, whose value in promoting harmony among the nations, in spreading a knowledge of useful inventions, and in stimulating a friendly emulation in the development of material resources, and the cultivation of the arts, can hardly be overestimated. They are the Crusades of the nineteenth century against universal ignorance.

The England of To-day. The reign of no English sovereign has been so prolific in measures for the public weal as that of Victoria. The England of to-day bears little resemblance to the England of even forty years ago. The removal of restrictions upon trade has led to a vast increase in commerce. Improved agricultural implements, and a practical knowledge of chemistry, have made the cultivation of the soil less burdensome and more remunerative. Improved machinery has increased immensely the products of manufactures. The construction of numerous railroads for the rapid transit of goods and passengers, the introduction of the electric telegraph facilitating the transaction of business, and the multiplication of swift ocean steamships, have placed England within reach of the markets of the world, and caused an immense and constantly increasing development of her resources.

But beneath all these evidences of material prosperity there is the basis of a wise legislation, which, recognizing the fact, that intelligence and virtue on the part of the people, form the only true foundation of national power and national prosperity, has sought in every way to elevate and enlighten the people. The criminal code has been shorn of its barbarities, and the death penalty abolished for all except the most heinous crimes. The cruel punishments of the navy have yielded to a milder and less brutalizing discipline. The horrors of prison life have been mitigated, and the poor and unfortunate of all kinds have been provided with comfortable asylums. Reformatory institutions have been established for juvenile delinquents and outcasts, where, far removed from circumstances of neglect or brutality, calculated to produce only paupers and criminals, they are trained, by a management, both wise and humane, to become good citizens. Sanitary precautions have left few lurking places in town or city for the pestilence that has so often wasted the population of England. Whatever concerns the physical, moral, and spiritual welfare of the English people, has engrossed English statesmanship, and become the subject of English legislation.

The British Government.

The Executive Department. The British government consists of three departments, the Executive, Legislative, and Judiciary. The Executive power is vested in a hereditary sovereign, who rules through a Ministry or Cabinet, composed of prominent officials, as follows :—

The First Lord of the Treasury, called Prime Minister or Premier; the Lord Chancellor; the Lord Privy Seal; the President of the Council; the Home Secretary; the Foreign Secretary; the Colonial Secretary; the Indian Secretary; the War Secretary; the Chancellor of the Exchequer; the First Lord of the Admiralty; the President of the Board of Trade; the President of the Poor Law Board; the Postmaster General; the Chancellor of the Duchy of Lancaster; and the Chief Secretary for Ireland.

The Cabinet Ministers form a standing committee of the Privy Council, a body of prominent men, selected by the sovereign as advisers in the administration of the government. The Cabinet holds frequent sessions, but the Privy Council is summoned only on important occasions. The Cabinet Ministers, usually called "the government," are held responsible for all the acts of the executive department, it being an established principle in the British government, that "The king can do no wrong." These Ministers remain in office only so long as they are sustained by a majority in the House of Commons. Whenever the vote of the House is cast against any important measure proposed by the ministry, it is accepted by the latter as expressing "a want of confidence in the government" on the part of the people. Two courses are now open to the ministry; they either resign at once, in which case the sovereign calls upon the leader of the opposite party to form a new ministry; or they can "appeal to the country," in which case the sovereign dissolves the Parliament, and issues writs for a new election. If the new House of Commons is in sympathy with the ministry, the latter remain in office; if not, they promptly resign, and a new ministry is formed of the opposite party. As the result of the election is readily ascertained, the ministerial question is usually settled before the meeting of the new Parliament.

An interesting fact may be mentioned in this connection, illustrating the authority attached in England to simple custom or usage. Although the Cabinet has existed as the real executive power, for more than a century and a half, it is an institution entirely unknown to the law, never having been recognized by any Act of Parliament. There is no official announcement of the names of its members, and no official record of its meetings is kept.

The prerogatives of the Crown are:—the right to make peace or war; to prorogue, dissolve, or summon Parliament; to give or withhold assent to Acts of Parliament; to send and receive ambassadors; to confer or create titles of nobility; to grant pardons; to coin money; to appoint judges and inferior magistrates; to give and revoke commissions in the army and navy; and, as head of the established church, to nominate to vacancies in the leading church offices.

The Legislative Department. The legislative power is vested in a Parliament consisting of the House of Lords, and the House of Commons.

The House of Lords. The House of Lords is composed of Lords spiritual and Lords temporal. The Lords spiritual are thirty in number,—twenty-six prelates of the Church of England, and four prelates (one Archbishop and three Bishops) of the Irish church, the latter holding office one year and then yielding their places to the next four. The number of Lords temporal in England is entirely unsettled, but there are sixteen Scottish, and twenty-eight Irish, nobles, who are elected by the nobility,—those from Ireland for life, and those from Scotland for a year. The English Lords are hereditary.

The House of Commons. The House of Commons consists of representatives of counties, cities, boroughs, and some of the Universities; England and Wales having about five hundred, Scotland about fifty, and Ireland about one hundred.

Bills may be proposed in either House, except those appropriating money, which can originate only in the House of Commons. The Lords can reject, but they cannot alter, money bills. Every bill must be read and passed by a majority vote, three times in each House, and receive the royal signature, before it can become law. Although the sovereign has the right to withhold the royal signature, this right has not been exercised since the reign of Queen Anne. By its control of the public funds, and by its ability, through a ministry necessarily in harmony with itself, to shape the entire policy of the government, the House of Commons is the chief ruling power.

The Judiciary Department. The Judiciary department consists, in England and Ireland, of the Courts of Chancery, Queen's Bench, Common Pleas, and Exchequer; in Scotland, of the Court of Sessions and the High Court of Justiciary. In the rural districts Circuit Courts are held twice a year by itinerant justices. The House of Lords is the highest law court in the empire. There are three kinds of law through which justice is administered in England; Common law, Statute law, and the law of Equity. Common law is based on custom, or precedents established by former decisions of the Courts; Statute law consists of Acts of Parliament; and the law of Equity is administered by the Lord Chancellor, in cases not covered by Statute law, and where justice cannot be secured by the Common law.

TOPICAL INDEX.

Preface,	3
Kings of England,	5
Names of Kings and Leading Topics,	6
Genealogical Table,	8
The British Empire,	10

CHAPTER I.

The Britons,	11
Druidism,	12
First Roman Invasion,	13
Second Roman Invasion,	13
Caractacus,	14
Slaughter of the Druids,	14
Boadicea,	14
The Roman Conquest,	15
The Saxon Conquest,	16
King Arthur,	17
The Heptarchy,	18
Introduction of Christianity,	18
Anglo-Saxon Religion,	19
Anglo-Saxon Government,	20

CHAPTER II.

Egbert. The Danish Invasions,	21
Alfred the Great. War with the Danes,	22
Alfred's Government,	23
Alfred's Successors,	24
Massacre of Danes,	24
The Danish Conquest,	24
Comparison between Saxon and Danish Conquests,	25

CHAPTER III.

Canute the Great. The Reign of Canute,	27

Canute and the Christian Church, . . . 28
Edward the Confessor. Character of Edward, 29
William, Duke of Normandy, ... 29
Battle of Hastings, A.D. 1066, ... 30

CHAPTER IV.

William the Conqueror. Rolf, the Dane, . 31
Revolt of the English, ... 31
Confiscation of English Estates, ... 32
The Feudal System Established, ... 33
The Doomsday Book, ... 34
The Curfew Bell, ... 34
The Norman Language, ... 34
Character of William the Conqueror, ... 34
William II. Rebellion of the Barons, . . . 37
Character of William II., ... 37
The Crusades, ... 38
The Benefits of the Crusades, ... 38
The System of Chivalry, ... 39
Henry I. First Charter of Liberties, . . . 40
Robert, Duke of Normandy, ... 41
Character and Reign of Henry, ... 42
The White Ship, ... 42
Stephen. Civil War, ... 43
Compromise between Stephen and Henry, . . . 44
The Robber Barons, ... 44
The Outlaws of the Forest, ... 45

CHAPTER V.

Henry II. The Condition of England, . . . 47
The Establishment of Order, ... 48
Contest between Church and State, ... 48
The Council of Clarendon, ... 49
Thomas à Becket and King Henry, ... 49
The Death of Thomas à Becket, ... 50
The Judiciary System, ... 50
Trial by Jury, ... 51
Conquest of Ireland, ... 52
Henry's Rebellious Sons, ... 52

TOPICAL INDEX.

Richard I. Slaughter of Jews,	53
Richard in the Holy Land,	54
Richard a Captive in the Tyrol,	54
War with France and Death of Richard,	55
Character of Richard,	55
John. Character of John,	56
Loss of Possessions in France,	57
John's Quarrel with the Pope,	57
The Papal Interdict,	58
John's Submission to the Pope,	58
Magna Charta, A.D. 1215,	59
Patriotism of the Bishops of England,	61
Henry III. The Regency,	62
Redress the Condition of a Vote of Supplies,	62
Henry's Attempt to Overthrow the Charter,	63
Rebellion of the Barons,	63
Simon de Montfort and the House of Commons, A.D. 1265,	64
Evesham,	65
Edward I. Conquest of Wales,	65
Arbitrary Taxation Forbidden,	66
Beginning of the Wars with Scotland,	67
Battle of Dunbar,	67
William Wallace,	68
Robert Bruce,	69
Character of Edward I.,	69
Edward II. Character of Edward II.,	70
Piers Gaveston,	70
Bannockburn, A.D. 1314,	71
Queen Isabella in France,	72
Deposition and Death of Edward,	72
Edward III. The Regency,	72
Treaty of Northampton,	74
Fall of Isabella and Mortimer,	74
Halidon Hill,	75
The "Hundred Years' War" with France,	75
Cressy, A.D. 1346,	76
Calais,	76
Neville's Cross,	77
Poictiers, A D. 1356,	77

Loss of French Possessions,	78
Internal Disorder,	78
The Good Parliament,	79
John Wickliffe,	79
The English Language,	80
The English People,	80
Change in the Methods of Warfare,	81
The Two Houses of Parliament,	81
Death of Edward,	82
Richard II. The Regency,	82
Causes of Wat Tyler's Rebellion,	83
Emancipation,	83
The Black Death,	84
The Statute of Laborers,	84
The Breaking out of the Rebellion,	84
Wickliffe and the First Reformation,	86
Otterburn and Chevy Chase,	87
Chaucer,	87
Tyranny of Richard,	88
Deposition of Richard,	88

CHAPTER VI.

Henry IV. Henry's Title,	90
The First Martyr at the Stake,	91
Revolt in Behalf of Richard II.,	91
Revolt of the Welsh,	92
Revolt of the Percies,	92
The Poet-King of Scotland,	93
Henry's Troubles,	93
Henry V. The Wise Beginning of Henry's Reign,	94
Suppression of the First Reformation,	95
Renewal of the "Hundred Years' War,"	97
Agincourt, A. D. 1415,	97
Siege of Rouen,	98
Conquest of France and Treaty of Troyes,	99
Beginning of the Navy,	99
Henry VI. The Dauphin of France Assumes the Crown,	100
Joan of Arc,	100
Loss of all France, except Calais,	103

English Discontent,	103
Jack Cade's Rebellion,	104
Events Preceding the Wars of the Roses,	105
Wars of the Roses,	106

CHAPTER VII.

Edward IV. Towton, A.D. 1461,	108
Tewkesbury, A.D. 1471,	109
Character and Government of Edward,	110
Results of the Wars of the Roses,	111
The Destruction of the Ancient Nobility,	111
The Loss of Constitutional Liberty,	113
The Decline of Civilization,	115
Edward V. Usurpation of Richard, Duke of Gloucester,	116
Richard III. The Elements of Opposition to Richard,	118
The Smothered Princes,	118
Bosworth Field,	119
Character of Richard,	120

CHAPTER VIII.

Henry VII. Union of York and Lancaster,	124
Lambert Simnel,	124
Perkin Warbeck,	125
The Statute of Allegiance,	126
The Discovery of America,	126
The Revival of Letters,	127
The Character and Policy of Henry,	128
Henry VIII. Character of Henry VIII.,	131
Foreign Affairs,	131
Divorce of Catherine of Arragon,	132
Cardinal Wolsey,	133
The Divorce of Catherine of Arragon Accomplished,	135
The Oxford Reformers,	135
Erasmus,	136
Thomas More,	137
Opposition to the Oxford Reformers,	137
Martin Luther and the Reformation,	138
The Reformation in England,	140
Bishop Fisher and Thomas More Executed,	141

TOPICAL INDEX.

Henry Supreme in Church and State,	141
The Suppression of the Religious Houses,	143
The Bloody Statute,	144
Henry's Wives,	144
Henry's Death,	145
Edward VI. The Regency,	146
Edward and Mary, Queen of Scots,	146
Peasant Revolts,	147
Progress of the Reformation,	147
Edward's Will,	148
Mary. Lady Jane Grey,	149
Catholicism Restored to England,	151
The Martyrs at the Stake,	151
Mary's Marriage with Philip of Spain,	152
Loss of Calais, A.D. 1558,	152
Extenuation of Mary's Cruelty,	153
Elizabeth. Protestantism Restored to England,	154
The Puritans,	155
The Dangers that Environed Elizabeth,	156
Elizabeth's Policy,	157
Mary, Queen of Scots,	159
The Maritime Growth of England,	163
Elizabeth's Defiance of Philip,	165
The Invincible Armada,	166
Great Names,	169
Death of Elizabeth,	169
Character of Elizabeth,	170

CHAPTER IX.

James I. Union of Scotch and English Crowns,	171
Persecution of Non-Conformists,	171
King James's Version of the Bible,	172
The Gunpowder Plot,	172
The Pilgrim Fathers,	173
James's Assumption in Matters of Religion,	174
James's Assumption in Matters of Government,	174
Foreign Affairs,	176
The Parliament of 1621,	176
Prince Charles,	177

Sir Walter Raleigh,	177
Character of James I.,	178

Charles I.

Constitutional Liberty at the Accession of Charles I.,	179
Renewal of the Constitutional Struggle,	181
Petition of Right, A.D. 1628,	183
The King Can Do No Wrong,	184
The Purpose of Charles to Rule Alone,	184
Laud, Strafford, and the Two Courts,	185
The High Commission and Puritan Emigration,	186
The Star Chamber and Illegal Taxation,	187
Ship Money and John Hampden,	187
The Attempt to Force Episcopacy upon the Scots,	188
The Short Parliament,	189
The Long Parliament,	189
The Attempt of Charles to Arrest the Five Members,	190
Civil War Inevitable,	190
Roundheads and Cavaliers,	191
Presbyterianism Made the National Religion,	191
Edgehill, A.D. 1642,	192
Naseby, A.D. 1645,	192
Struggle between Presbyterians and Independents,	192
Struggle between Parliament and the Army,	194
The Army Becomes Supreme,	194
The High Court of Justice,	195

The Commonwealth.

The Commonwealth and its Perils,	196
Worcester, A.D. 1651,	197
Parliament and the Army,	198
The Expulsion of the Rump Parliament.	199
Cromwell Made Lord Protector,	200
Cromwell Usurps the Government,	201
Prosperity under Cromwell's Rule,	202
Cromwell's Death,	203
Cromwell's Character and Motives,	203
Richard Cromwell,	206
The Restoration,	206
The Last Muster of the Puritan Army,	207

Charles II.

The Circumstances under which Charles Became King,	207

The Social Revolution,	208
The Convention Parliament,	210
The Restoration of the Episcopal Religion,	211
Attempt to Force Episcopacy upon the Scots,	211
Foreign Affairs,	212
The Plague in London,	213
The Great Fire of London,	213
Charles a Pensioner of Louis of France,	214
Declaration of Indulgence,	215
The Test Act,	215
The Popish Plot,	216
The Rye House Plot,	217
The Habeas Corpus Act, A.D. 1679,	217
The Merry Monarch,	218
James II. The Second Stuart Tyranny,	218
Rebellion of the Duke of Monmouth,	219
The English Reign of Terror,	220
Attempt to Restore Catholicism to England,	222
The Seven Bishops,	223
William of Orange Invited to Take the English Crown,	224
The Flight of James to France,	225
The Glorious Revolution Peacefully Accomplished,	226
William and Mary. The Grand Alliance,	227
Rebellion in Ireland,	228
Battle of the Boyne,	228
Peace of Ryswick,	229
The Bill of Rights, A.D. 1689,	229
The Constitution of England,	230
The Second Grand Alliance,	232
Death and Character of William,	233
Anne. The War of the Spanish Succession,	234
Marlborough,	235
Constitutional Union of England and Scotland,	236
Death of Good Queen Anne,	237

CHAPTER X.

George I. The Jacobites,	238
The Pretender,	239
The South Sea Scheme,	239

The Septennial Act,	241
George II. Robert Walpole,	241
War with Spain,	242
War of the Austrian Succession,	243
The Young Pretender,	244
Culloden,	244
The Last of the Stuarts,	245
The French and Indian War,	245
The Five Important Points,	246
The Battle of Quebec,	247
A Proud Year in English Warfare,	247
The Struggle for Dominion in India,	248
Plassey,	249
George III. The Peace of Paris,	250
Causes of the American Revolution,	251
The Repressive Policy of England,	251
Search Warrants,	251
The Stamp Act,	251
Boston Port Bill,	252
Battle of Lexington, April 19th, 1775,	252
The Declaration of Independence,	254
Surrender of Burgoyne and Alliance with France,	255
William Pitt, Earl of Chatham,	256
Yorktown, A. D. 1781,	257
Peace of Paris,	257
Causes of the French Revolution,	257
The Despotic Rule of Louis XIV.	257
The Corrupt Rule of Louis XV.,	258
The Inefficient Rule of Louis XVI.,	258
The French Sceptics,	258
The Influence of the American Revolution,	259
The States-General,	259
The Revolution Sweeps away Church and State,	260
The Reign of Terror,	260
Napoleon Bonaparte,	261
Admiral Nelson,	262
The Struggle on the Spanish Peninsula,	262
The Invasion of Russia,	263
The Battle of the Nations,	264

Napoleon at Elba,	264
Waterloo, A.D. 1815,	264
Napoleon at St. Helena,	266
Causes of England's Second War with the United States,	267
Right of Search and Impressment of Seamen,	267
"Decrees" of Napoleon and "Orders" of English Council,	268
Declaration of War by the United States,	268
Battle of New Orleans,	268
Peace of Ghent,	269
The Regency,	269
George IV. England after the Napoleonic Wars,	269
The Corn Law,	271
Agitation on the Subject of Reform,	271
The Repeal of the Corporation and Test Acts,	272
The Catholic Emancipation Bill,	273
Daniel O'Connell,	273
Navarino, A.D 1827,	274
Character of George IV.,	275
William IV.	
State of Feeling in England at the Accession of William,	276
The Reform Bill of 1832,	277
Results of Reform Legislation,	278
Abolition of Slavery in the Colonies,	279
Character of William IV.,	279
Victoria. Reform Legislation in the Reign of Victoria,	280
Repeal of the Corn Laws,	281
The Chartists,	282
The Disestablishment of the Irish Church,	285
The Irish Land Bill,	286
The Education Bill,	286
The Foreign Policy,	287
War with Egypt,	287
Wars with China,	288
The Balance of Power,	288
The Crimean War,	290
The Sepoy Rebellion,	291
Havelock and the Relief of Lucknow,	292
Campbell and the Second Relief of Lucknow,	293
The Affair of the Trent,	294

The Alabama Claims,	295
Queen Victoria,	296
Prince Albert,	297
The England of To-day,	298
The British Government.	
The Executive Department,	300
The Legislative Department,	302
The House of Lords,	302
The House of Commons,	302
The Judiciary Department,	303

INDEX.

Alabama Claims ... 295
Abyssinia ... 287
Acre (*a ker*) ... 288
Act of Settlement ... 230
Act of Supremacy ... 140, 141
Act of Uniformity ... 154, 211
Af-ghan-is-tan' ... 287
Ag'in-court (*ă-zhän-koor'*), Battle of 97
A-gric'o-la ... 15
Aix-la-Chapelle (*akes-lah sha-pel*), Treaty of ... 243
Al'bert, Prince ... 297
Alice Lisle (*lile*) ... 220
America, Discovery of ... 126
American Settlements ... 175, 186
Angles (*an'gls*) ... 16
An'gle-sey ... 12
Anne Boleyn (*bool'en*) ... 133, 135, 145
Anne of Cleves ... 145
Anti-Corn Law League ... 281
An'selm ... 36
Ar-a-bel'la Stuart ... 178
Arch-an'gel ... 164
Ar cot ... 249
Arthur, King ... 17
Arthur, Prince ... 57
As'ca-lon ... 54
Austrian Succession, War of ... 243
Balance of Power ... 288
Bal-ak-la'va ... 291
Bal'li-ol, Edward ... 75
Baliol, John ... 67
Ban'nock-burn, Battle of ... 71
Bar'net, Battle of ... 110
Becket, Thomas à ... 49, 50
Bede ... 19
Bel'gium ... 277
Benevolence ... 111, 129, 184
Bengal (*ben-gawl'*) ... 292
Bill of Rights ... 229
Black Death ... 84
Black Hole of Calcutta ... 249
Black Prince ... 76, 77, 80
Blake, Admiral ... 199
Blenheim (*blen'hime*), Battle of ... 234
Bloody Assize ... 220
Bloody Statute ... 144
Blucher (*bloo'ker*), General ... 265
Boadice'a, Queen ... 14
Bo'na-parte, Napoleon ... 261, 264, 246
Bo'na-parte, Louis Napoleon ... 281
Boston ... 187
Boston Port Bill ... 253

Bos'worth, Battle of ... 119
Both'well, Earl of ... 161
Boyne, Battle of the ... 228
Bretigny (*Breteen ye*) ... 78
Bright, John ... 280
British Constitution ... 230
British Empire ... 10
British Government ... 300
Brougham (*broo'am*), Lord ... 280
Bruce, Robert ... 67, 69
Brus'sels ... 277
Buck'ing-ham, Duke of ... 117
Bun'yan, John ... 215
Bur-goyne', General ... 255
Burgundy, Duchess of ... 125
By'ron, Lord ... 275
Ca-bal', The ... 214
Cabinet ... 300
Cab'lots ... 127
Cade, Jack ... 104
Cæ'sar, Julius ... 13
Calais (*kal'is*) ... 76, 152
Cal-cut'ta ... 249
Campbell, Sir Col'in ... 293
Campeg'gio ... 133
Ca-rac'ta-cus ... 14
Car-nat'ic ... 249
Car'o-line of Brunswick ... 275
Cath'e-rine of Ar'ra-gon ... 130, 135
Catherine of Bra-gan'za ... 248
Catherine Howard ... 145
Catherine Parr ... 145
Catholic Associations ... 273
Catholic Emancipation Bill ... 273
Cavaliers ... 191
Cavalier Parliament ... 211
Cawnpore' ... 292
Caxton, William ... 127
Chancery, Court of ... 66, 303
Charles Edward, the Pretender ... 244
Chartists ... 282, 283
Chaucer (*chaw'ser*) ... 87
Chev'y Chase ... 87
China, War with ... 282
Chivalry ... 30, 83
Church of England ... 140, 154
Churchill, Lord ... 224, 234, 235
Clive, Robert ... 249
Cob'den, Richard ... 280
Co-lum'bus ... 126
Common Prayer, Book of ... 148
Commonwealth ... 195
Com-pur-ga'tion ... 50

INDEX.

Constitution, British.............. 230
Constitutions of Clarendon...... 49
Convention, Parliament.......... 210
Corn-Laws.................. 281, 281
Corn-wallis, Lord............... 257
Corporation Act............ 211, 273
Court of High Commission... 185, 186, 190
Court of Star Chamber....185, 187, 190
Covenanters.............. 188, 213
Cranmer, Thomas... 135, 145, 147, 151
Cressy (*kres'se*), Battle of........ 76
Cri-me'a......................... 290
Cromwell, Thomas.......... 114, 115
Cromwell, Oliver........... 192, 200
Cromwell, Richard............... 206
Crusades......................... 38
Cul-lo'den, Battle of............. 241
Cumberland, Duke of............ 280
Curfew Bell................. 34, 42
Dane'geld......................... 24
Darn'ley, Lord.................. 160
"Decrees" of Napoleon........... 208
Declaration of Indulgence........ 223
De-i'ra................... 19, 32
De Ruyter (*ri'ter*)............... 199
Det'ting-en, Battle of............ 243
Dooms'day Book.................. 34
Drake, Sir Francis........... 165, 166
Dru'idism........................ 12
Dun'bar, Battles of.......... 67, 197
Dun'kirk................... 203, 214
Du Quesne (*kane*), Fort......... 246
East India Company........248, 294
Edgehill, Battle of.............. 192
Education Bill.................. 286
Egypt........................... 287
El'ba, Island of................. 254
Eleanor, [sister of Arthur]....... 57
Elgi'va.......................... 24
El'li-ot, Sir John............... 185
Elizabeth, Queen of Henry VII... 119
Empson and Dudley.............. 131
En-nis-kil'len.................. 228
E-ras'mus.................. 128, 136
Eugene, Prince.................. 234
Eves ham, Battle of.............. 65
Falkirk.......................... 68
Feudal System.................... 33
Field of Cloth of Gold........... 133
Fire of London.................. 213
Fisher, Bishop.................. 141
Flod'den Field, Battle of........ 132
Foth'er-in-gay Castle............ 163
French Revolution............... 237
Fro'bish-er, Martin......... 164, 167
Gas'coigne (*-koin*), Chief Justice. 94
Gav es-ton Piers................. 70
George, Prince of Denmark....... 237
Ghent, Treaty of................ 269
Gibraltar (*jib-rawl'ter*)....... 257
Glendower, Owen.................. 93
Godwin........................... 99
Grand Alliance.................. 227
Grand Alliance, Second.......... 232
Greece.......................... 274
Grey, Lord...................... 116

Grey, Lady Jane......... 132, 148, 149
Grouchy (*groo'she*), Marshal.... 265
Guiana (*ghe-ah'nah*)............ 173
Guise (*gweez*), Duke of........ 153
Gunpowder Plot.................. 172
Guth'rum......................... 22
Guy Fawkes...................... 172
Ha'be-as Cor'pus Act............ 217
Halidon Hill, Battle of.......... 76
Hampden, John............. 187, 192
Hanover......................... 290
Har'fleur (*har'flur*)........... 97
Hastings, Battle of.............. 30
Hastings, Lord.................. 116
Hastings, Warren................ 292
Hav'e-lock, General............. 292
Hawke, Admiral.................. 248
Haw'kins, Admiral.......... 164, 167
Hen'gist and Horsa............... 16
Henrietta Maria............ 177, 182
Heptarchy........................ 18
High Court of Justice........... 195
Hong Kong....................... 288
House of Commons....... 64, 81, 302
House of Lords......... 81, 195, 302
Howard, Lord.................... 167
Huguenots (*hu'ghe-nots*)....... 182
Hundred Years' War............... 97
Independents.................... 193
India........................... 248
Impressment of Seamen.......... 267
Ink'er-man, Battle of........... 291
Interdict.................... 57, 58
Invincible Armada............... 166
Irish Church.................... 285
Irish Land Bill................. 286
Isabella, Queen........... 72, 74, 76
Jac'o-bites..................... 238
Jamestown....................... 173
Jane Seymour.................... 145
Jeffries, Judge............ 220, 221
Jews............... 53, 60, 262, 285
Joan of Arc..................... 100
John of Gaunt................... 124
Joint High Commission........... 296
Judiciary System................. 50
Judiciary Department............ 303
Judgment of God.................. 51
King's Evil...................... 29
Kirke's Lambs................... 220
La Hogue (*hōg*), Battle of..... 229
Langside, Battle of............. 162
Lang'ton, Stephen............ 57, 61
Lat'i-mer, Bishop............... 151
Laud, Archbishop........... 185, 190
Leicester (*les'ter*), Earl of.. 165
Leipsic (*lipe'sik*), Battle of. 264
Lew'es (*lu'-is*), Battle of..... 64
Lexington, Battle of............ 252
Limoges, (*lee-mosh'*)........... 55
Llew-el'lyn...................... 65
Lochlev'en Castle............... 162
Lollards......................... 15
Londonderry..................... 228
Long Parliament............ 189, 206
Louis XIV. of France............ 257
Louis XV. of France............. 258

INDEX. 319

Louis XVI. of France... 258
Louis XVIII. of France... 264
Louis Philippe (*loo'e fe-leep'*)... 276
Louisburg... 243
Luck'now... 292, 293
Luther, Martin... 138
Magna Charta... 59
Mal'a-koff... 291
Malplaquet (*mal plah-ka'*), Battle of 234
Mar, Earl of... 239
Margaret of Anjou (*on-zhoo*)... 103
Maria Theresa (*te-re'zah*)... 243
Marl'bor-ough, Duke of.. 224, 234, 235
Marlborough, Duchess of... 235
Marston Moor, Battle of... 193
Mary, Queen of Scots... 146, 159
Mas'ham, Mrs... 237
Matilda, [wife of Conqueror]... 36
Matilda [wife of Henry I.]... 41
Matilda, [wife of Geoffrey Plantagenet]... 42
Mee'rut... 292
Milton... 218
Min'den, Battle of... 248
Monk, General... 206
Monmouth, Duke of... 210
Montcalm (*mont-kăm*), Marquis of 247
Montfort, Simon de... 64
More, Sir Thomas... 137, 141
Mortimer, Roger... 72
Mortimer's Cross, Battle of... 107
Nantes (*nants*), Edict of... 227
Napoleon... 261, 264, 265
Nase by, Battle of... 192
National Convention... 261
Navigation Laws... 198, 2-3
Navarino (*nah-vah-re'no*), Battle of 274
Navy, British... 89
Nelson, Lord... 262
Nana Sahib (*sah-eeb*)... 293
Neville's Cross, Battle of... 77
New Forest... 35
New Orleans, Battle of... 258
Nightingale, Florence... 291
Oates, Titus... 216
O'Connell, Daniel... 274
Oldcastle, Sir John... 95
Orangemen... 228
"Orders of English Council"... 258
Ovter-burn... 87
Ou'de-nar-de (*-deh*), Battle of... 234
Pakenham (*pak'n-am*), General... 268
Paris, Treaty of... 250, 257
Parliament... 81
Parliamentary Reform... 271, 277
Peel, Sir Robert... 284
Pembroke, Earl of... 62
Peninsular War... 265
Perkin Warbeck... 124
Peter the Hermit... 38
Petition of Right... 184
Philip II. of Spain... 150, 152, 157
Phil-ip pa, Queen... 77
Pilgrim Fathers... 173
Pilgrim's Progress, Bunyan's... 215
Pitt, William, Earl of Chatham... 256
Pitt, William, the Younger... 259

Plague, the Great... 213
Plantagenet, Geoffrey... 42
Plantagenet, Origin of Name... 46
Plas'sey, Battle of... 249
Poictiers (*poi-teerz'*), Battle of... 77
Pon-di-cher'ry (*-sher-*)... 249
Pop'ish Plot... 216
Presbyterians... 192
Preston Pans, Battle of... 244
Prince Albert... 297
Prince of Wales, Title of... 66
Printing... 127
Privy Council... 300
Protestants... 143
Puritans... 155
Purveyance... 175
Pym, John... 190
Quakers... 202, 212, 215
Que-bec, Battle of... 247
Quiberon Bay... 248
Raleigh (*raw'le*), Sir Walter... 177
Ram'il-lies, Battle of... 234
Reformation, First... 79, 83, 91, 95
Reformation, Great... 138, 140, 147
Regicides... 210
Reign of Terror... 260
Restoration... 206
Revolution of 1688... 226
Revolution, American... 251
Revolution, French... 257
Rheims (*reemz*)... 102
Richard, Duke of Gloucester... 116
Richelieu (*resh'ch-loo*)... 182
Ridley, Bishop... 151
Right of Search... 257
Rivers, Lord... 116
Rizzio (*reet'se-o*)... 151
Robert, Duke of Normandy... 41
Robert, Earl of Essex... 129
Robin Hood... 45
Rochelle (*ro-shel'*)... 182
Rouen (*roo'ang*)... 98
Roundheads... 191
Rump Parliament... 196, 199
Russell, Lord... 217
Rye-House Plot... 217
Rys'wick, Treaty of... 229
St. Alban (*awl'ban*)... 18
St. Alban's, Battle of... 107
St. Au gus-tine' (*-teen*)... 19
St. Brice, Massacre of... 24
St. He-le'na... 266
Sal'a-din... 54
Sal'ic Law... 79
Sar-a-to'ga... 253
Scone... 67
Scots and Picts... 15
Search Warrants... 251
Se-bas-to'-pol... 290
Sedgemoor, Battle of... 219
Sepoy Rebellion... 291
Serfdom... 29, 83, 85
Septennial Act... 241
Se-ve'rus... 16
Shakspeare... 169
Ship Money... 187
Short Parliament... 189

INDEX.

Sidonia, Medina.................... 166
Simnel Lambert 124
Sidney Algernon.................... 217
Slavery, Abolition of.............. 279
Somerset, Duke of................. 105
South Sea Scheme.................. 239
Spensers 72
Spurs, Battle of 131
Stafford, Lord.................... 216
Stamp Act 251
Star Chamber 129, 185, 187, 190
States-General..................... 259
Strafford, Lord.................... 185
Strongbow 52
Stuart, Charles Edward 244
Stuart, James Francis......... 232, 239
Sue-to ni-us (swe-)................ 14
Suffolk, Duke of................... 103
Suppression of Religious Houses ... 143
Supremacy..................... 140, 141
Supremacy, Oath of................. 154
Su-ra jah Dow'lah.................. 249
Sydney, Sir Philip................. 166
Syria 287
Tal-a-ve ra, Battle of............. 262
Test Act.......................215, 272
Tewkes'bury, Battle of............. 109
Toleration Act..................... 230
Tor-bay............................ 225
Tow'ton, Battle of................. 108
Traf-al gar', Battle of............ 262
Trent.............................. 234

Trial by Jury...................... 51
Triple Alliance.................... 214
Troyes (trwah), Treaty of.......... 99
Tudor, Owen 90, 127
Tyr-con'nel................... 225, 22f
Tyrrel, Walter..................... 38
Union of England and Ireland... 273
Union of Eng. and Scotland.. 171, 236
U'trecht, Treaty of................ 234
Van Tromp, Admiral................. 193
Victoria, Queen 2 46
Villiers (vil'yerz), George 176, 181, 184
Virginia 174
Wager of Battle.................... 51
Wakefield, Battle of............... 1 7
Wallace, William................... 68
Walpole, Sir Robert................ 241
Wars of the Roses.... 90, 105, 106, 111
War of the Spanish Succession... 234
Warwick (war'rik), Earl of... 105, 113
Washington, George 254
Wat Tyler.......................... 83
Waterloo, Battle of................ 264
Wel'lington, Duke of............... 263
Wick'liffe, John 79, 86, 96
Wilberforce, William 280
William, Prince [son of Henry I.] 42
Wit-an-ag'e-môt.................... 20
Wolfe, General..................... 247
Wolsey, (wool'-ze) Cardinal........ 13
Worcester, (woos'-ter) Battle of.. 194
Yorktown........................... 257

CARDINAL DATES OF ENGLISH HISTORY.

55 B.C. *Britain invaded by the Romans under Julius Cæsar*
43 A.D. Conquest of Britain begun by Emperor Claudius.
  78 Conquest completed by the Roman general Agricola.
 430 Britain evacuated by the Romans.
 449 Landing of the Angles, Saxons, and Jutes.
 607 Saxon conquest completed at the battle of Chester.
 827 *English Monarchy founded by Egbert.*
 871 Alfred the Great.
1002 Massacre of Danes by Ethelred the Unready.
1013 England conquered by Sweyn, king of Denmark.
1017 Canute the Great. Establishment of Danish Rule.
1041 Edward the Confessor. Saxon Line restored.
1066 *Battle of Hastings.*
    William I. Beginning of Norman Line.
1087 William II.
1100 Henry I. Union of Saxon and Norman Families.
1101 *First Charter of Liberties.*
1135 Stephen. Usurpation of Stephen.
1154 Henry II. Beginning of the Plantagenet **Family.**
1164 Constitutions of Clarendon.
1172 Conquest of Ireland.
1189 Richard I.
1199 John.
1215 *Magna Charta.*
1216 Henry III.
1264 Battle of Lewes.
1265 *First House of Commons.*
    Battle of Evesham.
1272 Edward I.
1282 Conquest of Wales.
1290 Banishment of Jews.
1296 *Arbitrary taxation forbidden.*
1297 Battle of Dunbar.
1307 Edward II.

CARDINAL DATES OF ENGLISH HISTORY.

- **1314** Battle of Bannockburn.
- **1327** **Edward III.**
- **1333** Battle of Halidon Hill.
- **1346** Battles of Cressy and Neville's Cross.
- **1347** Capture of Calais.
- **1356** Battle of Poictiers.
- **1360** Peace of Bretigny.
- **1377** **Richard II.**
- **1381** The Peasants' Revolt or Wat Tyler's Rebellion.
- **1399** **Henry IV. Beginning of the House of Lancaster.**
- **1401** First martyr at the stake.
- **1403** Battle of Shrewsbury.
- **1413** **Henry V.**
- **1415** Battle of Agincourt.
- **1420** Treaty of Troyes.
- **1422** **Henry VI.**
- **1429** Siege of Orleans.
- **1451** Loss of all France but Calais.
- **1455** Beginning of Wars of the Roses.
  First Battle of St. Albans.
- **1460** Battle of Wakefield
- **1461** Second Battle of St. Albans.
  Edward IV. Beginning of the House of York.
  Battle of Towton.
- **1471** Battles of Barnet and Tewkesbury.
- **1474** *Introduction of the Printing Press.*
- **1483** **Edward V.** Usurpation of Richard, Duke of Gloucester.
  Richard III.
- **1485** Battle of Bosworth and end of Wars of the Roses.
  Henry VII. Beginning of the Tudor Family.
- **1497** *Discovery of the Continent of North America.*
- **1509** **Henry VIII.**
- **1513** Battle of Flodden Field.
- **1517** Beginning of the Great Reformation in Germany.
- **1531** *Beginning of the Great Reformation in England.*
- **1534** The king made Supreme Head of the Church of England.
- **1547** **Edward VI.** Battle of Pinkie.
- **1553** **Mary.** The Catholic religion restored.
- **1558** Loss of Calais.
  Elizabeth. The Protestant religion restored.

CARDINAL DATES OF ENGLISH HISTORY.

1587 Death of Mary, Queen of Scots.
1588 Destruction of the Invincible Armada.
1603 **James I.** Beginning of the Stuart Family.
1605 The Gunpowder Plot.
1607 *Settlement of Jamestown.*
1611 Translation of the Bible.
1620 *Landing of the Pilgrims.*
1625 **Charles I.**
1628 *The Petition of Right.*
1630 Settlement of Boston.
1637 Levy of Ship Money.
1640 Meeting of the Long Parliament.
1642 Beginning of the Civil War.
Battle of Edgehill.
1645 Battle of Naseby.
1649 High Court of Justice, and Execution of Charles I.
1649 *Monarchy abolished—Commonwealth founded.*
1650 Battle of Dunbar.
1651 Battle of Worcester.
1653 Cromwell made Lord Protector.
1654 Cromwell usurps the Government.
1660 **Charles II.** *The Restoration of the Monarchy.*
1661 The Episcopal Religion restored.
1665 The London Plague.
1666 The London Fire.
1678 The Popish Plot.
1679 *The Habeas Corpus Act.*
1683 The Rye House Plot.
1685 **James II.** Battle of Sedgemoor.
1688 *The Glorious Revolution.*
1689 **William and Mary.** Accession of William and Mary.
1689 *The Bill of Rights.*
1690 Battle of the Boyne.
1697 Peace of Ryswick.
1701 *Act of Settlement.*
1702 **Anne.** War of the Spanish Succession.
1707 Constitutional Union of England and Scotland.
1713 Peace of Utrecht.

CARDINAL DATES OF ENGLISH HISTORY.

1714 **George I.**
1715 Landing of the elder Pretender.
1716 Septennial Act.
1727 **George II.**
1741 War of the Austrian Succession.
1745 Landing of the younger Pretender.
1746 Battle of Culloden.
1748 Peace of Aix-la-Chapelle.
1754 The French and Indian, or Seven Years', War.
1759 Battle of Quebec.
1760 **George III.**
1763 *Peace of Paris.*
1765 Stamp Act.
1774 Boston Port Bill.
1775 Battle of Lexington.
1776 *Declaration of Independence.*
1777 Surrender of Burgoyne at Saratoga.
1781 Surrender of Cornwallis at Yorktown.
1783 *Independence of the United States acknowledged.*
1789 The French Revolution.
1801 Constitutional Union of England and Ireland.
1805 Battle of Trafalgar.
1812 Second war with the United States.
1814 *Peace of Ghent.*
1815 Battle of Waterloo and fall of Napoleon.
1820 **George IV.**
1827 Battle of Navarino.
1829 Catholic Emancipation Bill.
1830 **William IV.**
1832 *The Reform Bill.*
1833 Abolition of Slavery in the Colonies.
1837 **Victoria.**
1846 Repeal of the Corn Laws.
1854 The Crimean War.
1857 The Sepoy Rebellion.
1858 The government of India assumed by the Crown.
1861 Death of Prince Albert.
1869 Disestablishment of the Irish Church.
1870 *The Education Bill.*

www.ingramcontent.com/pod-product-compliance
Lightning Source LLC
Chambersburg PA
CBHW030729230426
43667CB00007B/653